Anselm's Pursuit of Joy

Anselm's Pursuit of Joy

A COMMENTARY ON THE *PROSLOGION*

Gavin R. Ortlund

The Catholic University of America Press
Washington, D.C.

Copyright © 2020
The Catholic University of America Press
All rights reserved

Library of Congress Cataloging-in-Publication Data
Names: Ortlund, Gavin R., 1983– author.
Title: Anslem's pursuit of joy : a commentary on the *Proslogion* / Gavin R. Ortlund.
Description: Washington, D.C. : The Catholic University of America Press, [2020]
| Includes bibliographical references and index.
Identifiers: LCCN 2020009392 | ISBN 9780813232751 (cloth) |
ISBN 9780813232768 (ebook)
Subjects: LCSH: Anselm, Saint, Archbishop of Canterbury, 1033-1109. Proslogion. |
God—Proof, Ontological—Early works to 1800.
Classification: LCC B765.A83 P87227 2020 | DDC 212/.1—dc23
LC record available at https://lccn.loc.gov/2020009392

For Esther
My deepest friend

Contents

List of Figures	ix
Acknowledgments	xi
Note on Translations and Citations	xiii
Abbreviations	xv

Introduction

1

CHAPTER 1

The Method of the *Proslogion*: Getting beyond "The Problem of Anselm"

11

CHAPTER 2

The Interpretation of the *Proslogion*: Historical Reception and Contemporary Trends

46

CHAPTER 3

The Purpose of the *Proslogion*: *Excitatio* and *Argumentum* in Chapters 1–4

78

CONTENTS

CHAPTER 4

The Structure of the *Proslogion*: Spirals Upward from Chapter 5 to Chapter 22

125

CHAPTER 5

The Climax of the *Proslogion*: The *Visio Dei* in Chapters 23–26

173

Conclusion

223

Bibliography   231

Figures

FIGURE 1   Ms Bodley 271 30verso.
Reprinted with permission of The Bodleian
Libraries, The University of Oxford   50

FIGURE 2   Ms Bodley 271 31recto.
Reprinted with permission, as for figure 1   51

FIGURE 3   Anselm's Beatitudes   211

Acknowledgments

I am grateful to Dr. Oliver Crisp and Dr. John L. Thompson for their feedback and input during the course of my research and writing for this book. Both of them were consistently encouraging, and I have benefited greatly from their insights. I am indebted to Dr. David S. Hogg for his feedback on chapter 4. An earlier version of chapter 1 was read at the *Reading Anselm: Context and Criticism* international conference, organized under the aegis of the International Association for Anselm Studies, held at Boston College, July 27–30, 2015, and is set to appear in *Anselm of Canterbury: New Readings of His Intellectual Methods*, edited by Eileen Sweeney, John Slotemaker, and Thomas J. Ball. I am grateful for permission to reuse this material, updated slightly, here. Dave Lauer was kind enough to read an earlier draft of the entire manuscript and offer numerous textual corrections. John Martino and the entire editorial team at the Catholic University of America Press were a joy to work with and contributed to the final result of this project in many ways. Finally, my wife, Esther, has been a constant source of friendship, support, and encouragement, and I would not have been able to complete this book without her.

Note on Translations and Citations

All translations of Anselm are my own, but I have found particular help referencing those of Thomas Williams and Jasper Hopkins, as well as Ian Logan's translation of the *Proslogion*. I have also consulted with Walter Fröhlich's translations of Anselm's letters and Benedicta Ward's translations of Anselm's *Prayers and Meditations*. Translations of other Latin texts are my own, with the exception of Eadmer's *Vita Sancti Anselmi*, for which I have used Southern's translation. The translation used of other non-English sources is listed in the citation. In the case of previously untranslated French or German texts, I have supplied my own translation whenever they are cited.

References to Anselm's writings included in F. S. Schmitt's critical edition of Anselm's works are cited with the abbreviations listed below, followed by the relevant book/chapter/section citation of Anselm's work, and then subsequently the volume, page number, and line number in Schmitt. For instance, citation of the words *unam naturam* at the beginning of the *Monologion* would be as follows: M 1, Schmitt I 13:5.

Jasper Hopkins has identified three particular challenges involved in translating Anselm's writings: (1) the lack of a technical vocabulary, (2) the omission of possessive adjectives and of words that substitute for definite or indefinite articles, and (3) the presence of idiomatic locutions not easily captured in English.[1] As a result of these difficulties (particularly number 3), many of the existing translations of Anselm necessarily involve a kind of flexibility that, however helpful for carrying over Anselm's text into accessible English idiom, occasionally backgrounds his nuance or even obscures his meaning. Because my purpose in this study is to explore Anselm's meaning more than to generalize his ideas for a broader audience, I have aimed at translations that are more "literal," hoping that what is lost in readability may be gained by retaining some of the particularities of his language.

When carrying over the Latin text into the body of my writing, I have sought to strike a balance between translating everything (which can be cumbersome) and translating nothing (which makes the meaning less accessible) by translating Latin words or phrases that are longer or less known, while leaving well known or frequently repeated words and phrases untranslated so as to let the original wording retain its force whenever possible. In all cases, the appropriate citation of Schmitt's *Omnia Opera* is given so that readers who desire to do so may confer with the original.

1. Jasper Hopkins, "On Translating Anselm's Complete Treatises," in *Anselm of Canterbury, vol. 4: Hermeneutical and Textual Problems in the Complete Treatises of Anselm* (Lewiston, N.Y.: The Edwin Mellen Press, 1976), 11.

Abbreviations

CDH	Cur Deus homo
DC	De Concordia
DCD	De casu diaboli
DCV	De conceptu virginali et de originali peccato
DG	De grammatico
DIV	De incarnatione verbi
DLA	De libertate arbitrii
DPS	De processione Spiritus Sancti
DV	De veritate
Ep.	Epistola (using Schmitt's numerals)
Med.	Meditationes
Mem.	Memorials of St. Anselm
M	Monologion
Or.	Orationes
PL	Patrologiae cursus completus: Series Latina, ed. J.-P. Migne (Paris)
Pro Insip.	Quid ad haec respondeat quidam pro insipiente
P	Proslogion
Resp.	Quid ad haec respondeat editor ipsius libelli
R	The Rule of St. Benedict
V	Biblia Sacra Vulgata

Anselm's Pursuit of Joy

Introduction

The interpretation of Anselm of Canterbury's *Proslogion* has a long and rich tradition, beginning with Anselm's correspondence with his contemporary Gaunilo over the book's argument for God's existence in chapters 2–4. Across the centuries, interest in the *Proslogion* has tended to concentrate on this same portion of the book that concerned Gaunilo, the so-called ontological argument.[1] During and soon after Anselm's life, the *Proslogion* was used in monasteries and cathedral schools for educational and devotional purposes, along with his *Prayers and Meditations*. But from around the time of Thomas Aquinas, the medieval reception of Anselm's text came to be focused on its proof of God's existence, which itself was often associated with other similar arguments.[2] In the modern period as well, engagement with the *Proslogion* tended to rise and fall with

---

1. Indeed, as we will explore in chapter 2, the Anselm-Gaunilo debate contributed to this trajectory of interpretation, since it was circulated with the rest of the work.

2. Aquinas's rejection of the argument was highly influential, though he was likely not working with the text of the *Proslogion* itself, but with Anselm's argument as it had come to be used in association with a whole family of arguments asserting that God's existence is self-evident. St. Thomas Aquinas, *Summa Theologica* I, Q. 2, Art. 1, trans. Fathers of the English Dominican Province, Christian Classics (Notre Dame: Christian Classics, 1948), 11–12.

reformulations (Descartes, Spinoza, Leibniz, Wolff)[3] and critiques (especially Kant)[4] of the "ontological argument." After Kant's famous objection that existence is not a predicate, the argument was widely considered dead—and for many, the *Proslogion* was buried with it.[5]

Anselm scholarship made significant strides forward in the twentieth century, leading some scholars to speak of an "Anselm renaissance."[6] Amid these advances, interpretation of the *Proslogion* has entered newer and more complex territory. In the early 1930's, Karl Barth produced his famous work on the *Proslogion*, drawing atten-

---

3. For the most pivotal text, see René Descartes, *Meditations on First Philosophy*, in *The Philosophical Writings of Descartes*, vol. II, trans. John Cottingham, Robert Stoofhoff, and Dugald Murdoch, 2 vols. (Cambridge: Cambridge University Press, 1984), 24–36.

4. Immanuel Kant, *Critique of Pure Reason*, trans. J. M. D. Meiklejohn (1781; rpt, New York: Dutton, 1974), 346–52. It was Kant who named the argument the "ontological argument," though he was not working with Anselm's version of it.

5. M. J. Charlesworth claims that in post-Kantian philosophy the argument of *Proslogion* 2–4 "came to be viewed as a quaint and naïve medieval conundrum easily to be disposed of by rehearsing the Kantian axiom that existence is not a predicate" (*St. Anselm's "Proslogion"* [1965; rpt., Notre Dame: University of Notre Dame Press, 1979], 6–7).

6. F. S. Schmitt laid an essential foundation with his critical edition of Anselm works, published in six volumes from 1938 to 1961 (*S. Anselmi Cantuariensis Archiepiscopi Opera Omnia*, 6 vols. [1938; rpt., Edinburgh: Thomas Nelson and Sons, 1946]). R. W. Southern, *Saint Anselm: A Portrait in a Landscape* (Cambridge: Cambridge University Press, 1990), produced a definitive critical biography of Anselm's life, drawn in part from his earlier *Saint Anselm and His Biographer* (Cambridge: Cambridge University Press, 1963). Schmitt and Southern together edited the *Memorials of Saint Anselm*, Auctores Britannici Medii Aevi (Oxford: Oxford University Press, 1969). Gillian R. Evans edited a four-volume concordance of Anselm's works: *Concordance to the Works of St. Anselm* (Iola, WI: Kraus International Publications, 1983). Jasper Hopkins provided (along with Herbert Richardson) a four-volume work of translation and commentary from 1974 to 1976, along with his *A Companion to the Study of St. Anselm* (Minneapolis: University of Minnesota Press, 1972). D. P. Henry made significant advances in the understanding of Anselm's use of logic and grammar (and his *De Grammatico*) in *The Logic of St. Anselm* (Oxford: Clarendon Press, 1967), and "Saint Anselm's de 'Grammatico,'" *Philosophical Quarterly* 10 (1960): 115–26.

tion to the fiduciary and theological foundations of Anselm's project.[7] Soon after, Anselm Stolz produced an influential interpretation of the entire *Proslogion* as a work of mystical theology, not concerned with proving God's existence at all.[8] In the 1960's, interest in the "ontological argument" revived in philosophical circles, largely through the influence of Norman Malcolm and Charles Hartshorne, who argued that there are two different arguments in *Proslogion* 2 and 3, respectively, and sought to distinguish the latter from the Cartesian argument.[9] The late twentieth and early twenty-first centuries witnessed an explosion of Anselm scholarship, including a series of international conferences devoted to the study of his life and thought.[10] English-language readers may now choose from a number of different collections and translations of Anselm's works,[11] and the *Proslogion*, in particular, has benefitted from renewed interest its overall

---

7. Karl Barth, *Anselm: Fides Quaerens Intellectum: Anselm's Proof of the Existence of God in the Context of His Theological Scheme* (1931; rpt., Eugene, Ore.: Pickwick, 2009).

8. Anselm Stolz, "Zur Theologie Anselms im *Proslogion*," *Catholica: Veirteljahrschrift fur Kontroverstheologie* II (Paderborn: 1933): 1–24. Cf. also Stolz, "'Vere esse' im *Proslogion* des hl. Anselm," *Scholastik* 9 (1934): 400–409; and Stolz, "Das *Proslogion* des hl. Anselm," *Revue Benedictine* 47 (1935): 331–47.

9. Norman Malcolm, "Anselm's Ontological Arguments," *The Philosophical Review* 69 (1960): 41–62; Charles Hartshorne, *The Logic of Perfection: And Other Essays in Neo-classical Metaphysics* (Lasalle: Open Court, 1962), 28–117. They argued that *Proslogion* 3 deals with *necessary* existence, whereas *Proslogion* 2 (and the Cartesian argument) focuses on existence in general.

10. A good sample bibliography of recent Anselm scholarship (as well as a penetrating account of Anselm's thought) can be found in Eileen C. Sweeney, *Anselm of Canterbury and the Desire for the Word* (Washington D.C.: The Catholic University of America Press, 2012).

11. The translations provided by Thomas Williams, *Anselm: Basic Writings* (Indianapolis: Hackett, 2007) surpass earlier collections such as *Anselm of Canterbury: The Major Works*, ed. Brian Davies and G. R. Evans, Oxford World Classics (Oxford: Oxford University Press, 1998). A fuller collection of Anselm's treatises, including his *Meditation on Human Redemption* and four of his didactic letters, can be found in *Complete Philosophical and Theological Treatises of Anselm of Canterbury*, ed. Jasper Hopkins and Herbert Richardson (Loveland, Colo.: Arthur J. Banning Press, 2000), which rely on Hopkins and Richardson's older translations.

INTRODUCTION

theological program,[12] careful textual analysis,[13] and a deeper appreciation of the significance of its use of prayer (especially the introductory prayer of chapter 1).[14] Greater attention has been given to the later chapters of the *Proslogion*,[15] and several book-length French[16]

12. Much of the German literature particularly engages the *Proslogion* to explore the nature of theology. Thus, Reiner Wimmer, "Anselms *Proslogion* Als Performativ-Illokutionärer Und Als Kognitiv-Propositionaler Text Und Die Zweifache Aufgabe Der Theologie," in *Klassische Gottesbeweise in der Sicht der gegenwärtigen Logik und Wissenschaftstheorie* (Stuttgart: Kohlhammer, 1991), 174–201; Ingolf U. Dalferth, "*Fides Quaerens Intellectum*: Theologie Als Kunst Der Argumentation In Anselms *Proslogion*," *Zeitschrift Für Theologie und Kirche* 81, no. 1 (1984): 54–105.

13. Ian Logan translates and comments on the entire text of the *Proslogion* (*Reading Anselm's "Proslogion": The History of Anselm's Argument and Its Significance Today* [Farnham, Vt.: Ashgate, 2009]). In an earlier publication, Logan reflects on various weaknesses of existing translations of the *Proslogion*. Ian Logan, "'Whoever Understands This ...': On Translating the *Proslogion*," *New Blackfriars* 89:1023 (September 2008), 562.

14. For example, Klaus Kienzler, "*Proslogion* 1: Form Und Gestalt," in *Anselm* (Sheffield: Sheffield Academic Press, 1996), 38–55; Dom Jean-Charles Nault, "The First Chapter of St. Anselm's *Proslogion*," in *A Man Born Out of Due Time: New Perspectives on St. Anselm of Canterbury*, ed. Dunstan Robidoux, OSB (New York: Lantern Books, 2013), 33–41; Thomas A. Losoncy, "Chapter 1 of St Anselm's *Proslogion*: Its Preliminaries to Proving God's Existence as Paradigmatic for Subsequent Proofs of God's Existence," in *Greek and Medieval Studies in Honor of Leo Sweeney, SJ* (N.Y.: Peter Lang, 1995): 171–79.

15. A particularly illuminating interpretation of the *Proslogion* is offered by Louis Mackey, who argues that the proof of the *Proslogion* develops beyond chapter 4 and climaxes in chapter 22 ("Grammar and Rhetoric in the *Proslogium*," in *Peregrinations of the Word: Essays in Medieval Philosophy* [Ann Arbor: University of Michigan Press, 1997], 93–109). Mackey particularly draws attention to the dual grammatical and rhetorical strands of Anselm's text, emphasizing the paradoxical nature of its language in speaking of God. Unfortunately, Mackey's treatment of these later chapters is necessarily brief (sixteen pages) and has not been extended by many other interpreters. We will review other texts that have illumined *Proslogion* 5–26 in chapter 2.

16. Paul Gilbert, "Justice et miséricorde dans le *Proslogion* de saint Anselme," *Nouvelle Revue Théologique* 108 (March–April, 1986), 218–38; Gilbert, *Le "Proslogion" de S. Anselme: Silence de Dieu et joie de l'homme* (Rome: Pontifical Gregorian University, 1990); Gilbert, "Entrez dans la joie: Les ch. 24 à 26 du *Proslogion*," *Science et Esprit* 47, no. 3 (1995): 239–59; Gilbert, *Dire l'Ineffable: Lecture du "Monologion" de S. Anselme* (Paris: Éditions Lethielleux, 1984); Yves Cattin, *La preuve de Dieu: Introduction à la lecture du "Proslogion" d'Anselme de Canterbury*, Bibliothèque

and German[17] studies of the *Proslogion* have offered penetrating insights into how the *Proslogion* functions as an entire text. Nonetheless, the *Proslogion* is still too rarely studied and interpreted in its entirety. My own survey of monographs, dissertations, and scholarly articles published on the *Proslogion* since 1950 uncovered more works on chapters 2–4 than the rest of the book roughly by a ratio of roughly 25 to 1.[18] Much of the European literature—particularly the powerful works of Paul Gilbert, Yves Cattin, and Siegfried Karl—is untranslated and frequently goes unnoticed in the English-speaking world. In general, engagement with the *Proslogion* is often dominated by an interest in the "ontological argument" of its early chapters, and this circumstance has significantly

---

d'histoire de la philosophie (Paris: Librairie Philosophique J. Vrin, 1986); Cattin, "La prière de S Anselme dans le *Proslogion*," *Revue des Sciences philosophiques et théologiques* 72, no. 3 (1988): 373–96; Cattin, "Dieu d'amour, Dieu de colère: Justice et miséricorde dans le *Proslogion* (ch. VI–XI) d'Anselme de Canterbury," *Revue d'Histoire et de Philosophie religieuses* 69, no. 4 (1989): 423–50.

These are among the important writings of these authors as regards the *Proslogion*; a fuller bibliographic summary of all their work can be found in Hopkins's supplemental bibliography. Another significant French text is Michel Corbin, *Saint Anselme* (Paris: Éditions du Cerf, 2004), who seeks to establish that Anselm's argument does not proceed from a prior principle apart from faith and derives from the *Proslogion* many insightful comments concerning the nature and psychology of faith. Corbin draws his comments regarding the being of God (91–145) from *Proslogion* 2–4 and engages the later chapters of the book when discussing the event of God (146–96), but he neither explores the book as a whole nor analyzes its final chapters.

17. Siegfried Karl, *Ratio und Affectus: Zum Verhältnis von Vernunft und Affekt in den Orationes sive Meditationes und im Proslogion Anselms von Canterbury*, Studia Anselmiana (Rome: EOS Verlag, 2014). Another significant text is Georgi Kapriev, *Ipsa Vita et Veritas: Der "Ontologische Gottesbeweis" und die Ideenwelt Anselms von Canterbury*, Studien und Texte zur Geistesgeschichte des Mittelalters (Leiden: Brill, 1998).

18. I conducted this search by searching for dissertations, books, articles, and essays concerning Anselm's *Proslogion* in JStor, OATD.org, and the ATLA Religion Database. I supplemented this search by examining the list of Anselm publications in *25 Years of Anselm Studies*, ed. Fleteren and Schmitt, 32–55, and *The Saint Anselm Blog* (www.Anselm2009.blogspot.com), which is maintained by Ian Logan and for many years provided monthly updates of all noteworthy Anselm publications.

INTRODUCTION

shaped the book's interpretation, even among its abler commentators. Consider, as a representative example, Charlesworth's older but well-known translation and commentary on the *Proslogion*. His commentary on the text offers a sustained analysis on *Proslogion* 2–4, but provides no comment on *Proslogion* 8–11 because it "raises no points needing special mention."[19] It also skips over *Proslogion* 14 and offers no treatment of *Proslogion* 16–26 except for a quotation of its "very beautiful prayer."[20] While there is nothing inherently wrong with focusing on one portion of a text, that a work functioning as a *commentary* can contain such uneven interests is representative of a more general weakness in *Proslogion* scholarship. Too often, the significance of the *Proslogion* is sheerly equated to the "ontological argument" under the generic label of "Anselm's argument" or "the *Proslogion* argument" or "Anselm's *Proslogion* argument," which labels have no reference beyond the proof of God's existence.

Now, to be fair, a special interest in the argument of chapters 2–4 is understandable. For one thing, *Proslogion* 2–4 appears to be most directly related to the intellectual breakthrough that occasioned the *Proslogion* and set it apart as a distinct work from the *Monologion*, as he outlines in the *prooemium*.[21] Moreover, the sheer quantity of literature written about the argument of these chapters suggests its significance as an intellectual achievement in the history of Western thought. Readers of Anselm do well to give this argument special attention.

At the same time, if our interest in *Proslogion* 2–4 leads us to neglect the other parts of the book and the underlying unity of the whole work, something vital is lost. Anselm's driving interests are far from resolved in *Proslogion* 4—the same argument that

19. Charlesworth, *St. Anselm's "Proslogion,"* 80.
20. Charlesworth, *St. Anselm's "Proslogion,"* 82.
21. *P*, prooemium, Schmitt I 93:10–19. We will discuss the (complicated) relationship between the *Monologion* and the *Proslogion* more fully at the start of chapter 3.

proves God's existence is itself what leads into the meditations of the subsequent twenty-two chapters. Much of the real energy and genius of the *Proslogion* comes in its later movements and in the way Anselm carefully builds from his conception of God up into his vision of heavenly joy. Ultimately, for Anselm, God's identity as "that than which nothing greater can be thought" concerned far more than his mere existence but his position as the highest good of the human soul. Thus, we can only understand Anselm's proof of God in a limited and somewhat artificial way if we sever it from the larger spiritual effort in which Anselm placed it. We return to this theme repeatedly throughout chapters 3–5. For now it is sufficient to simply note that our interest in Anselm's pursuit of spiritual joy accords with both Anselm's own requests in the opening chapter of the *Proslogion*, as well as his stated purpose of the *prooemium*, which is "to prove that God truly is, that he is the highest good (*summum bonum*) needing no other and that which all things need for their being and well-being, and whatever else we believe about the divine substance."[22] My commentary will repeatedly stress the seriousness with which Anselm intends the final clause of this quoted statement. He thinks that his argument establishes not only *that* God is, but "whatever else" God is.

Many others, of course, have noticed the lopsided feel of *Proslogion* reception. But while it is commonplace to hear laments that Anselm's book is too infrequently studied on its own terms, it is surprising how little effort has been expended toward any kind of thorough correction of this deficiency. (In chapter 2 we will narrate the various advances that have been made in the interpretation of the *Proslogion* and situate our own effort in relation to them.) This book attempts to read the *Proslogion* particularly with attention to how it functions as a twenty-six-chapter book. It takes the prayerful supplications of *Proslogion* 1, recapitulated in *Proslogion* 14 and elsewhere—as well as the prayerful tone of the entire work—as

---

22. *P, prooemium*, Schmitt I 93:7–9.

INTRODUCTION

integral to its meaning. It traces the organic, incremental development of Anselm's doctrine of God as it proceeds throughout the *Proslogion*, culminating in the doctrine of heavenly joy in its final chapters. It suggests that *Proslogion* 24 and 25—those concerned with the infinite joy of the saints and angels in the heavenly vision of God—are the climax of the book. All that precedes, including chapters 2–4, plays a role in getting Anselm to this point, where his understanding of God as a being than which nothing greater can be thought finds its correlate in human faith as a *joy* than which nothing greater can be thought. Ultimately, then, the *Proslogion* is not just an argument for God's existence, but a spiritual pursuit of what his existence *entails* for the one who strives after Him in faith.

In the following chapters I offer a rationale for a more holistic reading of the *Proslogion* and seek to demonstrate some of the implications of such a reading. Some readers may wish to begin with chapters 3–5, which broadly comprise a commentary on Anselm's text. Before we engage the text of the *Proslogion*, however, it may be useful to approach it by considering several eccentricities that have characterized its historical reception and current interpretation. In the first two chapters we therefore explore two particularly common perceptions about the *Proslogion*—that it is essentially a work of what we today call philosophy (chapter 1) and that it essentially constitutes a proof of God's existence (chapter 2). It is hoped that the claim of consistency in both Anselm's thought generally, and in the procedure of the *Proslogion* specifically, will prepare for the commentary that follows and gain sympathy for the particular way the commentary proceeds—that is, reading the *Proslogion* as the prayer of a monk for the heavenly *visio Dei*.

Chapter 3 then initiates a sustained engagement with the text of the *Proslogion*. It explores Anselm's overall purpose in writing the book in light of the historical circumstances of its composition, its relationship to the *Monologion*, the opening prayer of *Proslogion* 1, and the particular kind of "ontological argument(s)" contained in *Proslogion* 2–4. It suggests that the most basic aim of the *Proslogion* is

INTRODUCTION

Anselm's pursuit of the soul's heavenly vision of God. Chapter 4 explores the logical development and flow of thought within the body of the *Proslogion*, particularly chapters 5–22. It detects there distinct "spiraling" movements (from chapter 1 to chapter 14, chapters 2–4 to chapters 15–17, and chapters 6–13 to chapters 18–22) in which Anselm transcends toward the beatific vision by recapitulating earlier themes in the book. The middle body of the *Proslogion* is thus interpreted as a carefully crafted progression of thought upwards toward a greater perception of the divine essence. Finally, chapter 5 explores Anselm's vision of heavenly joy in *Proslogion* 23–26. It develops Anselm's doctrine of heaven from his letters, from his *Prayers and Meditations*, and from the *Memorials* of his oral teaching. It then traces how Anselm's identification of the Trinity as the *summum bonum* of the soul in *Proslogion* 23 leads into his "conjecture" (*conjectatio*) in *Proslogion* 24–25 concerning the joy of those who possess this *summum bonum*, suggesting that this final section of the *Proslogion* represents the climax of the book, and the resolution of its earlier themes.

One final note. Readers who approach the *Proslogion* primarily out of curiosity about its proof for God's existence should be warned that they may find this book to be pursuing somewhat different interests. I do, of course, engage *Proslogion* 2–4 toward the end of chapter 3, and I am happy to reveal in advance that for my part, I regard Anselm's proof for God's existence to be both valid and sound within the context of Anselm's presuppositions. However, the ontological proof does not generate or organize my engagement with the *Proslogion*, and I recognize that some readers will be disappointed that there is not more commentary on this portion of Anselm's text.

In defense of my approach I offer two remarks. First, there has been and continues to be an enormous body of literature on the ontological argument, while other portions of the *Proslogion*, and the book as such, have received less attention. So I believe that there is a place for efforts that seek to balance the scales somewhat.

INTRODUCTION

But secondly and more basically, I would hope that the effort of my book, precisely because of its different angle of approach, would ultimately serve the best interests of Anselm's proof of God's existence. I have never been able to shake the feeling that analyses of Anselm's "ontological argument," however penetrating their technical insights into its logical coherence may be, cannot help missing Anselm's deepest intentions if they extract his proof from the prayerful movement of which it is but one part. It seems to me that a thoroughgoing effort to trace the course of thought by which Anselm rises from the misery of *Proslogion* 1 to the ecstasy of *Proslogion* 24–26 can only, in its own way, enhance our appreciation of the significance of *Proslogion* 2–4—just as a careful reading of the entire novel can only enhance the understanding of its most famous theme or most celebrated motif. Consider, for instance, how swiftly Anselm moves from establishing that God exists (*Proslogion* 2) to the further claim that God exists in an absolutely unique way such that God cannot be thought not to exist (*Proslogion* 3–4). Anselm has no interest at all in a God who shares generic existence with other things. He wants the God who is hidden in accessible light who alone can answer his plea, "I have come to you hungry; let me not leave unsatisfied."[23] It is only within the context of the entire book that we can appreciate why it is so vital for Anselm to prove *this* God particularly. If something more intriguing and more profound is happening throughout the *Proslogion* than a proof of God, we won't fully appreciate what Anselm is doing in *Proslogion* 2–4 until we have followed him on his journey from the despair of *Proslogion* 1 into the jubilation of *Proslogion* 25.

23. *P* 1, Schmitt I 100:1.

CHAPTER 1

The Method of the *Proslogion*

Getting beyond "The Problem of Anselm"

> No major Christian thinker has suffered quite so much as St. Anselm from the hit-and-run tactics of historians of theism and soteriology.
>
> —JOHN MCINTYRE

Modern views of Anselm of Canterbury are not always especially generous. Some critics seem to regard him as representative of all that is bad in theology, and even those who are sympathetic to his aims are often puzzled at how he pursues them. In particular, his theological method and epistemology have often been regarded as hopelessly inconsistent. Charlesworth's older commentary, for instance, opens with the claim that "on the whole matter of faith and reason St. Anselm's thought has a fluid, uncrystallized, or (blessed word!) ambivalent character."[1] Charlesworth contrasted the *sola ratione* ("by reason alone") of *Monologion* 1 with the *fides quaerens intellectum* ("faith seeking understanding") of *Proslogion* 1, arguing that these "two sides of Anselm's thought" entailed a contradiction that Anselm

---

1. Charlesworth, *St. Anselm's "Proslogion,"* preface (1965; rpt., Notre Dame: University of Notre Dame Press, 1979).

never resolved,[2] although he was "groping his way confusedly" toward the distinction between faith and reason that Aquinas would make a century after him.[3] For Charlesworth, Anselm's inconsistency on issues of faith and reason explained why his interpreters have reached such wildly different views about his epistemology. As examples, Charlesworth was able to cite assertions as flatly contradictory as those of Gordon Leff, "[Anselm] allowed reason no independent validity,"[4] and Henri Bouliard, "the *Proslogion* proof ... is meant to work independently of faith."[5]

It is almost monotonous how consistently interpreters of Anselm approach him in these same terms. A decade earlier than Charlesworth, John McIntyre opened his classic study of Anselm's *Cur Deus Homo* by contrasting the *credo ut intelligam* ("I believe in order to understand") of the book's *commendatio* with the *remoto Christo* ("Christ being set aside") of the book's *praefatio*, claiming that these two principles raised a difficulty in the interpretation of Anselm that his numerous commentators have confused more than clarified.[6] In the decades since Charlesworth and McIntyre, not only has this "rationalism/fideism" construct continued to dominate discussions of Anselm's epistemology, but many of the leading texts on Anselm have used it as a rubric by which to en-

---

2. Charlesworth, *St. Anselm's "Proslogion,"* 34. Cf. 36–37, "if we stress the one side of his thought we can easily make Anselm into a rationalist for whom not only the 'preambles' or presuppositions of faith are rationally demonstrable, but also the mysteries of faith themselves. On the other hand, if we stress the other side of Anselm's thought we can easily make him into a quasi-fideist, maintaining that nothing can be known about God save on the basis of faith."

3. Charlesworth, *St. Anselm's "Proslogion,"* 38; cf. 39.

4. Gordon Leff, *Medieval Thought: From St. Augustine to Ockham* (London: Humanities Press, 1958), 99, as quoted in Charlesworth, *St. Anselm's Proslogion,"* n37.

5. Henri Bouillard, "La preuve de Dieu dans le *Proslogion* et son interpretation par Karl Barth," as quoted in Charlesworth, *St. Anselm's "Proslogion,"* 45n.

6. John McIntyre, *St. Anselm and His Critics: A Re-Interpretation of the Cur Deus Homo* (Edinburgh: Oliver and Boyd, 1954), 2–7. Cf. 15–38, where he surveys Webb, Gilson, Taylor, Baillie, and Barth. Ultimately, McIntyre seeks to extricate Anselm from the charge of inconsistency or contradiction (e.g., 51, 55).

gage the whole of his thought. So, for instance, with the influential works by McGill,[7] Hopkins,[8] Evans,[9] Southern,[10] Holopainen,[11] Kapriev,[12] Adams,[13] Corbin,[14] Logan,[15] Visser and Williams,[16] and many others.[17] In a recent study, Eileen Sweeney labels this

---

7. McGill, "Recent Discussions in Anselm's Ontological Argument," in *The Many-Faced Argument: Recent Studies on the Ontological Argument for the Existence of God*, ed. John Hick and Arthur C. McGill (N.Y.: Macmillan, 1967), 1–69.

8. Hopkins, *A Companion to the Study of St. Anselm*, 38–66.

9. Gillian R. Evans, "The Cur Deus Homo: The Nature of St. Anselm's Appeal to Reason," *Studia Theologica* 31 (1977): 33–50.

10. Southern, *Saint Anselm*, 123–27.

11. Toivo J. Holopainen, *Dialectic and Theology in the Eleventh Century* (N.Y.: E. J. Brill, 1996), 119–55.

12. Kapriev, *Ipsa Vita et Veritas: Der "Ontologische Gottesbeweis" und die Ideenwelt Anselms von Canterbury. Studien und Texte zur Geistesgeschichte des Mittelalters* (Leiden: Brill, 1998), 17–167.

13. Marylin McCord Adams, "Anselm on Faith and Reason," in *The Cambridge Companion to Anselm*, ed. Brian Davies and Brian Leftow (Cambridge: Cambridge University Press, 2004), 32–60.

14. Michel Corbin, *Anselme* (Paris: Éditions du Cerf, 2004), 45–90.

15. Ian Logan, *Reading Anselm's "Proslogion": The History of Anselm's Argument and Its Significance Today* (Farnham: Ashgate, 2009), 19–24.

16. Sandra Williams and Thomas Visser, *Anselm*, Great Medieval Thinkers (Oxford: Oxford University Press, 2009), 13–25.

17. Schufreider approaches Anselm as a rational mystic, with his rationalism and his mysticism as "two sides of a single face" (*Confessions of a Rational Mystic, Anselm's Early Writings* [West Lafayette, Ind.: Purdue University Press, 1994], 13). Katherin A. Rogers sets up her treatment in terms of Anselm's "contradictory" statements about faith and reason, ultimately arguing for a rationalistic Anselm over and against an "intrafideistic" Anselm (her term, 459) ("Can Christianity Be Proven? St. Anselm of Canterbury on Faith and Reason," in *Anselm Studies: An Occasional Journal II*, ed. Joseph C. Schnaubelt, Thomas A. Losoncy, et. al. [White Plains, N.Y.: Kraus International Publications, 1988], 447–79).

For a classic example of the "rationalistic Anselm," see Étienne Gilson, *Reason and Revelation in the Middle Ages* (N.Y.: Scribner, 1946), 23–27. The most influential reactions against the rationalistic interpretation of Anselm remain 1) Karl Barth, *Anselm: Fides Quaerens Intellectum: Anselm's Proof of the Existence of God in the Context of His Theological Scheme* (1931; reprint, Eugene, Ore.: Pickwick, 2009); and 2) Anselm Stolz, "Zur Theologie Anselms im *Proslogion*," *Catholica: Vierteljahrschrift fur Kontroverstheologie* 2 (Paderborn: 1933), 12–21. Ermanno Bencivenga uses tensions in Anselm's epistemology to explore the nature of logic (*Logic and Other Nonsense: The Case of Anselm and His God* [Princeton: Princeton University Press, 1993]).

challenge "the problem of Anselm." The problem, briefly stated, concerns how to correlate Anselm's "unparalleled" and "seemingly boundless" rationalism with the emotional fervor of his writings and his stated method of "faith seeking understanding."[18] Sweeney observes that these seemingly discrepant aspects of his thought have made the study of Anselm for modern readers "a study in contradictions" and that "philosophers and systematic theologians carry off parts of his corpus, while those interested in spirituality take others."[19]

It will be helpful, before embarking on our sustained engagement with the text of Anselm's *Proslogion*, to see if we can make some sense of these seemingly strange juxtapositions that characterize his thought. It would be difficult, actually, to attempt any substantive reading of the *Proslogion* without addressing the "problem of Anselm," because, historically, rationalistic portraits of Anselm have tended to go hand in glove with philosophical readings of the *Proslogion*, and claims of inconsistency in his epistemology have tended to run along with piecemeal engagements of his works. This, of course, is not particularly surprising—the perception of confusion in the thought of an author rarely motivates readers to harmonize their statements. If Anselm had not sorted in his own mind out how *ratio* and *fides* work together, why should we correlate them in his argument? If he himself was divided, why should the study of his text not be?

In this chapter, I suggest that "by reason alone" was a statement of method, not an alternative epistemology. That is to say, in a medieval context where florilegia were among the most common

---

18. Eileen Sweeney, *Anselm of Canterbury and the Desire for the Word* (Washington, D.C.: The Catholic University of America Press, 2012), 1.

19. Sweeney, *Anselm of Canterbury and the Desire for the Word*, 2, 5. In the rest of the book, Sweeney interprets tensions in Anselm's epistemology within the larger framework of Anselm's search for the union of opposites, evident in all of his writings throughout their chronological development. Ultimately, she argues that Anselm's "rational and spiritual projects are elements of an integral whole: reason serving spirituality and spirituality giving value to reason" (369).

theological documents—and the citation of theological authorities (like Augustine and Scripture) was considered standard theological argumentation—*sola ratione* meant reason apart from theological authority, not reason apart from faith. What it excluded was not the approach of *fides qua* (the faith by which we believe) but an appeal to *fides quae* (the faith which is believed).[20] This method of argumentation no more involved an audacious rationalism than C. S. Lewis's lack of biblical quotations in *Mere Christianity* entailed a thoroughgoing natural theology. In sum, Anselm's theological epistemology operates consistently in accordance with the prayer of the first chapter of *Proslogion* and is well encapsulated in its climactic assertion from Isaiah 7:9: "unless I believe, I shall not understand."[21]

To show that *sola ratione* did not entail *fides remota*, we will explore four different areas: first, Anselm's definitions of *sola ratione* and *remoto Christo*; second, Anselm's actual procedure in the works described by these phrases; third, Anselm's insistence on the futility of reason apart from faith; and fourth, Anselm's historical context, in which a contrast between reason and authority would have been more meaningful than a contrast between reason and faith. We will conclude by summarizing several implications for Anselm's engagement with the unbeliever and for the interpretation of the *Proslogion*.

Anselm's Definition of *sola ratione*

The word *sola* in the phrase *sola ratione* implies the exclusion of a possible conjunction. By comparison, in the context of the Prot-

---

20. This does not mean that Anselm will not cite or allude to such authorities when using this method (there are many such allusions in *Proslogion*; he derives the term "the fool" from Psalm 14:1/53:1, for example). It means he does not assume their *authority* in his argumentation.

21. P 1, Schmitt I 100:19. This is a paradigmatic text for Anselm from which he also quotes at crucial junctures in *Cur Deus Homo* and *On the Incarnation of the Word*. *DIV* 1, Schmitt II 7:11–12, *CDH* Commendatio, Schmitt II, 40:8.

estant Reformation, *sola fide* entailed the exclusion of works.²² Approaching Anselm after more than 900 years of further development in the realm of religious thought, it is all too easy to assume he is operating in the same epistemological categories of a contemporary *Philosophy of Religion* textbook: faith and reason. In a modern context, "rationalism" typically refers to a methological preference of reason over religious authority or experience in the realm of thought and/or life, and *faith versus reason* is a common construct in religious and philosophical discourse. But if we are to understand Anselm, we must enter into his world, not drag him into ours—and that means paying close attention to the categories in which *he* is operating. Anselm predates not only the faith versus reason discussions in the split of philosophy and religion after the rise of modernity but also Aquinas's famous distinction between the "preambles of faith" (proved by reason) and the "mysteries of faith" (taken by faith).²³ What Anselm means by terms like *ratio*²⁴

---

22. In fact, Barth's comparison of Anselm's *sola ratione* and Luther's *sola fide* presents some helpful initial categories of thought: "this formula [*sola ratione*], which as we have explained precludes collision with authority, is as liable to be understood or misunderstood as was Luther's *sola fide* in its context. It cannot be understood as if Anselm has written *solitaria ratione*. Authority is the necessary presupposition of Anselm's *ratio*, just as works are the necessary consequence of Luther's *fides*" (Barth, *Anselm: Fides Quaerens Intellectum*, 44). He develops his discussion of the meaning of *ratio* in Anselm's writings on the following pages.

23. Corbin protests against reading later Thomistic/Aristotelian categories back onto Anselm, pointing instead to Boethius as the most significant source for Anselm's understanding and use of logic (*Anselme*, 46–47).

24. The Latin word *ratio* has a large and complex semantic range in both its classical and medieval usage. *The Oxford Latin Dictionary* lists fifteen broad headings for the term, including (4) "the act or process of reasoning or working out, reckoning" (ed. P. G. W. Glare [Oxford: Oxford University Press, 1976], 1575–76). Charlton T. Lewis and Charles Short list thirteen different possible meanings of *ratio*, organized under several more basic headings (*A New Latin Dictionary: Founded on the Translation of Freund's Latin-German Lexicon, Revised, Enlarged, and in Great Part Re-Written* [New York: American Book Company, 1879], 1525–27).

Anselm's usage of the term *ratio* reflects this complexity (according to my search in *PL*, Anselm uses the term over 1,000 times in his writings). Lexically, it is certainly possible for *ratio* in the phrase *sola ratione* to mean something like "argumentation"

and *fides*,²⁵ therefore, cannot be assumed in advance but must be considered in the context of his eleventh-century monastic world.

The phrase *sola ratione* first occurs in chapter 1 of the *Monologion*, which was Anselm's first major work after more than four decades of life and almost two decades of quiet obscurity within the peaceful confines of a monastery.²⁶ Two especially important features of this long, relatively inactive period in Anselm's life were the intimate friendships he formed with other monks (as revealed in his early letters) and the intensity of his spiritual life (as revealed in his *Prayers and Meditations*). It was in this context that the seeds of the *Monologion* germinated; without this historical background in view, the *purpose* of Anselm's *sola ratione* remains obscure. When Anselm's interpreters rush into analysis of the first paragraph of *Monologion* 1 without sufficient reflection on the book's prologue, *sola ratione* is often brought into modern contexts before it is seen in Anselm's. In the prologue, Anselm narrates what circumstances led an unknown, middle-aged monk suddenly to write for a larger audience:

Some of the brothers have often and studiously entreated me, that I should describe some of the things I have offered to them in our talking together by frequent conversation concerning how one ought to meditate on the divine essence, and about certain other things relating to such a meditation, as a sort of pattern for meditating on these things. More according to their own desire than according to the ease of the task or my ability, they

---

or "a process of reasoning," but its precise meaning in each occurrence in Anselm obviously depends upon a close exegesis of its usage in context. For further discussion of Anselm's use of the term *ratio*, see Yves Cattin, *La preuve de Dieu*, 98–105.

25. *Fides* likewise has a whole range of meanings, in Anselm and elsewhere (the *Oxford Latin Dictionary* lists thirteen meanings [697–98]). In this paper, when I speak of faith as not excluded by Anselm's *sola ratione*, I am obviously using it in the subjective sense of the individual's belief in God, i.e., *fides qua* (as is customary in discussions of faith and reason).

26. Richard Southern dates *De Grammatico* early on in Anselm's career but notes that the only other writings during this long stretch of silence were the *Prayers and Meditations* (*Saint Anselm*, 62–65).

prescribed this form to me in writing this meditation: absolutely nothing in it would be established by the authority of Scripture, but whatever the conclusion of each investigation would assert, the necessity of reason would concisely prove, and the clarity of truth would manifestly show that it is the case by plain style, common arguments, and simple disputation.[27]

Several things are noteworthy in this paragraph. First, the method or "form" (*forma*) of Anselm's *Monologion* was not his own invention, but the request of his fellow monks, following from their theological discussions. Second, the kinds of discussions that led to the *Monologion* concerned "how one ought to meditate on the divine essence," and his book aimed at providing "a sort of pattern for meditating (*meditationis exemplo*) on these things." Indeed, the original title of the *Monologion* was *A Pattern for Meditation on the Reason of Faith* (*Exemplum Meditandi De Ratione Fidei*).[28] Anselm's *sola ratione* project must also be interpreted in light of this essentially spiritual purpose. Third, "the necessity of reason" (*rationis necessitas*) is here conjoined with "the clarity of truth" (*veritatis claritas*). It also corresponds to a particular style of argumentation that aimed for simplicity and straightforwardness ("plain style, common arguments, and simple disputation"). These are *methodological* descriptions, indicating the manner of argumentation which Anselm would employ in this work. Fourth and most significantly, reason is not here set against faith as an epistemology; rather, reason is set against Scripture as a methodology (or "form" [*forma*]). The "form" of Anselm's meditation is such that it would establish its claims by plain reasoning, *as opposed to* establishing them by an appeal to Scripture. From this opening paragraph alone, it is already a bit awkward to conceive of the *Monologion* as rationalistic project operating apart from faith. Indeed, it is the product of theological discussions in a monastery, and its purpose is to assist *meditation* upon the divine nature.

27. *M, prologus*, Schmitt I 7:2–11.
28. *P, prooemium*, Schmitt 94:6–7.

Later in his writing career, Anselm continued to reflect back on the *sola ratione* methodology of the *Monologion* (and, significantly, the *Proslogion*) as excluding not faith but an appeal to the authority of Scripture. In his letter *On the Incarnation of the Word*, for example, he referenced "my two little works, namely, *Monologion* and *Proslogion*, which were made mainly for this purpose, that what we hold by faith concerning the divine nature and his persons, except the incarnation, could be proved by necessary reasons, without the authority of Scripture."[29] Not only does Anselm here qualify what it means to prove by "necessary reasons" with the additional clause, "without the authority of Scripture," but he also stipulates that the conclusions which are "proved" here are those which are *already* held "by faith."

Eadmer, Anselm's first biographer, understood the method of Anselm's *Monologion* in a similar way: "here [in the *Monologion*], putting aside all authority of Holy Scripture, [Anselm] enquired into and discovered by reason alone (*sola ratione*) what God is, and proved by invincible reason that God's nature is what the true faith (*vera fides*) holds it to be."[30] Here also, *sola ratione* is defined as the absence of an appeal to Scripture, and the conclusions which reason establishes are those *already* held by the true faith. In these passages, reason is not an alternative to faith but its tool; *sola ratione* is not at odds with *fides quaerens intellectum* but a method employed within it.

While these three statements refer specifically to Scripture, it is evident from Anselm's broader writings that when he refers to theological authority, he has in mind several other sources of authority as well. Looking at the thirty-six usages of the term *auctoritas* in Anselm's writings (other than his letters), Colomon Viola observes that Anselm uses the term sometimes with reference to specific phenomena such as papal magisteria on doctrinal matters,

29. *DIV* 6, Schmitt II 20:16–19.
30. Eadmer, *Vita Sancti Anselmi* I:19, ed. R. W. Southern (1962; rpt., Oxford: Clarendon Press, 1979), 29.

the apostolic authority of the papal legate, or the authority of Lanfranc—while in other instances it has a more generic reference to the authority of Scripture, *auctoritas Christiana, omnis veritatis auctoritatis,* and so forth.[31] In *De Concordia,* Anselm will expound on his view of the relationship of authority and Scripture more thoroughly, prioritizing Scripture over reason and identifying it as the font of all of the church's proclamation: "for we proclaim nothing useful for spiritual salvation which the Holy Scriptures, made fertile by a miracle of the Holy Spirit, have not offered or do not contain within themselves."[32]

If the *sola ratione* of the *Monologion* is intended to exclude an appeal to Scripture, rather than the approach of faith, what about the *remoto Christo* of *Cur Deus Homo*? *Cur Deus Homo* may be particularly relevant to our study because it comes later in Anselm's career and in a different context than the *Monologion* and the *Proslogion.* The *remoto Christo* of *Cur Deus Homo* must be seen as roughly equivalent to the *sola ratione* of the *Monologion.* If one posits a discontinuity between them, one must posit a discontinuity within *Cur Deus Homo,* for Anselm can alternate back and forth between the two phrases in this book.[33] For example, at the end of the book, Boso will reflect that Anselm's argument is sufficiently sound that, even if he omitted several particular items, "you would satisfy not only Jews but also pagans by reason alone (*sola ratione*)."[34] Similarly, when Boso quotes Scripture in 1.20 to establish the firmness of his hope in the forgiveness of sins, Anselm reminds him:

But this is spoken only to those who either waited for Christ before he came or believe in him after he came. But when we set out to investigate

---

31. Colomon Étienne Viola, "Authority and Reason in Saint Anselm's Life and Thought," in *Anselm: Aosta, Bec and Canterbury: Papers in Commemoration of the Nine-Hundredth Anniversary of Anselm's Enthronement as Archbishop, 25 September 1093,* ed. D. E. Luscombe and Gillian R. Evans (Sheffield, UK: Sheffield Academic Press, 1996), 175–80.

32. *DC* 3.6, Schmitt II 721:26–28.

33. As Hopkins observes, *A Companion to the Study of St. Anselm,* 63.

34. *CDH* 2:22, Schmitt II 133:8.

whether his coming was necessary for the salvation of men, we agreed to proceed by reason alone (*sola ratione*), as though Christ and the Christian faith had never existed.[35]

This second quote suggests not only that Anselm saw *remoto Christo* and *sola ratione* as roughly identical; it also clarifies what Anselm *means* by these phrases, for once again *sola ratione* is contrasted with the biblical revelation of Christ as an alternative method of argumentation, not with faith as an alternative epistemology. Anselm's parallel use of *sola ratione* and *remoto Christo* supports our interpretation, for the latter is more clearly a methodological description—Anselm is arguing *as if* Christ had not come. Anselm is, as in the *Monologion*, adopting a role or *persona*.[36]

Anselm's statements about faith and reason at the start of *Cur Deus Homo* further clarify that he does not intend for *sola ratione* or *remoto Christo* to exclude faith. In the book's commendation to Pope Urban II, Anselm presents the book as part of the "reason of faith" (*ratio fidei*), which refutes unbelievers and nourishes believers who have already attained the "certainty of faith" (*certitudinem [fidei]*).[37] As with *Proslogion* 1 and *On the Incarnation of the Word*, he quotes from the Vulgate of Isaiah 7:9, "unless you believe, you will not understand," arguing that it is possible to proceed into understanding only after one has arrived at faith.[38] Anselm then begins the book by explaining that, like the *Monologion*, it is written in response to the requests of other believers for an explanation concerning certain articles of the faith—an explanation which "they do not ask for in order to achieve faith through reason, but in order to

---

35. *CDH* 1.20, Schmitt II 88:3–6. This is the second of the four occurrences of the phrase *sola ratione* in Anselm's writings. The other two are in *DC* III.11 and *DIV* 1, where he speaks of reason *sola* and *pura* (to be discussed below). For discussion of these latter phrases, see Colomon Étienne Viola, "Authority and Reason in Saint Anselm's Life and Thought," in *Anselm: Aosta, Bec and Canterbury*, 190.

36. We will discuss in the next chapter the nature of Anselm's personae and their important bearing on the interpretation of his books.

37. *CDH* Commendatio, Schmitt II 39:3.

38. *CDH* Commendatio, Schmitt II 40:8.

delight in the understanding and contemplation of the things they already believe."[39] Boso's early comment provides confirmation that this indeed is how Anselm wants *Cur Deus Homo* to be read: "right order requires that we believe the deep matters of Christian faith before we presume to examine them by reason."[40] It is clear from these statements that Anselm views this work as embracing both *sola ratione* and *fides quaerens intellectum*. It is difficult to see that he could have advanced such flatly contradictory claims if these principles indeed represented different epistemologies. Furthermore, in articulating his hesitancy at taking on the task requested of him, Anselm relegates the certainty of the conclusions he arrives at by reason to a provisional status until they are confirmed by greater theological authorities: "if I say something that a greater authority does not confirm, even if I appear to prove it by reason, let it be accepted with certainty only as what seems to me to be the case in the meantime, until God should in some way reveal it to me better."[41]

What about Anselm's other works? A weakness that is sometimes found in those who charge Anselm with inconsistency is a failure to note the methodological diversity of his different works. Charlesworth, for example, assumes that Anselm's epistemology operates in the same way across his writings, drawing the majority of his discussion from *Cur Deus Homo*.[42] Likewise, McIntyre operates under the assumption that *remoto Christo* is representative of all Anselm's writings, leading him to the erroneous assertion that Anselm does not assume the authority of Scripture in his writings.[43] Visser and Williams go so far as to claim that "the dating of Anselm's works, the progression of his career, is of very little relevance to interpreters."[44] It may be true that Anselm's thought

---

39. *CDH* 1.1, Schmitt II 47:8–9.
40. *CDH* 1.1, Schmitt II 48:16–17.
41. *CDH* 1.1, Schmitt II 50:7–10.
42. Cf. *Saint Anselm's "Proslogion,"* 30–31.
43. McIntyre, *St. Anselm and His Critics*, 20, 50.
44. Visser and Williams, *Anselm*, 5.

remained relatively stable throughout his writing career (especially in comparison to an Augustine or Luther or Barth), but it does not follow that there are no important differences among his works that bear on their interpretations. The general rubric of *sola ratione* appears in the *Monologion*, the *Proslogion*, *Cur Deus Homo*, and Anselm's letter *On the Incarnation of the Word*, as outlined in their respective prologues/introductions.[45] Though there are important differences in the methodology of each work, they all make an effort to avoid assuming the authority of Scripture in their argumentation.

Anselm's other writings, however, do frequently appeal to Scripture and theological authority: for instance, his string of quotations proving original sin in *On the Virginal Conception, and Original Sin* 7 or his biblical argument that God can predestine bad things to happen in *De Concordia* 2.2. That this methodology is self-consciously different from *sola ratione* becomes evident in Anselm's preface to *On Truth, On the Freedom of the Will*, and *On the Fall of the Devil*. These were the first works Anselm wrote after the *Monologion*, the *Proslogion*, and his response to Gaunilo, composed sometime in the early 1080s, after he became abbot of Bec. In the first sentence of their preface, Anselm calls these three works "treatises pertaining to the study of Holy Scripture" and then explains that they belong together as a unit because they were all written in similar form.[46] What is interesting is that, though Anselm occasionally appeals to Scripture in them,[47] on the whole they evidence very little biblical

---

45. *DIV* 1 does frequently appeal to Scripture in the introductory section of the letter, but at the start of *DIV* 2, where his disputation with Roscelin begins, Anselm explains that he will proceed by rational argumentation: "the response to this man should not be by the authority of Holy Scripture, because either he does not believe it or he interprets it in a perverse sense. For what does Holy Scripture say any more clearly than that there is one and only one God? Therefore his error should be exposed by reason, by which he tried to defend himself." See *DIV* 2, Schmitt II 11:5–8. Note once again the Scripture/reason contract (not faith/reason).

46. *DV praefatio*, Schmitt I 173:2–5.

47. For example, his quotation of I Corinthians 4:7 is significant in the early chapters of *On the Fall of the Devil*.

quotation and exegesis. Rather, sometimes called "philosophical dialogues," they consist of a dialogue between a teacher and student in which a particular doctrine or truth is searched out through rational investigation. What Anselm seems to mean by "treatises pertaining to the study of Holy Scripture" is that these works assume the trustworthiness of biblical revelation in their argumentation—this is their shared form, the "similarity of reasoning" (*similitudo disputationis*) that Anselm appeals to in order to explain why he clumps them together.[48]

What changes in Anselm's different writings, therefore, is neither an unwavering starting point in faith nor a strong reliance on logic and rational argument. Anselm's epistemology is not weaving back and forth between rationalist and fideist tendencies from the *Monologion* in the 1070s to *On the Fall of the Devil* in the 1080s and then to *Cur Deus Homo* in the 1090s. Rather, throughout his career, *fides quaerens intellectum* remains an apt description of Anselm's general theological epistemology, while *sola ratione* (or *remoto Christo*) is an occasional method employed by him within this framework that does not assume theological authorities.

Anselm's Procedure in Works Designated *sola ratione* or *remoto Christo*

The *sola ratione* of *Monologion* 1 comes into even clearer focus when it is interpreted in light of his actual procedure in the book's remaining seventy-nine chapters. In the early chapters of the *Monologion*, Anselm draws out God's necessary, supreme existence (chapters 1–6); creation, and sustenance of all other existing things (chapters 7–14); ineffability, spirituality, and inherent superiority to all other reality (chapter 15); simplicity (chapters 16–17); eternality (chapters 18–19, 24); omnipresence and penetration of all things (chapters 20–23); immutability (chapter 25); complete otherness

---

48. *DV praefatio*, Schmitt I 174:4.

(chapter 26); substantiality and spirituality (chapter 27); and utterly unique existence (chapter 28). The middle and lengthiest section of the book then focuses upon God's Triune relations (chapters 29–63). Here, Anselm attempts to prove that God's utterance, or Word, is the same thing as himself; that they are not two things but one; that all things exist through God's Word; that the Word is begotten; that the begetter and begotten are as a Father and Son; that they share the divine essence; that the mutual love between the begetting Father and begotten Son is the Spirit of the Father and Son; that the Spirit shares the divine essence; and that each is distinct, and yet the three are one God. Finally, Anselm seeks to demonstrate a host of conclusions regarding human knowledge of God, including that the rational mind can know God, that the soul is immortal, that human happiness exists in loving God, and that God should therefore be hoped and believed in (chapters 66–80).

Anselm teases out all these doctrines, including the thorough Trinitarianism that forms the book's core, within the boundaries of the *sola ratione* principle of *Monologion* 1. Were this principle intended as to exclude faith, Anselm would be a stark rationalist indeed, since he would evidently believe that all these intricacies of theology proper (including the precise nature of the relations of the divine persons) lie available to naked reason, apart from faith. Does this sound like the Anselm who can confess with bewilderment, "how can I approach an unapproachable light?"[49] The sheer *scope* of the *Monologion* already suggests that Anselm conceives its rational meditation as an expression of, rather than alternative to, his faith.

Several specific passages in the later sections of the *Monologion* add further weight to this point. In *Monologion* 64, for example, Anselm insists upon the inherent mystery of divine things and the necessity of faith in the face of this mystery. The chapter is titled, "that although this is inexplicable, it must nevertheless be believed."[50] He opens the chapter with the assertion, "it seems to me that the

---

49. *P* 1, Schmitt I 98:5.
50. *M* 64, Schmitt I 74:29.

mystery of so sublime a thing transcends every power of human understanding," and then he argues that the limitations of our knowledge of God should in no way inhibit the certainty of our faith in him.[51] Not only does Anselm's insistence upon divine mystery and his stress on the inability of human language to attain to God (cf. *Monologion* 65) counterbalance concerns that he overestimates the power of words and argumentation, but his insistence on faith in the midst of this mystery demonstrates that he perceives no friction between *sola ratione* and *fides quaerens intellectum*. Then, in *Monologion* 76–78, Anselm stipulates that believing (*credere*) and striving (*tendere*) are inseparable. He claims that believing in God entails striving unto the divine being and that striving is impossible apart from faith: "no one is able strive for him unless he believes him."[52] Thus, Anselm is so far from excluding faith in the *Monologion* that he can insist upon its utter necessity. For Anselm, faith is not an alternative to rational meditation on God but its prerequisite.

The structure and vocabulary of the *Monologion* also suggest that its presuppositions are those of faith. Assent to the data of revelation is assumed in the initial paragraph of *Monologion* 1, for example, where the book's stated goals concern not a bare and generic theism but various aspects of a distinctively Christian doctrine of God, such as God's uniquely self-sufficient eternal happiness.[53]

51. *M* 64, Schmitt I 74:30–31.
52. *M* 77, Schmitt I 84:11–12.
53. *M* 1, Schmitt I 14:5–9. Anselm also states here that the book seeks to prove God's supremacy, his creation and sustenance of all things, and "a great many other things that we necessarily believe about God or his creation." The "we" in this sentence corresponds to Anselm's monastic community, in which the book developed. What Anselm envisions in his opening paragraph as a person who is ignorant of God "either by not hearing or not believing" appears to be a movement from ignorance to knowledge more than the movement from unfaith to faith. How faith might precisely relate to such a scenario is not here specified, but it is noteworthy that the individual conceived in this way is seeking to convince *himself* of the reality of God (and through silent meditation, no less). Anselm uses this construct as a tool for meditation in his monastic context. We will say more about the *persona* of the *Monologion* in the next chapter.

THE METHOD OF THE *PROSLOGION*

Anselm will cite and allude to Scripture throughout the book, and his terminology is biblical (e.g., Father, Son, and Spirit). Moreover, Anselm concludes the book in *Monologion* 80 urging love, worship, and prayer to the one whose existence he has established, calling God the one "whom all other natures ought to lovingly worship and worshipfully love with all their power, from whom alone they ought to hope for good things, to whom alone they ought to flee from troubles, to whom alone they ought to pray for anything."[54] From the presuppositions, procedure, and conclusion of the *Monologion*, it is evident that Anselm does not set out from a neutral state, ready to be blown wherever reason may happen to lead him. He is on a clearly defined trajectory, seeking to establish certain doctrines of Christian orthodoxy; and, having done so, he worships.

In addition to its content and presuppositions, the book's meditative, introspective tone militates against the thesis that *sola ratione* excludes faith. In our own day, rationality and spirituality are often implicitly contrasted. But for Anselm, living as a monk in the eleventh century, rationality was spiritual faculty, and *sola ratione* in particular involved a turn inward in contemplation and prayerful thought, rather than outward to theological authorities.[55] *Sola ratione* corresponded to Anselm's determination to seek knowledge "by thought alone" (*sola cogitatione*) at the end of the *prologus* of the *Monologion*, by which he indicated a method of meditative inquiry, not an epistemology apart from faith.[56] Anselm attached particular importance to rational meditation on the divine essence because he held that "the rational mind is the only thing among all creatures that can rise up to the search of [God]."[57] This helps explain why

---

54. *M* 80, Schmitt I 87:9–12.
55. Southern draws attention to the introspective, meditative aspect of Anselm's early writings, insisting that *Monologion* and *Proslogion* "must be viewed as they evolved from prayer and meditation" (*Saint Anselm*, 116).
56. *M prologus*, Schmitt I 8:18.
57. *M* 66, Schmitt 77:17–19.

elsewhere Anselm could contrast "bodily imaginations" (*imaginationibus corporalibus*) with "reason itself, alone and unmixed" (*ratio ... ipsa sola et pura*).[58] Whereas *ratio* "should be the ruler and judge of everything in a human being" (*princeps et iudex debet omnium esse quae sunt in homine*), the souls of some arrogant and wicked men have been so covered over by "bodily imaginations" that they cannot raise themselves to see how there can be three persons "in that that most hidden and exalted nature" (*ilia secretissima et altissima natura*).[59] Anselm seems to conceive of reason as operating on a higher plane than bodily sensation, uniquely capable of certain kinds of divine and spiritual apprehension.

For Anselm, then, rational meditation can yield spiritual knowledge—but never apart from a posture of faith in the one meditating. Rather, rational meditation is a tool to be employed by one in the posture of faith. Thus Eadmer will describe Anselm's efforts upon arriving at Bec as follows: "he applied his whole mind to this end, that according to his faith he might be found worthy to see with the eye of reason (*mentis ratione*) those things in the Holy Scriptures which, as he felt, lay hidden in a deep obscurity."[60] Southern has translated *mentis ratione* a bit loosely here; it is not clear why *percipere* should be given a visual thrust. One might instead render *mentis ratione mereretur percipere* more strictly as "worthy to understand by the reason of the mind"—which, although a bit clunky, brings into greater view the role of *ratio* in relation to *fides* and *scriptura* that is presupposed in Eadmer's language. Anselm seems to regard reason not only as a meditative tool to be employed by faith but also as a tool to be employed for understanding those truths of Scripture that remain hidden in *multa caligne* ("great darkness"). In other words, *ratio* functions for Anselm within the boundaries of both *fides* and *scriptura*.

This subordination of reason to faith is even clearer in the *Pro-*

---

58. *DIV* 1, Schmitt II 10:2–4.
59. *DIV* 1, Schmitt II 10:1–6.
60. Eadmer, *Vita Sancti Anselmi* 1:7, 12.

slogion, which Anselm claims is written from a particular *persona*, specifically that of one "under the role (*sub persona*) of someone trying to raise his mind to contemplating God and seeking to understand what he believes."[61] This assertion corresponded to the original title of the book, which was simply *Fides quaerens intellectum*,[62] and the entire book represents the unpacking of this principle. That is why Anselm can write, in what justly his most famous statement concerning epistemology, "I do not seek to understand in order to believe; I believe in order to understand."[63] We will draw out further implications from Anselm's epistemology with respect to how to read the *Proslogion* toward the end of this chapter, and in chapter 3 we will explore this book's relation to the *Monologion*, an often-overlooked point that also bears on our interpretation of that book.

Anselm's Strictures on the Futility of Speculative Reason

Perhaps the most significant portion of Anselm's writings for determining his views on the relation of faith and reason, yet one that is often overlooked, is his letter *On the Incarnation of the Word*. Anselm opens this work, addressed to Pope Urban II and occasioned by Roscelin's heretical view that the Father and the Spirit were incarnate with the Son, by protesting his own unworthiness to defend the Christian faith. Quoting Daniel 2, he writes:

> For if other men were to see me loaded with pegs and ropes and other things, by which we often stabilize and bind wavering things, working around Mount Olympus to establish it, lest it totter or be overturned by the force of something—it would be amazing if they restrained themselves from mockery and derision. How much more with the stone which was cut from the mountain without hands that struck and breaks the statue,

---

61. *P, prooemium*, Schmitt I 93:21–94:1.
62. *P, prooemium*, Schmitt I 94:7.
63. *P* 1, Schmitt I 100:18.

which Nebuchadnezzar saw in his dream, which has now become a great mountain that filled the whole earth, if I were to endeavor to prop it up with my reasons and stabilize it, as if it were wavering.[64]

Such an awareness of the precariousness of his own efforts already raises question marks against some rationalistic interpretations of Anselm. When Étienne Gilson claims, for instance, "Anselm's confidence in reason's power of interpretation is unlimited,"[65] we start to feel a tension between the ambitious Anselm depicted in Gilson's interpretation and the more tentative Anselm we find here. Far from adopting a use for reason that reflects an unlimited confidence, Anselm worries that he is engaged in a foolish enterprise that godly Christians would attribute to "frivolous boasting" (*iactantiae levitati*).[66] Then, before Anselm continues to engage with the teaching of Roscelin, he spends several pages castigating those who divorce reason from faith. Here the tension with rationalistic interpretations becomes unavoidable. Anselm speaks of the "presumption of those who with wicked rashness dare to argue against one of the things the Christian faith confesses, since they cannot understand it with their intellect."[67] Anselm makes clear that he sees no place for reason questioning faith:

> Indeed, no Christian ought to argue that something the Catholic Church believes with her heart and confesses with her lips is not the case, but by always holding the same faith without doubting, by loving it and living according to it, he should humbly seek as much as he can the reason of how it is. If he is able to understand, let him give thanks to God. If he is not ... let him bow his head toward that which is to be venerated.[68]

Here Anselm makes it clear that he conceives of reason as functioning as the servant of faith, seeking only what it professes and

---

64. *DIV* 1, Schmitt II 5:10–17.
65. Étienne Gilson, *History of Christian Philosophy in the Middle Ages* (N.Y. : Random House, 1995), 129.
66. *DIV* 1, Schmitt II 5:19.
67. *DIV* 1, Schmitt II 6:6–8.
68. *DIV* 1, Schmitt II 6:10–7:4.

THE METHOD OF THE *PROSLOGION*

staying strictly within its boundaries. Quoting a text that will function significantly throughout his writings, Isaiah 7:9, Anselm further excoriates those who presume to approach the knowledge of divine truth apart from the "ladder of faith" (*fidei scalam*).[69] In a vivid metaphor, he writes, "it is as if bats and owls, which do not see the sky unless at night, should dispute concerning the rays of the midday sun against eagles, who look upon the sun itself with un-repelled vision."[70] Rather than giving reason unlimited power, it would seem that Anselm assigns it quite definite boundaries and that he regards straying outside of these boundaries as hopelessly foolish—like a bat or owl disputing about the sun.

This emphasis on the primacy of faith was Anselm's consistent posture on matters of theological epistemology throughout his career. In an important letter from 1089, for instance, in the context of his dispute with Roscelin, Anselm further stipulates that not only is reason futile apart from faith, but even within faith it enjoys only a very modest goal:

> Our faith has to be defended by reason against the impious, not against those who confess rejoicing in the honor of being called Christians. For it is just to demand from these that they hold unshaken the pledge made in baptism; but to the former it must be shown by reason (*rationabiliter*) how irrationally (*irrationabiliter*) they scorn us. For a Christian ought to advance through faith to understanding, not reach faith through understanding or, if he is not able to understand, fall away from faith. But when he is able to reach understanding, he should rejoice; but when he cannot, he should venerate what he is not able to understand.[71]

This claim sounds quite similar to his arguments in *On the Incarnation of the Word*, and throughout this letter much of his imagery is similar to that found there (e.g., the Christian faith as *firmam petram*, unbelief as *nutantium*). But what emerges more clearly in this

---

69. *DIV* 1, Schmitt II 7:11.
70. *DIV* 1, Schmitt II 8:4–6.
71. Ep. 136, Schmitt III 280:34–281:41.

passage is the restrained, modest role that Anselm regards reason to have for the believer. Where reason can bring understanding, the result is joy. Where it cannot, the result is mystery and veneration. But at no point does the thought of reason imparting or even confirming faith arise; instead, it is limited to a more defensive role in relation to the unbeliever. And though elsewhere Anselm will speak of the *ratio fidei* as nourishing the believer and resulting in joy, this passage makes clear he is also perfectly content to recognize and live within the limitations of what the believer will be able to understand in this life.[72]

This more modest view of the power of reason is similar to that taken in Anselm's reply to Gaunilo, where he applies his argument "to refute a fool who does not accept the sacred authority,"[73] while for believers, he simply commands them to believe Romans 1:20. To be sure, reason does have a role for the believer—but it seems to be a spiritual, meditative role, as a tool by which the believer can grow and be nourished. This is the role of reason in *Cur Deus Homo* as well, where Anselm appeals to reason not to strengthen the believer's faith so much as to nourish them in it and give them joy.[74] It is significant here that Boso, Anselm's dialogue-partner throughout the work, is not an unbeliever, nor even a wavering believer seeking confirmation of his faith—instead, he is a believer seeking the joy of understanding that his faith accords with reason.[75] Thus, Boso will request rational explanation "not in order to confirm me in faith, but in order that the one already confirmed would delight in the understanding of this truth."[76] Furthermore, even in its "apologetic" use, Anselm is not so much hoping to convert the unbeliever as silence and mute the force of his objection. Thus, he says the argument of *Cur Deus Homo* is "for confuting the foolishness and breaking down

72. *CDH Commendatio*, Schmitt II 39:4–6.
73. Resp. 8, Schmitt 1 137:28–138:3.
74. *CDH Commendatio*, Schmitt II 39:4–6.
75. Cf. Hopkins, *A Companion*, 40.
76. *CDH* 2.15, Schmitt II 116:11–12.

the hardness of unbelievers,"[77] and his argument in *On the Incarnation of the Word* is to "curb the presumption" of those who arrogantly object to articles of the Christian faith they cannot understand.[78]

Why is it so important for Anselm that faith operate within the boundaries of faith? *On the Incarnation of the Word* makes it clear that the reason is Anselm's high view of spiritual *experience*. Faith must precede understanding because understanding flows from experience, and faith *also* precedes experience.[79] In a lengthy paragraph sprinkled with nine biblical quotations, Anselm insists that true knowledge of God is dependent on inward cleansing, illumination, childlike obedience, and being filled with the Holy Spirit. He concludes by asserting:

He who has not believed will not understand. For he who has not believed will not experience, and he who has not experienced will not know. For as much as experiencing a thing is superior to hearing about it, so much does the knowledge (*scientia*) of someone who experiences surpass the understanding (*cognitionem*) of someone who hears.[80]

Anselm's emphasis on the necessity of spiritual illumination and cleansing for knowing God undermines charges of rationalism. When Richard Campbell calls Anselm "the most uncompromising rationalist which the Church has ever produced,"[81] for instance, one wonders how such a claim can withstand a sympathetic reading of

---

77. *CDH* Commendatio, Schmitt II 39:3–4.

78. *DIV* 1, Schmitt II 6:5–6. Translating *cognitio* as "understanding" here distinguishes it from *scientia* as well as draw out some of the nuances inherent in the term; e.g., Lewis and Short, *A New Latin Dictionary*, qualify "knowledge" with "as a consequence of perception or of the exercise of our mental powers" (361).

79. Hopkins also draws attention to the phrase *corde intelligere* in De Concordia ("to understand with the heart"), as an important component of Anselm's epistemology (*A Companion*, 43).

80. *DIV* 1, Schmitt II 9:5–8.

81. Richard Campbell, "Fides Quaerens Intellectum - Deo remoto," in *Saint Anselm—A Thinker for Yesterday and Today: Anselm's Thought Viewed by Our Contemporaries*, ed. Colomon Viola and Frederick Van Fleteren, Texts and Studies in Religion 90 (Lewiston, N.Y.: The Edwin Mellen Press, 2002), 169.

On the Incarnation of the Word or the first chapter of the *Proslogion*. And even those arguing for a fideistic or mystical Anselm often overlook this intermediary role of experience in Anselm's epistemology. Spiritual experience is, for Anselm, the middle step between faith and spiritual knowledge: *fides quaerens intellectum via experentia*.

Anselm's Historical Context

The uniqueness of Anselm's *sola ratione* project in its historical context is frequently observed. Southern notes that "the most striking characteristic which separated [the *Monologion*] from other contemporary writings was its lack of quotation of authorities."[82] Elsewhere, he claims that this method "sets him apart from all his contemporaries, except those who came under his immediate influence."[83] Similarly, after noting Anselm's method in the *Monologion* of not citing any authorities, Evans claims, "it is hard to emphasize sufficiently how unusual this was. All of Anselm's contemporaries, and his predecessors for many generations, had proceeded by commenting on a text or by quoting a series of passages and perhaps linking them closely together."[84] Because Anselm lived at the start of the transition from the monasteries to the cathedral schools as the center of theological education, it is easy to read later Scholastic developments back onto him. But in his own day, Anselm's *sola ratione* method was highly innovative. Adams even claims that "Anselm is the pioneer-representative of a methodological translation that came to full flower in the thirteenth and fourteenth-century universities, moving from the lecture (*lectio*) which focused on the assimilation and exegesis of texts, to the methods of question and disputation."[85]

But what was it that made *sola ratione* unique? What did Scho-

---

82. Southern, *Saint Anselm*, 120.
83. Southern, *Saint Anselm and His Biographer*, 52.
84. Gillian R. Evans, *Anselm*, Outstanding Christian Thinkers Series (New York: Bloomsbury Academic, 2005), 38.
85. Adams, "Anselm on Faith and Reason," in *The Cambridge Companion to Anselm*, 32–60, at 47.

lasticism—and the revival of speculative thought associated with it—replace? Early medieval education tended to rely on *florilegia* (compilations of quotations from theological authorities), and theological argumentation placed heavy emphasis on the citation of authority. Ninth-century disputations about the meaning of the Eucharist, for example, often consisted of batteries of quotations from Scripture and Augustine.[86] Beryl Smalley notes that during the Carolingian period, theological study was devoted almost entirely to the task of compilation.[87] Thus, "to study the commentaries of Alcuin, Claudius of Turin, Raban Maur and Walafrid Strabo his pupil, to mention outstanding names, is simply to study their sources."[88] Eventually, during the eleventh and twelfth century, glosses became the standard source for theological education in monastic and cathedral schools. Though glosses went beyond *florilegia* in offering running comments on a text, the focus was still on the authority of the text cited. In many cases, the comments occupied a much smaller space than the actual text; and rarely did the comments stray far from the text into speculative theology.[89] Thus, in the centuries leading up to Anselm, theological argumentation was generally rooted in the exegesis of sacred texts.

In this context, Anselm's *sola ratione* project represented a sharp departure from custom—but its uniqueness lay in its method. Anselm's views on faith and reason, by contrast, were not exceptional in his time. Both Abelard and Richard of St. Victor, for instance,

---

86. As examples, consider the use of Scripture and Augustine in Paschasius Radbertus of Corbie's *The Lord's Body and Blood* or Ratramnus of Corbie's *Christ's Body and Blood*, in *Early Medieval Theology*, vol. ix, ed. George E. McCracken and Allen Cabaniss, The Library of Christian Classics (Philadelphia.: The Westminster Press, 1957). The editors note that in theological writings from this period, "recourse to support from the sacred writings is constant" (16).

87. Beryl Smalley, *The Study of the Bible in the Middle Ages* (N.Y.: Philosophical Library, 1952), 51.

88. Smalley, *The Study of the Bible in the Middle Ages*, 37–38.

89. Smalley draws attention to Robert of Melun's twelfth-century commentary on Paul as an example (*The Study of the Bible in the Middle Ages*, 73). Lanfranc's glosses of Scripture provide another good representative example.

shared Anselm's belief that faith preceded understanding and that reason could not penetrate all doctrines of faith by itself.[90] Nor did Anselm consider the *content* of his theology to be novel. He frequently claimed that he sought to establish nothing that was not found in Scripture and Augustine, and throughout his writings one can detect Anselm self-consciously seeking to stay within Catholic boundaries. At the start of *Cur Deus Homo*, for instance, he links his defense of the *ratio fidei* to the previous efforts of "many of our holy fathers and teachers" (*sancti patres et doctores nostri multi*).[91] One perhaps detects a slight nervousness in Anselm's protest in *On the Incarnation of the Word* that the *Monologion* and the *Proslogion* advance only what is harmonious with what the church fathers taught, even if they did not explicitly state it.[92]

Anselm's eagerness to establish his Catholicity comes into clearer light when viewed in relation to his teacher Lanfranc's early discomfort with the *Monologion*. In about 1076, Anselm sent a copy of the *Monologion* to Lanfranc to ask for him for critical feedback.[93] Lanfranc, who had preceded Anselm as prior of Bec and now served as the Archbishop of Canterbury, criticized the book for its lack of citation of authorities.[94] In his letter response, Anselm mentioned how Lanfranc had advised him that the content of the *Monologion* should be pursued in dialogue with those learned in Scripture and that "when reasons fails, it should be equipped by divine authorities."[95] Anselm was careful to draw attention to the *Monologion*'s implicit Augustinian roots, claiming that its points were already

---

90. Jaroslav Pelikan, *The Christian Tradition: A History of the Development of Doctrine, vol. 3: The Growth of Medieval Theology* (Chicago: University of Chicago Press: 1980), 255–67, especially 259, 262.

91. *CDH Commendatio*, Schmitt II 39:2.

92. *DIV 6*, Schmitt II 20:22–24.

93. Ep. 72, Schmitt III 193–94.

94. Ep. 77, Schmitt III 199–200. Sweeney suggests that the Trinitarian language of *Monologion* may have been an additional concern of Lanfranc's (*Anselm of Canterbury*, 61–63, 116).

95. Ep. 77, Schmitt III 199:13–16.

established in *De Trinitate* and even that he wrote the *Monologion* "trusting in the authority" of *beatus Augustinus*.[96] Nonetheless, Anselm ultimately neglected to add biblical and patristic quotes to the text, despite Lanfranc's concerns. The episode may have damaged Anselm's relationship with Lanfranc,[97] and Anselm expressed great hesitancy in sending a copy of the *Monologion* to Abbot Reginald of Saint Cyprian of Poitiers, fearing that its lack of explicit grounding in theological authorities would cause its Trinitarian language to be seen as unorthodox rather than as strictly Augustininian.[98]

What made the *Monologion* so controversial for Lanfranc and others was its argumentative strategy of using reason apart from authoritative texts. Throughout his writings, Lanfranc was suspicious of theological efforts that lacked sufficient witness to theological authorities. In his *De Corpore et sanguine Domini*, he had contrasted theological argumentation based on "dialectical reasons" with theological argumentation based on "sacred authorities."[99] One of the key issues in the dispute over the Eucharist between Lanfranc and Berengar was whether dialectical reasoning could function apart from the citation of authority. In a letter to Reginald, abbot of S. Cyprien and one of the *Monologion*'s first readers, Lanfranc criticized Berengar for daring to disagree with Hilary of Poitiers. His method of critique is fascinating, because the bulk of his response consists not in engagement with the content of Berengar's position but with citations from Pope Gelasius, canon law, Augustine, and Jerome, establishing Hilary's status and authority.[100] Anselm's *Monologion* came in the larger context of these eleventh-century disputes concerning the relative roles of reason and authority.

These eleventh-century discussions concerning the relation of

96. *Ep.* 77, Schmitt III 199:24–26.
97. See Southern's account of the episode in *Saint Anselm*, 119–20.
98. *Ep.* 83, Schmitt III 207:3–6.
99. As noted by Holopainen, *Dialectic and Theology in the Eleventh Century*, 119.
100. Letter 46, *The Letters of Lanfranc Archbishop of Canterbury*, ed. and trans. Helen Clover and Margaret Gibson (Oxford: Oxford University Press, 1979), 142–51.

reason and authority were, in turn, an extension of earlier patterns of thought in the Western tradition Anselm inherited. Gregory the Great's *Moralia*, which was present in the library at Bec, anticipated some of the concerns we find in later discussion: "Holy Church in her teaching makes no demand on the ground of authority, but persuades by reason. So she says plainly that she is not believed because of authority, but her assertions are weighed by reason in order to discover whether they are true."[101] Even prior to this, in Augustine, the phrase *sola ratione* is employed in *De quantitate animae* in the context of a warning against the use of solitary reason, where it is evident that both reason and authority both stand upon *credere*.[102] The powerful influence of Augustine on Anselm, especially in terms of his views of faith and reason, has been frequently noted,[103] despite the fact that Anselm only quotes Augustine six times in his writings.[104] Already in the twelfth century Anselm was called *alter Augustinus*.[105] But Anselm also inherited the subsequent Augustinian *tradition* and, in particular, Boethius's transmission of Aristotelian logic.[106] Thomas Aquinas would distinguish Boethius's

---

101. Gregory the Great, *Moralia*, as quoted in Charlesworth, *St. Anselm's "Proslogion,"* 29. Sally Vaughn argues that Anselm absorbed Gregory's philosophy of education, noting similarities in their letters so striking that they almost appear as paraphrase ("The Monastic Sources of Anselm's Political Beliefs: St. Augustine, St. Benedict, and St. Gregory the Great," in *Anselm Studies: An Occasional Journal II*, 71–74). Anselm may also have had a relatively broad exposure to the Greek Fathers in translation at the library in Bec. See Giles E. M. Giles, *Saint Anselm of Canterbury and His Theological Inheritance* (Burlington, Vt.: Ashgate, 2004).

102. See the discussion in Colomon Étienne Viola, "Authority and Reason in Saint Anselm's Life and Thought," in *Anselm: Aosta, Bec and Canterbury*, 191–97.

103. For example, see the particularly influential and extended discussion of Southern, *Saint Anselm*, 71–87. It is not easy to detect influence on Anselm because Anselm rarely cites others, but Southern builds an impressive case from similarities of both style and substance.

104. Sally N. Vaughn, "The Monastic Sources of Anselm's Political Beliefs," in *Anselm Studies: An Occasional Journal II*, 53.

105. G. Stanley Kane, "*Fides Quaerens Intellectum* in Anselm's Thought," in *The Scottish Journal of Theology* 26 (1973): 41.

106. As pointed out, for instance, by Tadeusz Grzesik, "What Anselm Owes

use of reason in *De Trinitate* from that of Augustine in his work of the same name precisely in terms of this reason-authority contrast:

The method used in treating the Trinity is twofold, as Augustine says: authority and reason. Augustine combined both of these methods, as he himself states. Some of the holy Fathers, like Ambrose and Hilary, made use of only one of them, namely authority. Boethius, however, chose to pursue the other method, that of reasoning, taking for granted what the others had investigated by authority.[107]

Boethius' writings were widely known and read in eleventh-century France. His discussion of Aristotle's *Categories* was highly influential, and his own theological tractates (bound together with his *On the Consolation of Philosophy*) had become a standard text in schools several centuries prior.[108] Boethian logic was certainly taught in Anselm's day at Bec,[109] and its influence is clearly discernable in Anselm's writings.[110] Of these two influences pouring

---

to Boethius and Why He May Be Regarded as the Initiator of the Boethian Age," in *Studia Anselmiana* 128, *Cur Deus Homo* (Rome 1999), 179. Cf. D. P. Henry: "attempting to comprehend the logic of Anselm without a thorough acquaintance with the doctrines of Boethius is rather like trying to become a proficient pianoforte performer by practicing on a paper keyboard" (*The Logic of Saint Anselm* [Oxford: Clarendon Press, 1967]).

107. Thomas Aquinas, *Faith, Reason, and Theology: Questions I-IV of His Commentary on the* De Trinitate *of Boethius*, trans. Armand Maurer, Medieval Sources in Translation 32 (Toronto: Pontifical Institute of Medieval Studies, 1987), 5–6.

108. Douglas C. Hall, *The Trinity: An Analysis of St. Thomas Aquinas'* Expositio of the De Trinitate *of Boethius* (New York: Leiden, 1992), 35. That Boethius's influence was not confined to his transmission of Aristotelian logic but also concerned his own theology is evident from the fact that some twenty commentaries were written on his *De Trinitate* between 1120 and 1200. See Hall, *The Trinity*, 36.

109. Marcia L. Colish, *Medieval Foundations of the Western Intellectual Tradition: 400–1400* (1997; rpt., New Haven: Yale University Press, 2002), 164, 167; and Glynnis M. Cropp, "The Medieval French Tradition," in *Boethius in the Middle Ages: Latin and Vernacular Traditions of the* Consolatio Philosophiae, ed. Maarten J. F. M. Hoenen and Lodi Nauta (New York: Brill, 1997), 245.

110. Osmund Lewry draws attention to similarities in the technical language of the *Monologion* and the *Isagoge*, *Perihermeneias*, and *Topica Ciceronis*, suggesting further that the influence of Boethian logic (and especially Aristotle's Praedicamenta

into Anselm's thought, an Augustinian/Platonic ontology and a Boethian/Aristotelian dialectic, the latter is particularly relevant to understanding Anselm's method of arguing apart from the citation of authority. It is in the context of noting the influence of both Augustine and Boethius upon Anselm that Kapriev emphasizes the uniqueness of Anselm's thought, calling him "a beginning without immediate precursors."[111]

Anselm and the Unbeliever

We may both clarify and test our conclusions with reference to an important and potentially difficult issue: how Anselm's principle of *fides quaerens intellectum* relates to the unbeliever. This has arguably been one of the leading causes for confusion in understanding Anselm's epistemology. It can be put as a question: if reason operates *within* the boundaries of faith, what is its relevance to unbelievers? If the only ladder to true knowledge of God is the ladder of humble faith (picking up on Anselm's image in *On the Incarnation*),[112] why bother to defend the faith by reason at all? Some interpreters of Anselm, in their admirable protest against the notion of a rationalistic Anselm, have downplayed the extent to which Anselm allows reason to operate within faith and yet also *influence* those outside of faith. Barth's study on Anselm, for example, despite its numerous merits, goes too far in downplaying a contact point between

---

in Boethius's commentary) can be detected throughout Anselm's writings in his use of paronyms and in his treatment of universals and modality ("Boethian Logic in the Medieval West," in *Boethius: His Life, Thought, and Influence*, ed. Margaret Gibson [Oxford: Basil Blackwell, 1981], 100–102). D. P. Henry gives thorough treatment of the influence of Boethian logic in Anselm's *De Grammatico* (*Commentary on De Grammatico: The Historical-Logical Dimensions of a Dialogue of St. Anselm's* [Boston: D. Reidel, 1974]); Grzesik goes so far as suggesting that Anselm is largely responsible for subsequent interest in Boethius in the medieval period ("What Anselm Owes to Boethius," 188–90).

111. Kapriev, *Ipsa Vita et Veritas*, 5: "ein Anfang ohne unittmelbare Vorganger".
112. *DIV* 1, Schmitt II 7:10–12.

the believer and the unbeliever. Drawing from Anselm's quip about bats and owls and eagles, he speaks of the gulf between the believer and the fool, over which no help can pass, and in light of which "all discussion with [the fool] is pointless and meaningless."[113] Barth's book on Anselm still has great value in spite of the fact that at times it is not always clear where he is exegeting Anselm and where he is working out his own theology *via* Anselm.[114] But we must resist casting Anselm as an eleventh-century Barthian, and it is a mistake to disregard the genuine dialogue Anselm seeks with the unbeliever. For example, see not only his assertion Ep. 136, quoted above, but his statement at the beginning of *Cur Deus Homo* that the purpose of the book is "to refute the foolishness of unbelievers and break down their obstinacy."[115] Even the *Monologion* is written in part to "convince" (*persuadere*) the one who is ignorant of God "either by not hearing or not believing."[116] We should not pit meditative inquiry against apologetic interest, since in Anselm's monastic context a Christian meditation must reflect charity to all.[117]

A crucial aid to resolving this dilemma comes into view when we ask what *kind* of knowledge the believer and the unbeliever can have. So, for example, in Anselm's familiar phrase, *fides quaerens intellectum*, what precisely does *intellectum* mean? In *Cur Deus Homo* Anselm explains, "since I understand that the understanding we achieve in this life is the intermediate between faith and sight, I think that as much as someone moves toward it, to that extent he draws near to that sight for which we all long."[118] Thus, for Anselm,

---

113. Barth, *Anselm: Fides Quaerens Intellectum*, 64–65.

114. Barth also fails to appreciate the significance of *Proslogion* 1, calling it merely an introductory invocation and failing to explore its relation to the later sections of the book.

115. *CDH Commendatio*, Schmitt II 39:3–4.

116. *M* 1, Schmitt I 14:9.

117. Cf. Andre Hayen, "The Role of the Fool in St. Anselm and the Necessarily Apostolic Character of True Christian Reflection," in *The Many-Faced Argument*, 162–82, at 165.

118. *CDH Commendatio*, Schmitt II 40:10–12.

the *intellectum* that faith seeks is the intermediate step between faith and the beatific vision; it stands between seeing in a mirror dimly and seeing face to face; it is a rung on the ladder of the believer's movement up to heaven. This kind of experiential, partial-sight knowledge (which results from grace and issues in joy) is as distinct from the knowledge of the unbeliever as eagle's knowledge of the sun is distinct from that of bats and owls. It may be worth noting that when Anselm describes the kind of knowledge he expects the fool to have in *Proslogion* 4, he omits the term *vere* (truly).[119] Anselm would probably have been perfectly comfortable to put it in terms of Jonathan Edwards's famous analogy: it is one thing to know theoretically that honey is sweet; it is another to taste the honey.[120] So also, for Anselm, it is one thing for faith to seek understanding by reason, and it is another thing for reason to defend the faith to the unbeliever.

And yet, while insisting on the distinctness of the knowledge of faith and unfaith, Anselm still allows for a contact point between the two. They are separate domains, but it does not follow that they are *non-overlapping* domains. Indeed, for Cattin, much of the unique value of the *Proslogion* consists in the diversity and subtlety by which it gives joy and strength to the believer and at the same time listens carefully to the questions of the unbeliever.[121] An analogy may help elucidate Anselm's meaning here: a husband and wife know their marriage and their love in a way that no one outside the marriage ever can. Their knowledge is utterly distinct. Nevertheless, a rational and credible case for the marriage's sincerity and integrity could still be made to those outside the marriage. The husband need not divorce his wife or step outside the knowledge he enjoys *within* the marriage in order to make this rational case

---

119. As noted by Hogg, *Anselm of Canterbury*, 101.

120. Jonathan Edwards, "A Divine and Supernatural Light," in *The Sermons of Jonathan Edwards: A Reader*, ed. Wilson H. Kimnach, Kenneth P. Minkema, and Douglas A. Sweeney (New Haven, Conn.: Yale University Press, 1999), 127–28.

121. Cattin, *La preuve de Dieu*, II.

to outsiders, even if the knowledge that the rational case yields is qualitatively different from the knowledge he himself knows from within the marriage. In the same way, eagles may seek to convince bats of the existence of the sun, and those who have tasted honey can describe the experience to those who have not. Such secondhand knowledge is qualitatively inferior to firsthand knowledge, but that does not entail that secondhand, theoretical knowledge has no value or that communication is impossible between the bat and the eagle. So, also, Anselm holds that a believer may start and end with the knowledge of faith and yet employ reason to make a certain rational defense to those outside of the faith. As Visser and Williams put it, "the fool cannot grasp the reason of faith in the same way as someone who has the 'experience' that comes from belief; yet there is always something the believer can say to the fool that the fool can understand."[122]

What does all this entail for the interpretation of the *Proslogion*? In the first place, having gained an understanding of Anselm's faith, reason, and authority, we will be better prepared to appreciate the interplay of rationality and spirituality in his *Proslogion*. Interpreters of the *Proslogion* have often been perplexed at how it proceeds from the densest threads of technical logic on one page to the most poignant expressions of spiritual yearning on the next. The tendency has been to interpret one of these qualities through the other. Anselm is either inconsistent mystic or lapsing rationalist. But for Anselm, there was no tension between logic and love, emotion and argument, desire and dialectic. Rational meditation was an essentially spiritual exercise by which he sought to explore more of the divine essence. *Sola ratione* was a strategy employed within the boundaries of *fides quaerens intellectum*. We must read the *Proslogion* with sensitivity to how its diverse qualities not only functioned in harmony with each another but amplified each another.

Having surveyed Anselm's epistemology, we can also more

---

122. Visser and Williams, *Anselm*, 24.

readily appreciate that the *Proslogion*, though it uses biblical language and evidences Augustinian-Boethian influence, will avoid appealing to theological authorities. That the *Proslogion* falls under the same *sola ratione* method of argumentation as the *Monologion* is evident, for instance, in his later reference to the shared methodology of the two works.[123] This does not entail that there are no differences between these works; in chapter 3 we will explore their relationship, which we suggest is more complicated than often thought. But the works share the general characteristic of not assuming theological authorities. This also may help us appreciate the scope and ambition of the book. In one movement, Anselm pursues both a theistic proof and the beatific vision—he engages in both disputation with the fool as well as meditation on heaven. He writes in a monastery for monks, but academics in philosophy classrooms are among his readers. Keeping in mind the harmony of *sola ratione* and *fides quaerens intellectum* may help us appreciate, rather than work around, these seeming incongruities. If Anselm's method is *sola ratione*, he must start with a goal as basic as proving God's existence; but if his epistemology is *fides quaerens intellectum*, he may proceed to an end as ambitious as beholding God's beauty. Setting aside authority, Anselm must start at the very foot of the mountain; proceeding by faith, he may climb to its highest peak.

Finally, we must read the *Proslogion* according to the particular *persona* Anselm adopts in it. Anselm defines this *persona* as *fides quaerens intellectum*, and, as we will draw out in chapter 3, the particular kind of *intellectum* that Anselm pursues is that which he defines as the intermediate step between faith and the heavenly vision of God.[124] In other words, Anselm is concerned with attaining as much as he can of the taste of the knowledge of God in this life prior to its full realization of heaven; this desire has been aroused

---

123. *DIV* 6, Schmitt II 20:16–19.
124. *CDH Commendatio*, Schmitt II 40:10–11.

by his spiritual experience during matins and is informed at every step by his faith. The *Proslogion* must therefore be read in light of Anselm's high doctrine of spiritual experience, which we have summarized as *fides quaerens intellectum via experentia*.[125] But before we embark into the text itself, we must consider how it has been read by others—for, as we shall see, the *Proslogion* has been pulled apart in ways analogous to Anslem's *ratio* and *fides*.

---

125. This is drawn from Anselm's assertion in *DIV* 1, Schmitt II 9:5–8.

CHAPTER 2

The Interpretation of the *Proslogion*

Historical Reception and Contemporary Trends

> The remaining things of this book are argued so truly, so clearly and excellently, filled with such usefulness,... that they should in no way be condemned on account of those things in the beginning which are indeed perceived rightly, but argued less strongly.
>
> — GAUNILO, PRO INSIP. 8

Arguably the most significant event in the history of the interpretation of the *Proslogion* came within its author's lifetime. When Anselm's fellow monk Gaunilo critiqued the book's argument for God's existence in chapters 2–4, Anselm not only wrote a rejoinder but then requested that both Gaunilo's objections and his replies be circulated with the book. Thus, from its earliest days the *Proslogion* tended to be read in relation to this particular dispute concerning its proof for God's existence. It is not surprising, when a book contains a kind of built-in commentary on one particular portion of its contents, that greater interest might cluster around that portion of the book. But in the case of the

Proslogion, the trajectories of interpretation established by the Anselm-Gaunilo interchange have so marked its subsequent reception that *Proslogion* 1 and 5–26 have at times been altogether ignored. In many respects, engagement with the *Proslogion*, both medieval and modern, never fully broke away from Gaunilo's interests.

Now, granted, the recurrent interest in *Proslogion* 2–4 and Anselm's own eagerness to respond to Gaunilo testify to the significance of these chapters. At the same time, their importance does not justify their isolation, and we will argue that Anselm's argument for God's existence is itself best understood only in the context of the entire book. It is a historical irony that, while Anselm and Gaunilo focused on *Proslogion* 2–4 precisely because they agreed on the rest of the book, subsequent interpreters have often focused on these same chapters at the expense of the rest of the book. Not many philosophical critiques of Anselm's "ontological argument" can join Gaunilo in praising the rest of the book for its "profound aroma of devout and holy feeling."[1]

In this chapter we attempt to narrate something of the *Proslogion*'s story, from the initial response of Anselm's contemporary Gaunilo up to present day views. First, we draw attention to various historical and codicological circumstances throughout the medieval and into the early modern era that contributed to the isolation of Anselm's proof for God's existence from the rest of the book. We then chart out some more recent advances that have been made in the interpretation of the *Proslogion*, focusing especially on the French and German literature and situating our effort in the rest of this book in relation to them. Our survey, though not exhaustive, will demonstrate the need for further holistic engagement with the *Proslogion* and, in particular, greater sensitivity to the book's organic development into its climactic vision of the soul's heavenly enjoyment of the Trinity in *Proslogion* 23–26.

---

1. *Pro Insip.* 8, Schmitt 129:21–22.

The Interchange with Gaunilo

As noted above, Gaunilo's response, entitled *Quid Ad Haec Respondeat Quidam Pro Insipiente* ("how someone might reply to these [words] on behalf of the fool," often simply shortened to *Pro Insipiente*), concerned the argument for God's existence in *Proslogion* 2–4. Gaunilo's critique makes a number of points, several of which have been carried over into later discussion of the argument—for instance, his preference for *intelligi* ("understood") over *cogitari* ("thought") in the divine formula[2] or his earlier (accidental?) reshuffling of this formula to *illud omnibus quae cogitari possint maius* ("that which is greater than everything which can be thought").[3] But at the heart of his response appears to be a more basic ambivalence about the inference from God's existence in the mind to his actual existence.[4] He posits his famous "lost island" analogy to demonstrate that one cannot deduce the actual existence of an object on the basis of its possessing maximal greatness.[5] Anselm's *Responsio* deals with Gaunilo's various arguments, and he explicitly points out Gaunilo's misquotation of the divine formula.[6] A number of times his rebuttal focuses on the insight that God is utterly unique in that he cannot be thought not to exist—at one point, Anselm confidently promises to give the famous "lost island" to anyone who can find any other object that his inference applies to other than that than which nothing great can be thought.[7]

But the influence of the Gaunilo-Anselm interaction has not been limited to particular issues involved in the book's argument

---

2. *Pro Insip.* 7, Schmitt 129:11–12.
3. *Pro Insip.* 4, Schmitt 126:30.
4. For instance, *Pro Insip.* 2, Schmitt 125:15–17.
5. *Pro Insip.* 6, Schmitt 128:14–32.
6. *Resp.* 5, Schmitt 134:27–28.
7. *Resp.* 3, Schmitt 133:6–9.

for God's existence. More basically, albeit more subtly, Anselm's interchange with Gaunilo served to generate focus on *Proslogion* 2–4. Anselm's request that Gaunilo's objection and his response be circulated with the book was not completely fulfilled: of the nineteen extant manuscripts that contain *Proslogion* 2–4, nine also contain Gaunilo's *Pro Insipiente* and Anselm's *Responsio*.[8] Nonetheless, in one of the earliest and most significant medieval manuscripts, MS Bodley 271, *Proslogion* 2–4 was recopied at the end of book, immediately preceding *Pro Insipiente* and Anselm's *Responsio*— after having already been included within the earlier 26 chapters. This manuscript, probably written between 1107 and 1114 at Christ Church Priory, Canterbury, possibly in connection with an edition of Anselm's work with which Anselm was involved,[9] thus contains a recapitulation of *Proslogion* 2–4 (with only minor changes in punctuation) at the end the book. The recapitulation is introduced at folio 30 verso, at the top of the left-hand column, with the explanatory text: *explicit Proslogion liber Anselmi Cantuariensis Archiepiscopi* ("[thus] ends the *Proslogion*, the book of Anselm, Archbishop of Canterbury"). It then continues: *sumptum exeodem libello* ("excerpt from the same little book") before launching into the text of *Proslogion* 2–4 once again (*ergo domine*). At the end of the *sumptum*, Gaunilo's *Pro Insipiente* is introduced with the familiar title: *quid adhaec respondeat quidam pro insipiente*.

Schmitt also retains this *sumptum* between *Proslogion* 26 and Gaunilo's *Pro Insipiente* in his critical edition of Anselm's works.[10] Not many other documents in Western literature have had one por-

---

8. McGill, "Gaunilo and Anselm: Criticism and Reply," in *The Many-Faced Argument*, 9.

9. Ian Logan, "Ms Bodley 271: Establishing the Anselm Canon?" *The Saint Anselm Journal* 2 (2004): 67–80. Logan notes that Ms Bodley 271 is virtually identical to the critical edition of Anselm's works produced by Schmitt and suggests that Ms Bodely 271 "represents the closest things we have to a definitive edition of Anselm's works" (*Reading Anselm's "Proslogion,"* 4).

10. Schmitt I 123–24.

[Facsimile of manuscript: Bodleian Libraries, Oxford, MS Bodley 271, fols. 30v-31r]

Note: This and the following image have been used with permission from the Bodleian Libraries, the University of Oxford, Ms Bodley 271, fols. 30v-31r.

tion of text abstracted out of its original context and then repeated later in the text in this manner, and it is not difficult to imagine how such a procedure would influence its subsequent interpretation. The fact that Anselm himself approved of the inclusion of this interchange suggests that its influence in focusing attention on *Proslogion* 2–4 would have been powerful both for those sympathetic to, as well as those skeptical of, Anselm's argument.

These codicological data confirm that it is specifically *Proslogion* 2–4 with which Gaunilo's response was concerned, providing a textual basis for later interpreters to prioritize these chapters above the rest of the book.

THE INTERPRETATION OF THE *PROSLOGION*

Further Isolation of *Proslogion* 2–4 in Medieval and Modern Reception

There appears to have been some neglect of the *Proslogion* following the dispute with Gaunilo, although conventional Anselm scholarship seems to have exaggerated the extent of this neglect.[11] Charlesworth's claim, for instance, probably goes too far but nonetheless makes the point vividly: "St. Anselm's *Proslogion* might have fallen stillborn from the scriptorium for all the influence it had upon his own intellectual milieu."[12] A. Daniels's definitive work on medieval reception of the *Proslogion* argued that it was almost completely neglected in the twelfth century, and even in the thir-

11. As noted by Giles E. M. Gasper and Ian Logan, "Anselm: A Portrait in Refraction," in *Saint Anselm of Canterbury and His Legacy*, ed. Giles E. M. Gasper and Ian Logan, Durham Medieval and Renaissance Monographs and Essays 2 (Durham: Institute of Medieval and Renaissance Studies, 2012), 8, 10–11.

12. Charlesworth, *St. Anselm's "Proslogion,"* 3.

teenth century the argument of chapters 2–4 was extracted from its context and mixed together with a number of other isolated arguments that God's existence is self-evident.[13] There is a growing recognition of the influence of the *Proslogion*, however, already in the twelfth century, particularly in monastic contexts and for devotional purposes.[14] Margaret Healy-Varley argues that the fourteen beatitudes listed in *Proslogion* 25 became a commonplace, even within Anselm's lifetime.[15] Nonetheless, it is surprising how little engagement with the *Proslogion* there was in the generations following Anselm's death. Anselm seems to have had greater influence through his spiritual and devotional writings following his death—there are far more manuscripts of his devotional writings from this time period than of his speculative works. There are also many more spurious, imitative works of a devotional nature than a speculative one.[16]

Part of the reason for this neglect may lie in the fact that in the generations following Anselm's death, the cathedral schools that would eventually become universities made heavy use of florilegia for educational purposes. As Gillian Evans notes, Anselm's works "did not fit the practical teaching needs of the working schools" because they were "not easy to lecture on or to divide up satisfac-

---

13. A. Daniels, "Quellenbeitrage und Untersuchungen zur Geschichte der Gottesbeweise in Dreizehnten Jahrhundert," as summarized in Arthur C. McGill, "Recent Discussions of Anselm's Argument," in *The Many-Faced Argument*, (1967, rpt; Eugene, Ore.: Wipf & Stock, 2009), 33–110, at 38.

14. Margaret Healy-Varley, "Anselm's Fictions and the Literary Afterlife of the *Proslogion*," (PhD diss., Harvard University, 2011). Jay Diehl, "Harmony between Word and World: Anselm of Canterbury, Aelred of Rievaulx and Approaches to Language in Twelfth-Century Monasticism," in *Saint Anselm of Canterbury and His Legacy*, 95–113, explores the influence of Anselm's philosophy of language on tewlfth-century monasticism.

15. Margaret Healy-Varley, "Anselm's Afterlife and the Middle English *De Custodia Interioris Hominis*," in *Saint Anselm of Canterbury and His Legacy*, 241.

16. Gillian Evans, "Anselm's Life, Works, and Immediate Influence," in *Cambridge Companion to Anselm*, 5–31, at 25.

torily for quotation or extract in *florilegium* or commentary."[17] Frequently, however, *Proslogion* 2–4 (often with the interchange with Gaunilo) was isolated from the rest of the work and reproduced in florilegia.[18] In light of this, it is not surprising that the title of the book was occasionally altered in the medieval era from *Proslogion* to *Alloquium de Dei Existentia*, an alternative that occasionally persists today.[19] There is no basis for this title in Anselm's text—the word *alloquium* is used by Anselm in the preface to qualify the meaning of the term *proslogion*, but Anselm nowhere describes the *Proslogion* as a work *de dei existentia*. The insertion of the words *de dei existentia* into the title of the work both reflected and doubtless reinforced the predominance of chapters 2–4 in its legacy.

Later into the medieval period, the *Proslogion* received more attention.[20] However, not only did an interest in the argument of *Proslogion* 2–4 tend to dominate its reception, but the usage of this argument often had a loose grounding in Anselm's text. For instance, Bonaventure's engagement with Anselm's proof for God's existence appears to be working not with the *Proslogion* directly but with citations from its early chapters (along with other works),

---

17. Evans, "Anselm's Life, Works, and Immediate Influence," 24.

18. As noted by Gregory Schufreider, *Confessions of a Rational Mystic: Anselm's Early Writings* (West Lafayette, Ind.: Purdue University Press, 1994), 168. Thomas Williams and Sandra Visser note that the argument of *Proslogion* 2–4 has been perennially "extracted and anthologized" (*Anselm*, Great Medieval Thinkers [Oxford: Oxford University Press, 2009], 73). In addition, Margaret Healy-Varley notes that "Anselm's writings were prone to fragmentation by selective reading, excerption and incomplete transmission" ("Anselm's Afterlife and the Middle English *De Custodia Interioris Hominis*," 244).

19. In many catalogues of Anselm's doctrinal works, the title is still listed as "*Proslogion*" *seu alloquium de Dei existentia*. Thus, it appears, for instance, in Migne's classic collection. More recently, see José Rosa's translation: *Santo Anselmo, "Proslogion" seu Alloquium de Dei existentia* Textos Clássicos de Filosofia (Covilhã: LusoSophia, 2008).

20. For a particularly helpful overview of the historical reception of Anselm's argument, see Logan, *Reading Anselm's "Proslogion*," 149–67.

designed to show that God's existence was self-evident.[21] Bonaventure's treatment of the *Proslogion* does contain a reference to *Proslogion* 5, but it is subsumed into his summary of the proof for God's existence in *Proslogion* 2–4.[22] At times, Anselm's argument appears to have been employed for even broader purposes—for instance, William of Auxerre used Anselm's proof of God's existence to establish God's absolute simplicity in his *Summa Aurea*.[23] Even Aquinas, whose rejection of Anselm's argument was highly influential, was likely interacting not with the text of the *Proslogion* but rather with Bonaventure's use of Anselm's argument.[24] Aquinas's criticism of the argument did not prevent its subsequent rearticulation, but its continued legacy grew more complicated—for instance, John Duns Scotus introduced his own qualifications to the argument, which were carried forth by later thinkers such as William of Ockham.[25]

In the late medieval and Reformation eras, interest in the *Proslogion* tended to wane along with interest in proofs for God's existence more generally. It was René Descartes in the seventeenth century who revived interest in the *Proslogion* by developing his own "ontological argument" (again, this was a subsequent his-

---

21. Donald Dixon Wood, "Anselm's Contribution to Barth's Doctrine of the Knowledge of God," PhD diss., Fuller Theological Seminary, 1974, 72.

22. Bonaventure, *Disputed Questions on the Mystery of the Trinity*, in *Works of St. Bonaventure* III, trans. Zachery Hayes (1979, rpt.; N.Y.: The Franciscan Institute, 2000), 112.

23. Walter Henry Principe, *William of Auxerre's Theology of the Hypostatic Union*, Studies and Texts 7 (Toronto: Pontifical Institute of Mediaeval Studies, 1963), 41. Cf. William's treatment in *Summa Aurea*, included in Principe's text, 293–302.

24. Aquinas, *Summa Theologica* I, Q. 2, Art. 1, 11–12. Cf. Logan, *Reading Anselm's "Proslogion*," 138; Charlesworth, *St. Anselm's "Proslogion*," 4.

25. John Duns Scotus, "The Existence of God," in *John Duns Scotus, Philosophical Writings: A Selection*, ed. and trans. Allan Wolter (Indianapolis: Hackett, 1987), 73–76; William Ockham, "The Proof of God's Existence," in *William Ockham, Philosophical Writings: A Selection*, ed. Stephen F. Brown, trans. Philotheus Boehner (Indianapolis: Heckett, 1990), 125–26; cf. Logan's discussion in *Reading Anselm's "Proslogion*," 146.

torical label).²⁶ Descartes did not interact with Anselm at all; he claimed that he formed his argument independently. But when Johannes Caterus sought to rebut Descartes by appealing to Aquinas's objection to Anselm's argument, the medieval heritage behind Descartes's argument was brought into the discussion. Gottfried Leibniz identified Descartes's argument with Anselm's, arguing that it established that if God is possible, God exists.²⁷ Baruch Spinoza and (later) Christian Wolff soon followed with their own versions of "ontological argument."²⁸ Wolff specifically associated the argument with that of Descartes and Anselm.²⁹

The link between the argument of Anselm and Descartes was thus well established by the time of Immanuel Kant's objection. Although Kant was interacting with Wolff's argument and had little (if any) contact with Anselm,³⁰ his argument was largely considered decisive over all varieties of ontological argument, including Anselm's. Post-Kantian critics of the "ontological argument," such as Schelling and Hegel, often treated the *Proslogion* as a precursor to Descartes. Widespread feeling about the argument could be represented by Arthur Schopenhauer's assertion that, "considered by daylight, however, and without prejudice, this famous Ontological Proof is really a charming joke."³¹ Even those who defended Anselm's argument, however, such as Robert Flint, now considered it one kind of an "ontological argument," clumped together with the arguments of Descartes, Spinoza, etc. Thus, throughout the early modern era, the

26. Descartes, *Meditations on First Philosophy*, 24–36.
27. Gottfried Leibniz, *New Essays on Human Understanding* IV.10.7, ed. and trans. Peter Remnant and Jonathan Bennett, Cambridge Texts in the History of Philosophy (Cambridge: Cambridge University Press), 435–39.
28. Baruch Spinoza, *Ethics*, in *The Collected Works of Baruch Spinoza*, vol. 1, ed. and trans. Edwin Curley (Princeton: Princeton University Press, 1985), 408–46.
29. Logan, *Reading Anselm's "Proslogion,"* 156.
30. Hopkins, *A Companion to the Study of St. Anselm*, 70.
31. Arthur Schopenhauer, "On the Fourfold Root of the Principle of Sufficient Reason and On the Will in Nature," in *The Ontological Argument: From St. Anselm to Contemporary Philosophers*, ed. Alvin Plantinga (Garden City, N.Y.: Anchor Books, 1965), 66.

significance of Anselm's *Proslogion* was often reduced to its proof of God's existence, which was in turn engaged in relation to the family of ontological arguments originating with Descartes.

In sum, the frequent textual isolation of *Proslogion* 2–4 in the medieval era and the association of Anselm with the "ontological argument" of Descartes and others in the modern era have contributed to an overfocus on Anselm's proof for God's existence, so much so that we can appreciate Evans's label for the historical interpretation of the *Proslogion* as "a patchy and piece-meal business."[32]

Advances in Twentieth and Twenty-first Century Reception of the *Proslogion*

Amidst the twentieth-century and early twenty-first-century "Anselm renaissance," interpretation of the *Proslogion* has been decisively reoriented. We might break down the key stages of advance in four phases.[33] First, several German-language studies of the *Proslogion* in the 1930's, most notably those of Karl Barth and Anselm Stolz, advanced "theological" readings of Anselm's text that generated enormous interest in the *Proslogion* and advanced a new range of concerns among its interpreters.[34] Anselm was particularly significant for Barth's theological development. Looking back at his work on Anselm in his 1958 preface to the second edition, Barth stated, "my interest in Anselm was never a side-issue for me.... In this book on Anselm I am working with a vital key, if not the key, to an understanding of that whole process of thought that has im-

---

32. Gillian Evans, *Anselm and Talking about God*, 2.

33. Here I just briefly touch on several major developments as illustrative of more general tendencies. I outline *Proslogion* scholarship more fully, though still not exhaustively, in Gavin Ortlund, "Ascending toward the Beatific Vision: Heaven as the Climax of Anselm's *Proslogion*," PhD diss., Fuller Theological Seminary, 2016.

34. Barth, *Anselm: Fides Quaerens Intellectum*; Anselm Stolz, "Zur Theologie Anselms im *Proslogion*," *Catholica: Vierteljahrschrift fur Kontroverstheologie* II (Paderborn: 1933); Stolz, "'Vere esse' im *Proslogion* des hl. Anselmi," 400–9; Stolz, "Das *Proslogion* des hl. Anselm," 331–47.

pressed me more and more in my *Church Dogmatics* as the only one proper to theology."[35] It is ironic, however, in light of Barth's more comprehensive interest in the *Proslogion*, that his treatment of the *text* is confined chapters 2–4, which he refers to as "the whole passage (*Pros.* 2–4) which is to be regarded as the main text."[36] After all, Barth's stated reason for dissatisfaction with previous interpreters of the *Proslogion* is that they fail to "assess Anselm's Proof of the Existence of God ... within the series of the other Anselmic Proofs, that is, within the general context of his 'proving,' the context of his own particular theological scheme."[37] Barth's admirable effort to read Anselm theologically and contextually was probably not well served by limiting his textual commentary to *Proslogion* 2–4.

Soon after Barth's work, the Benedictine monk Anselm Stolz went even further in protesting against rationalistic interpretations of Anselm. He categorized the *Proslogion* as a fundamentally different kind of project than the *Monologion*, describing it as a work of mystical theology that attempts to attain a vision of God by exploring what is affirmed by faith.[38] Stolz particularly emphasized the programmatic importance of *Proslogion* 1, claiming that it "outlines the plan of the whole work" and faulting even Barth for neglecting it.[39] (Barth had called this chapter a "long introductory invocation," and it had not featured in a central way to his discussion of the *Proslogion*.) Stolz denied that the *Proslogion* contained any proofs of God's existence; rather, *Proslogion* 2–4 serve to establish

---

35. Barth, *Anselm: Fides Quaerens Intellectum*, 11. Even more strongly, in Karl Barth, *Church Dogmatics* II.1, ed. Geoffrey Bromiley and T. F. Torrance, study edition (London: T&T Clark, 2009), 2: "I learned the fundamental attitude to the problem of the knowledge and existence of God ... at the feet of Anselm of Canterbury, and in particular from his proofs of God set out in *Pros.* 2–4."

36. Barth, *Anselm: Fides Quaerens Intellectum*, 8.

37. Barth, *Anselm: Fides Quaerens Intellectum*, 8.

38. Stolz, "Zur Theologie Anselms im *Proslogion*," 2–4. The translations used here are those of Arthur C. McGill, *The Many-Faced Argument*, 183–206. Cf. also Stolz, "'Vere esse' im *Proslogion* des hl. Anselm," 400–9; and Stolz, "Das *Proslogion* des hl. Anselm," 331–47.

39. Stolz, "Zur Theologie Anselms im *Proslogion*," 5.

the *kind* of existence God enjoys, with a view to the *experience* of the one who already believes in Him.[40] Accordingly, he argued, "nothing is more absurd than to see a philosopher in the author of the *Proslogion*."[41] Stolz's work is sometimes dismissed by those who think it obvious that Anselm sought to prove God's existence. But it is not necessary to agree with all of Stolz's larger theological claims in order to benefit from his numerous textual insights, which we will utilize throughout our commentary in the following chapters.

A second advance in the interpretation of the *Proslogion* came during the revival of interest in the ontological argument in philosophical circles during the early 1960's. Charles Hartshorne and Norman Malcolm, in two independent but similar works, popularized a distinction between the argument of chapter 2 and the argument of chapter 3.[42] According to Hartshorne, *Proslogion* 2 was burdened to prove God's existence, while *Proslogion* 3 was concerned with his necessary existence. He called *Proslogion* 2 a "blundering preamble" to the real argument of *Proslogion* 3.[43] Hartshorne believed that weaknesses reflected in the first argument were not present in the second, and many subsequent interpreters have shared this intuition.[44] Generally speaking, this development in the interpretation of the *Proslogion* has been more philosophical than theological, tending to approach Anselm from the angle of the "ontological argument" as a theistic proof, including both its Anselmian and Cartesian streams.[45]

---

40. Stolz, "Zur Theologie Anselms im *Proslogion*," 12–21.

41. Stolz, "Zur Theologie Anselms im *Proslogion*," 6.

42. Malcolm, "Anselm's Ontological Arguments," 41–62; Hartshorne, *The Logic of Perfection*, 28–117.

43. As cited in Logan, *Reading Anselm's "Proslogion*," 180.

44. Similarly, all the way to the present day, drawing from previous publications, Richard Campbell defends Anselm's proof of God's existence by arguing that its critics, ancient and modern, wrongly locate the argument in *Proslogion* 2 (*Rethinking Anselm's Arguments: A Vindication of His Proof of the Existence of God*, Anselm Studies and Texts 1 [Leiden: Brill, 2018]).

45. A good representation of this vein of literature would be Alvin Plantinga,

THE INTERPRETATION OF THE *PROSLOGION*

A third development in the interpretation of the *Proslogion* has come with the gradual development of English-language scholarship in the second half of the twentieth century and early twenty-first century, which has witnessed greater concern for Anselm's medieval context, more sensitivity to his theological method and aims, and subtler analysis of his logic and grammar. If the tendency to approach the *Proslogion* primarily for its proof of God in the middle decades of the twentieth century can be represented by the influential texts of Charlesworth (previously discussed) or Hopkins,[46] English-language scholarship on the *Proslogion* in the 1970's, 1980's, and 1990's witnessed a gradually emerging protest against the isolation of *Proslogion* 2–4, often combined with an interest in particular aspects of Anselm's thought in the work, most notably his theological method. Benedicta Ward emphasized Anselm's monastic context for understanding the *Proslogion*, as well as its meditative and prayerful qualities and the longing for heaven that energizes it.[47] Gillian Evans lamented the tendency for *Proslogion* 2–4 to be

---

The Nature of Necessity (Oxford: Clarendon Press, 1974), 197–98. Here, as well as in subsequent publications, Plantinga develops a modal version of the ontological argument, interacting particularly with Kant's objection.

46. *Anselm of Canterbury: Works*, ed. and trans. Jasper Hopkins and Herbert Richardson, 4 vols. (New York and Toronto: The Edwin Mellen Press, 1974–1976). A number of these translations are revised in the more recent Jasper Hopkins and Herbert Richardson, *Complete Philosophical and Theological Treatises of Anselm of Canterbury* (Minneapolis: Banning Press, 2000). Hopkins's *A Companion to the Study of St. Anselm* is an eloquent and useful introduction to the basic contours of Anselm's thought, following on the heels of this earlier four-volume study. It represents the common trend to engage the *Proslogion* basically for its proof of God's existence (chapter 3), although it also uses the *Proslogion* to explore Anselm's epistemology. Hopkins's preface to his translation (along with Herbert Richardson) of the *Proslogion* also summarizes the significance of the book in terms of its "ontological argument." See Jasper Hopkins and Herbert Richardson, *"Monologion," "Proslogion," and Meditation on Human Redemption*, in *Anselm of Canterbury: Works*, vol. 1, vii–viii.

47. Benedicta Ward, *Anselm of Canterbury: A Monastic Scholar*, Fairacres 62 (Oxford: Sisters of the Love of God, 1973); Benedicta Ward, *The Prayers and Meditations of Saint Anselm with the "Proslogion"* (London: Penguin Books, 1973), 77–81. In her more recent introduction to Anselm's life and legacy, Ward commends the Barth-Stolz interpretation of the *Proslogion* over the rationalist interpretation of

dealt with in isolation, arguing that the if *unum argumentum* were concerned exclusively with *Proslogion* 2–4, then it is difficult to account for the prayer of chapter 1 or the content of chapters 5 and following.[48]

These laments about the interpretation of the *Proslogion*, however, have not generally produced the kind of sustained, integrated analysis that would function to correct this imbalance. *Proslogion* 5–26 get gestured at more than explored. R. A. Herrera's *Anselm's Proslogion: An Introduction*, which appeared in the year in between Evans's two major works, notes how many studies altogether omit later chapters from the *Proslogion*, and he attempts a brief description of the *Proslogion*'s twenty-six chapters in chapter 2 of his book.[49] But his interests appear primarily directed toward the "demonstration proper" (i.e., *Proslogion* 2–4), and he stipulates that it is reasonable to omit certain later chapters of the *Proslogion* from discussion because they "simply carry out a lengthy and at times thematically uninteresting unpacking of 'that-than-which-nothing-greater-can-be-thought' into the domain of the divine attributes."[50] Schufreider's 1994 book, similarly, insists that the book's proof of God's existence is not over after chapters 2–4,[51] but nonetheless devotes his book to *Proslogion* 1–4, in line with his cautionary comment that "we do not want to let the theological issues distract us

---

Étienne Gilson precisely because of its focus on the entirety of the book, as well as its emphasis on the *Proslogion* as a prayer (*Anselm of Canterbury: His Life and Legacy* [London: Society for Promoting Christian Knowledge, 2009], 2). For Ward, the *Proslogion* is "not concerned to 'prove' anything, in a modern sense." Rather, the book is "a prayer of desire and longing, in the best monastic tradition of longing" (25).

48. Gillian R. Evans, *Anselm and Talking about God* (Oxford: Clarendon Press, 1978), 2, 47. She also draws attention to Anselm's stated intention in his preface, suggesting that the book as a whole represents the unfolding of his three stated purposes. Cf. also her *Anselm and a New Generation* (Oxford: Oxford University Press, 1980).

49. Robert A. Herrera, *Anselm's "Proslogion": An Introduction* (Washington D.C.: The Catholic University Press of America, 1979), 73–75.

50. Herrera, *Anselm's "Proslogion,"* 25.

51. Schufreider, *Confessions of a Rational Mystic*, 205.

from our ultimate object of interest, namely, the ontological conception of God."[52]

Twenty-first century English-language scholarship on the *Proslogion* carried these concerns still further. It is now common for introductory texts on Anselm's thought to lament neglect of the later chapters of the *Proslogion*[53] and to engage them in relation to Anselm's method or view of divine attributes.[54] Ian Logan has provided richer textual analysis of the *Proslogion*, as well as a fuller account of the book's history of reception, than have yet appeared in the English language.[55] He, with others, laments the neglect of the work as a whole.[56] Eileen Sweeney traces all of Anselm's works along their development, detecting his search for unity amidst opposites, especially the union of the human soul with God, as the uniting thread amidst seemingly disparate strands of thought.[57] She offers a more penetrating account of the relation of the *Monologion* and *Proslogion*, emphasizing their particular *persona* by which they are both written.[58] Many other examples could be provided to establish that the *Proslogion* is increasingly valued for purposes beyond merely possessing an argument for God's existence; at the same time, engagement with the *Proslogion* 1 and 5–26 still tends to be piecemeal; summations of the whole book are, if present at all, very brief; the logical progression throughout the book remains underexplored; and Anselm's doctrine of heavenly joy at the climax of the book in *Proslogion* 24–25 is neclected.

A fourth development in the interpretation of the Proslogion has arrived with several European texts that have provided surpassing accounts of the *Proslogion*'s unity, direction of thought, and spiritual

---

52. Schufreider, *Confessions of a Rational Mystic*, 209.
53. David S. Hogg, *Anselm of Canterbury: The Beauty of Theology*, Great Theologians Series (Burlington, Vt.: Ashgate, 2004), 2.
54. Williams and Visser, *Anselm*, 3–10.
55. Logan, *Reading Anselm's "Proslogion."*
56. Logan, "'Whoever Understands This …': On Translating the *Proslogion*," 562.
57. Sweeney, *Anselm of Canterbury*, 7–12.
58. Sweeney, *Anselm of Canterbury*, 110–74.

profundity—in particular, the French-language scholarship of Yves Cattin and Paul Gilbert and the German-language work of Siegried Karl (and, to a lesser extent, Georgi Kapriev). Because these works have yet to make significant inroads into the English-language scholarship, we provide a summary of each of them in turn.

Georgi Kapriev (1998)

Georgi Kapriev stipulates at the start of his book that his interest in the *Proslogion* is philosophical.[59] As a result, he defines the focus of his engagement with the *Proslogion* as the celebrated argument of chapters 2–4, although his interest is not this argument in itself so much as this argument as a window into Anselm's broader world of ideas.[60] He notes the long history of dispute concerning the argument of these chapters and the frequent misrepresentation and mistreatment of this argument, arguing that in light of this history the best way to proceed is a careful and word-for-word study of *Proslogion* 2–4.[61] Thus, in his opening statement of the problem his book seeks to address, he reproduces the Latin text of *Proslogion* 2–4.[62]

At the same time, Kapriev denies that Anselm's *unum argumentum* is restricted to these chapters. He regards it as involving the whole *Proslogion*, following Holopainen on the definition of the term *argumentum*.[63] He therefore expressly protests the reduction of Anselm's argument to a proof of God's existence, insisting that "all 26 chapters of the entire text must be taken into account and not merely the traditionally used three chapters."[64] Specifically, he

---

59. Kapriev, *Ipsa Vita et Veritas*, 7–8.
60. Kapriev, *Ipsa Vita et Veritas*, 10.
61. Kapriev, *Ipsa Vita et Veritas*, 13–14.
62. Kapriev, *Ipsa Vita et Veritas*, 14–15.
63. Kapriev, *Ipsa Vita et Veritas*, 172. We will discuss Holopainen on this point in chapter 3.
64. Kapriev, *Ipsa Vita et Veritas*, 171. Earlier he protests the more general restrictive focus upon Anselm in which most of what is written about him is devoted

stipulates that the prayer of chapter 1 is more than "edifying prelude" to the argument but an organic part of the work and that the new formula in chapter 15 is more than a rhetorical move within the book's further development.[65] Ultimately, Kapriev denies that Anselm's aim is to produce an "ontological argument" as such, interpreting the book fundamentally as a search for the origin and boundary of thought. He wants to defend Anselm from the typical charge that his argument leaps from the mere analysis of a concept to its extramental existence.[66] The *Proslogion*, in his view, is not the answer to an externally posed question; rather, it is driven internally by the spiritual desperation of its author.[67] Already in *Proslogion* 1 it is clear that Anselm believes that the highest truth and good can be perceived *sola mente*.[68] Accordingly Anselm's proof of God's existence is not a generic appeal to reason but rather employs reason within the specific context of the only manner that God can be known by humans, through the inward striving of faith.[69] Kapriev believes Anselm has been frequently misportrayed, and so he devotes the fourth and final section of his book to exposing the "imaginary Anselm" (*ausgedachte Anselms*) so often portrayed in the history of philosophical interpretation, both medieval and modern.[70] He believes that Anselm's ultimate goal in the *Proslogion*—and ultimately in all his writings— is to produce Christian wisdom, which is a spiritual faculty beyond every human knowledge or ability.[71]

Surprisingly, at the very climax of his protest against reductionistic readings of Anselm, Kapriev further emphasizes his focus on *Proslogion* 2–4, arguing that these 34 sentences represent Anselm's

---

to the so-called ontological argument (in philosophy) and Anselm's doctrine of satisfaction (in theology) (10).

65. Kapriev, *Ipsa Vita et Veritas*, 15–16.
66. Kapriev, *Ipsa Vita et Veritas*, 309.
67. Kapriev, *Ipsa Vita et Veritas*, 171.
68. Kapriev, *Ipsa Vita et Veritas*, 172–73.
69. Kapriev, *Ipsa Vita et Veritas*, 174–78.
70. Kapriev, *Ipsa Vita et Veritas*, 309–68.
71. Kapriev, *Ipsa Vita et Veritas*, 378–80.

system of thought and that to understand them is to penetrate into "the whole of Anselm" (*das Ganze Anselms*).[72] Accordingly, *Proslogion* 2–4 become the textual focus of the book: after the first introductory section, followed by an examination of Anselm's method and epistemology (section 2), he proceeds into a detailed, line-by-line exploration of the argument of *Proslogion* 2–4, with each sentence numbered and commented on in detail (section 3). It is not clear why, after insisting upon the importance of *Proslogion* 1 and 5–26, Kapriev should then proceed in his actual engagement of the text to focus strictly on *Proslogion* 2–4. Kapriev's important insights into the nature of the *unum argumentum* would likely have been put to better use had they treated *Proslogion* 2–4 less as a window into "the whole of Anselm" and more as a step into the whole of the *Proslogion*. Nonetheless, Kapriev's work offers a substantial contribution to *Proslogion* scholarship, particularly for its insights into Anselm's use of faith and reason, its emphasis on the spiritual subcurrent of the *Proslogion*, and its protest against traditional philosophical readings of Anselm's arguments.

Yves Cattin (1980s–1990s)[73]

Cattin's work is virtually unknown in the English-speaking world. Even the most thorough and careful studies of Anselm rarely mention it.[74] Yet Cattin's work yields a number of unique insights about the *Proslogion* that are all the more important to summarize here because they cut against the grain of the typical readings of the work. In chapter 4 we will also return to further, more detailed engagement with Cattin as we explore the structure of the *Proslogion*.

72. Kapriev, *Ipsa Vita et Veritas*, 16. Corbin also engages *Proslogion* 2–4 in its 34 distinct sentences, divided into six larger sections (*Anselme*, 91–145).

73. Cattin, *La preuve de Dieu*; Cattin, "La prière de S Anselme dans le *Proslogion*," 373–96; Cattin, "Dieu d'amour, Dieu de colère," 423–50.

74. For instance, Logan's book on the *Proslogion*, despite its rich historical overview of the reception of the book, makes no mention of Cattin in the text or bibliography.

Cattin opens his book expressing his regard for the entire *Proslogion* and lamenting that, in most interpretations of the book, chapters 2–4 tend to dominate the focus:

> We willingly recognize that these three chapters are essential. But the *Proslogion* is not a work that limits itself only to establishing a proof of the existence of God, it is a genuine treatise "on God" (*veritable traite "De Deo"*). And even if one is interested only in the proof of the existence of God, one has no chance of entering the meaning of the Anselm's argument in chapters 2–4, unless one includes a study of the entire *Proslogion*, possibly even situating this study within the whole works of Anselm. Also one must study these chapters in relation to the entire argument of Anselm in the *Proslogion*.[75]

In his later publications, Cattin furthers this complaint of the neglect of the *Proslogion*'s later chapters, devoting his efforts to analyze specific portions of the later text, such as the relation of divine mercy and justice in *Proslogion* 6–11.[76] Cattin perceives "a certain injustice in the history of thought toward Anselm of Canterbury" in the broader reception of Anselm's works, on account of the dominance of his satisfaction theory of atonement and ontological argument over other aspects of his legacy.[77] But an even more serious problem in the interpretation of Anselm, for Cattin—at least in its consequences—is that so many commentators skim lightly over the text, rather than performing a work of thorough exegesis. Therefore, they find evidence for their own particular interpretation of Anselm here or there, rather than submit their interpretations to the entirety of what Anselm has written. As a result, according to Cattin, Anselm is "at once very well known and completely unrecognized."[78]

Cattin agrees with Karl Barth that Anselm is fundamentally a theologian, and thus the *Proslogion* must be interpreted first and

---

75. Cattin, *La preuve de Dieu*, II. All translations of French and German texts throughout are my own.
76. Cattin, "Dieu d'amour, Dieu de colère," 423–50.
77. "La prière de S Anselme dans le *Proslogion*," 373.
78. Cattin, *La preuve de Dieu*, III: "à la fois très connu et tout à fait méconnu."

foremost theologically.[79] Like Barth, he believes that the vitality and richness of Anselm's thought far exceeds what most studies see in it.[80] Nonetheless, like Stolz, Cattin sees the *Proslogion* as involving a kind of mystical theology. He calls the work "the speculative translation of a lived experience, at once reflecting research and the testimony of faith."[81] Part of what accounts for the unique juxtapositions of the *Proslogion* is the profound religious experience that the book aims to express. He identifies three aspects to the book, philosophical, theological, and mystical, but he argues that "the mystical aspect, the testimony in and for faith, does not locate itself at the same level as these other aspects."[82] While the book's philosophical and theological aspects appear directly in its content, "the mystical aspect translates itself especially at the level of language and literary form."[83] Elsewhere, Cattin stresses the role of love and desire in Anselm's thought[84] and raises protests against the tendency of interpreters to divorce his rigorous argumentation from the living faith (*foi vivante*) that undergirds it.[85]

Perhaps Cattin's greatest contribution to the interpretation of the *Proslogion* lies in a number of insights into the structure of the book, a topic to which he devotes considerable space.[86] Cattin considers the style and structure of the *Proslogion* to be essential in order to determine its genre. He claims that the book is "extremely diverse" (*extrêmement diverse*) in that it is both spontaneous and yet also highly structured.[87] Cattin suggests that the prayer of *Proslogion* 1 initiates a section that continues essentially until chap-

---

79. Cattin, *La preuve de Dieu*, 139–40.
80. Cattin, *La preuve de Dieu*, 206.
81. Cattin, *La preuve de Dieu*, 129. Cf. the similar emphasis in "La prière de S Anselme dans le *Proslogion*," 373.
82. Cattin, *La preuve de Dieu*, 130.
83. Cattin, *La preuve de Dieu*, 130.
84. Cattin, "Dieu d'amour, Dieu de colère," 450.
85. Cattin, "La prière de S Anselme dans le *Proslogion*," 373–74.
86. Cattin, *La preuve de Dieu*, 8–59.
87. Cattin, *La preuve de Dieu*, II.

ter 13. Then, in chapter 14, Anselm considers the result of his searching and launches into another prayer, patterned after the same style as that of chapter 1, which initiates a section that continues until chapter 23.[88] Cattin thus sees a similar basic structure to the *Proslogion* as Stolz, emphasizing *Proslogion* 14 as the most significant transition within the book. Whereas Stolz saw in the *Proslogion* two thirteen-chapter halves, Cattin appears to perceive *Proslogion* 23 as the terminus of the prayer initiated in *Proslogion* 14, then claiming that "the final three chapters, 24–26, are at once both successive meditation (24–25) and prayer (26)."[89] Cattin also draws attention to what he calls the "double structure" in *Proslogion* 1, 14, and 24–25—those chapters where Anselm speaks both to himself and God. For Cattin, therefore, it is not merely the content but also the literary patterns and structure of the *Proslogion* that indicate that Anselm's purpose is broader than simply proving God's existence.[90]

Following the observation of F. S. Schmitt, Cattin detects two distinct styles in the Latin text of the *Proslogion*: (1) a more "objective" prose, tightly ordered and designed to translate with precision the logical labor of his work; and (2) a "poetical" style characterized by parallelisms, the constant joy of antithesis, and an abundance of "sparkling images" (*images chatoyantes*).[91] He identifies as characterized by this latter, more poetical style all of *Proslogion* 1; *Proslogion* 9 lines 20–48; *Proslogion* 14 lines 25–46; *Proslogion* 16 lines 9–20; all of *Proslogion* 17; *Proslogion* 23 lines 1–27; *Proslogion* 24 lines 8–19; *Proslogion* 25 lines 1–54; and *Proslogion* 26 lines 22–48.[92] For Cattin, the location of these different styles is not accidental or arbitrary but deliberate and strategic to Anselm's purpose—in

88. Cattin, *La preuve de Dieu*, 9.
89. Cattin, *La preuve de Dieu*, 9. Elsewhere, as we will discuss in chapter 4, Cattin will identify three stages of prayer in the *Proslogion*, chapters 1, 14–18, and 24–26, at the beginning, middle, and end of the book, respectively ("La prière de S Anselme dans le *Proslogion*," 377).
90. Cattin, *La preuve de Dieu*, 9–10.
91. Cattin, *La preuve de Dieu*, 13.
92. Cattin, *La preuve de Dieu*, 14–15.

particular, Cattin is interested in how these different styles relate to the two different forms he detects in the *Proslogion*, the "*allocutive*" and "*impersonnelle.*"[93] What is strikingly absent, as he notes, is the lack of a relationship between the *impersonelle* and the poetic. The *allocutive*, by contrast, is often objective. As a consequence of this, Cattin posits the presence of three stages in the *Proslogion*, not chronological, but structural:

1. personal form + objective prose
2. impersonal form + personal form + objective style
3. impersonal form + personal form + objective style + poetic style[94]

The upshot of all this is a more deliberate and incremental structure in the *Proslogion* than is commonly detected. Cattin detects three fundamental movements within the *Proslogion*:

1. *Proslogion* 2–4: The existence of God (*L'existence de Dieu*)
2. *Proslogion* 5–22: The being of God (*L'être de Dieu*)
3. *Proslogion* 23: The Trinity (*Dieu un et Trine*)

Section 2 is subdivided into two further subsections: the first step (chapters 5–12) and second step (chapters 13, 18–22), with chapters 14–17 set within as a "reflexive rupture"[95] within this second step. Chapter 1 is then set apart as a general introduction (*introduction générale*) and chapters 24–26 as general conclusion (*conclusion générale*), both of which are indented and set outside the three larger sections (2–4, 5–22, and 23). Cattin then examines in more detail the "poetic" parts of the *Proslogion*: chapters 1, 9, 14, 16, 17–18, 24–25.[96] His analysis of the final three chapters, just one paragraph in length, emphasizes their speculative character.[97]

---

93. Cattin, *La preuve de Dieu*, 16.
94. Cattin, *La preuve de Dieu*, 16.
95. Cattin, *La preuve de Dieu*, 47–48.
96. Cattin, *La preuve de Dieu*, 50–55.
97. Cattin, *La preuve de Dieu*, 54.

Cattin has provided a massive contribution to the interpretation of the *Proslogion*, particularly with respect to its structure, as well as the various levels of "style" and "form" that are operative within it. Many of his insights are unparalleled in other literature on Anselm's book and reflect a studied insight into the Latin text. Nonetheless, for all its insights into *Proslogion* 5–23, Cattin's work falls short of providing a commanding interpretation of the book *as a whole* insofar as *Proslogion* 1 and *Proslogion* 24–26 are set in the background and exert minimal influence in the interpretation of the significance of the book. From Cattin's account of the *Proslogion* it is not clear how Anselm's reflection on the *visio dei* in *Proslogion* 24–26 provides a fitting resolution to the book, and one wonders if many of Cattin's insights into the structure of the book could have carried him further into an analysis of these chapters.[98] For example, it is not clear why, in his summary of the first word of each chapter, Cattin has passed over the important term *coniectatio* in *Proslogion* 24 and listed instead the next words, *Quale et quantum*.[99] His insight into the significance of the chapter titles with respect to the structure of the book is an important contribution to *Proslogion* scholarship, but in this case he may not have followed this insight consistently. One wonders, more generally, if it is possible to see the prayer of *Proslogion* 14 as realized in *Proslogion* 23— and if such an interpretation is not in danger of slicing off as peripheral those openings and concluding chapters that in fact bookend the whole movement of the text. More needs to be said regarding how Cattin's important contribution can be taken up into a more comprehensive account of the entire *Proslogion*. We will return to engagement with Cattin's work particularly in chapters 4–5.

---

98. This is similar to the challenge represented by Mackey, who briefly attempts a holistic reading of the *Proslogion* but ultimately slices off *Proslogion* 23–26 as a mere "denouement of sorts" that requires no further discussion or analysis (*Peregrinations of the Word: Essays in Medieval Philosophy* [Ann Arbor, Mich.: University of Michigan Press, 2000], 93–100, at 99). Cf. my discussion at the start of chapter 5.

99. Cattin, *La preuve de Dieu*, 19.

Paul Gilbert (1980s–1990s)[100]

The scholarship of Paul Gilbert, like that Yves Cattin, has been almost completely overlooked in the English-speaking world.[101] In his 1986 article, Gilbert lamented the restrictive focus on the "ontological argument" in Anselm studies, noting that this famous argument actually fills only three pages of Schmitt's entire critical edition.[102] He calls for a new approach to the *Proslogion*, one that is more respectful to its size and design and more careful to situate each of its themes in relation to whole work.[103] For Gilbert, neglect of the broader text of the *Proslogion* is related to various misrepresentations of Anselm's broader thought, particularly the depiction of divine justice in *Cur Deus Homo*. He sought to resolve the apparent tension between divine mercy and justice in Anselm's thought by correlating *Proslogion* 5–11 to the parallel chapters in the *Monologion* and analyzing them in relation to Anselm's broader writings.[104]

But Gilbert's interest is broader than just *Proslogion* 5–11. In subsequent publications, particularly his 1990 monograph, Gilbert continued his lament of the restrictive focus on *Proslogion* 2–4. Like Cattin, he drew attention to the relatively small amount of space Anselm's proof takes up in the book, noting that *Proslogion* 2–4 occupy only 50 lines in Schmitt's critical edition, with an average of eleven words per line (excluding the titles).[105] He claimed that despite the abundance of works treating the "ontological argument,"

---

100. Paul Gilbert, "Justice et miséricorde dans le *Proslogion* de saint Anselme,"; Gilbert, *Le "Proslogion" de S. Anselme: Silence de Dieu et joie de l'homme*; Gilbert, "Entrez dans la joie: les ch. 24 à 26 du *Proslogion*." Gilbert has also written several works that are not specifically on the *Proslogion*.

101. Several of Gilbert's works are listed in Jasper Hopkins's thorough bibliography, and one of his articles is in Sweeney's, but beyond that it is difficult to discern any awareness or engagement with his work in the English-language texts on Anselm.

102. Gilbert, "Justice et miséricorde," 218.
103. Gilbert, "Justice et miséricorde," 218.
104. Gilbert, "Justice et miséricorde," 219, 237–38.
105. Gilbert, *Le "Proslogion" de S. Anselme*, 7.

the *Proslogion* itself is a relatively unknown work and studies that treat Anselm's work merely for its proof of God's existence result in a very superficial understanding of Anselm's thought.[106] The ultimate aim of the *Proslogion*, for Gilbert, is not the mere affirmation of God's existence but "the demand for a greater participation in the divine life."[107]

For Gilbert, the *Proslogion* concerns the most fundamental questions of human existence—questions pertaining not only to the furthest limits of human thought but also to the deepest desires of human love. For Gilbert, our lives, in both thought and desire, are conducted under a sense of divine transcendence—and the *Proslogion* engages its readers at this deep, existential level. Gilbert emphasizes that the subject matter of the *Proslogion* ultimately transcends human language and understanding, although he will later put strictures upon Stolz's "mystical" reading of Anselm as too dominated by modern categories.[108] Nonetheless, for Gilbert, studying the *Proslogion* requires more than intellectual abilities and is ultimately a spiritual exercise, drawing us into the silent and secret desire of humanity.[109]

Because of the dominance of interest in the so-called ontological argument, Gilbert notes, "the entirety of the *Proslogion* has almost never been studied for itself."[110] Interestingly, Gilbert cites as one exception Cattin's *Le preuve de Dieu*, which he calls "completely excellent and accurate" (*tout à fait excellent et précis*) before faulting Cattin for reading the entire *Proslogion* in order to interpret the "ontological argument."[111] This is a revealing comment with respect to where Gilbert understands his own work to surpass Cattin's. For Gilbert, the *Proslogion* must be interpreted *on its own terms*. It is

---

106. Gilbert, *Le "Proslogion" de S. Anselme*, back cover.
107. Gilbert, *Le "Proslogion" de S. Anselme*, 7: "la demande d'un plus grande participation à la vie divine."
108. Gilbert, *Le "Proslogion" de S. Anselme*, 8, 32–33.
109. Gilbert, *Le "Proslogion" de S. Anselme*, 8–9.
110. Gilbert, *Le "Proslogion" de S. Anselme*, 7.
111. Gilbert, *Le "Proslogion" de S. Anselme*, 7n2.

therefore insufficient to widen our focus to *Proslogion* 1 and *Proslogion* 5–26 if we do so simply to better understand *Proslogion* 2–4. It is debatable whether Cattin actually does this, and it is a bit surprising that Gilbert only mentions Cattin once more in the book, for a brief supportive quotation in a footnote.[112] His more consistent dialogue partners are Karl Barth, Anselm Stolz, Étienne Gilson, and Henri Bouillard.

Gilbert's work deals much with the structure of the *Proslogion*. He seeks to go through the text of the *Proslogion* step by step, arguing that the entire work represented the overflow of Anselm's famous formula, "that than which nothing greater can be conceived." He draws special attention to the divine attributes as they unfold in the *Proslogion*.[113] He also highlights the book's destination of the joy of heaven, claiming that this ending flavors the entire work.[114] His work proceeds in five stages, corresponding to his five-fold division of the structure of the *Proslogion*:

1. Anselm's method, especially as the preface and *Proslogion* 1 compare to the *Monologion*.
2. The "ontological argument" of *Proslogion* 2–4.
3. The divine essence in *Proslogion* 5–12, especially the mercy and justice of God.
4. *Proslogion* 13–22, especially God's eternality.
5. *Proslogion* 23–26, with their discussion of Trinity as the happiness and joy of humanity.[115]

Gilbert calls this fourth section on divine eternality, *Proslogion* 13–22, the "real center" (*centre réel*) of the book. The new divine name given in *Proslogion* 15 is especially important to his interpretation of the structure of the book.[116]

---

112. Gilbert, *Le "Proslogion" de S. Anselme*, 245.
113. Gilbert, *Le "Proslogion" de S. Anselme*, 111–94.
114. Gilbert, *Le "Proslogion" de S. Anselme*, 197–242.
115. Gilbert, *Le "Proslogion" de S. Anselme*, 8.
116. Gilbert, *Le "Proslogion" de S. Anselme*, 8.

In his 1995 article, Gilbert went further in his exploration of the conceptual organization of the final chapters of the *Proslogion*.[117] Interpreting them as a meditation on the spiritual fulfillment of humankind, he argued that in these chapters Anselm expresses in ethical terms what is expressed earlier in the book in theoretical terms. Gilbert suggested that the entire work could be understood as a dialectic outgrowth from the idea of perfection.[118]

Gilbert has provided a great service in advancing understanding of the structure of Anselm's book. No previous work provided such as a thorough, step-by-step analysis of the structure of the *Proslogion*. Furthermore, Gilbert's work contains many unparalleled insights into the logical development and overarching meaning of the book, particularly in the heightening of both tone and content that occurs from the earlier portions of the book (what I regard as continuing through *Proslogion* 13, and what he regards as continuing through *Proslogion* 12) to the middle and later portions of the book. Gilbert's work contains an even stronger emphasis than Cattin's on the unified nature of the entire *Proslogion*.[119] We will be engaging with Gilbert's work throughout chapters 4 and 5, thereby consistently benefitting from his insights.

At the same time, on a few points we will seek to go beyond Gilbert. In the first place, in Gilbert's account of the structure of the *Proslogion*, he places so much emphasis on the new divine formula in *Proslogion* 15 as the "axis" (*l'axe*) of the book that the surrounding material in the middle section of the book tends to get filtered through this insight. It is not clear that Anselm intended as much of a disjunction between *Proslogion* 12 and *Proslogion* 13 as Gilbert's structure implies; and one wonders if the controlling influence Gilbert allows for the new divine formula in *Proslogion* 15 at times downplays the significance of the recapitulative prayers of *Proslogion* 14 and 18. This becomes especially clear in his comparison of

117. Gilbert, "Entrez dans la joie," 239–59.
118. Gilbert, "Entrez dans la joie," 239.
119. Gilbert, *Le "Proslogion" de S. Anselme*, 197.

the structure of the *Monologion* and the *Proslogion* later on, which we will engage at some length in chapter 4. In terms of the book's overarching themes, Gilbert's exegesis of *Proslogion* 24–26 contains many helpful insights, and he does make efforts to relate this section to the preceding flow of the book.[120] At the same time, he tends to give this section of the book less emphasis than the earlier parts of the book on divine eternality. In later chapters we will go further to suggest that the heavenly beatific vision is a more fitting apex to the book than divine eternality.

Siegried Karl (2014)

Siegfried Karl's 2014 tome *Ratio und Affectus* explores the relation of reason and affect in human knowledge of God, particularly as seen through Anselm's *Prayers and Meditations* and his *Proslogion*.[121] This focus, essentially the analysis of the nature and role religious feeling, is the driving interest by which he approaches the *Proslogion* and Anselm more generally. He emphasizes that for Anselm, in contrast to modern philosophy, religious feeling and reason are harmonious.[122] The *Proslogion* is explored in the third section of his book (Part C).[123] Karl characterizes the *Proslogion* as "entirely a spiritual exercise"; its employment of rational argumentation is entirely to this end, and it is therefore inseparable from prayerful meditation.[124] Karl argues that the deepest impulse driving Anselm's *unum argumentum* is the deep existential need for God within fallen humanity,[125] as articulated by Anselm in his state of sinful need in

---

120. For instance, Gilbert does observe at one point that the final four chapters of the *Proslogion* fulfill the desires of the first chapter (*Le "Proslogion" de S. Anselme*, 197).

121. E.g., Karl, *Ratio und Affectus: Zum Verhältnis von Vernunft und Affekt in den Orationes sive Meditationes und im Proslogion Anselms von Canterbury (1033/4–1109)* (Rome: Studia Anselmiana, 2014), xxi, li–liii. I am grateful to Eileen Sweeney for directing my attention to Karl's work.

122. E.g., Karl, *Ratio und Affectus*, 1007.

123. Karl, *Ratio und Affectus*, 721–1006.

124. Karl, *Ratio und Affectus*, 1005.

125. E.g., Karl, *Ratio und Affectus*, 736.

Proslogion 1.[126] Significantly for our purposes, Karl devotes the final section of his treatment of the *Proslogion* to the fulfillment of human desire in the heavenly knowledge of God in *Proslogion* 24–26.[127] For Karl, it is the beatific vision, lost in *Proslogion* 1 and regained in *Proslogion* 24–26, that provides the basic orientation for the book. The goal of the whole *Proslogion*, he states, is the perfect unity of knowledge, love, and affection that Anselm achieves at the end of the book, which fulfills both the intellectual and affective aspects of his pursuit of God. The *Proslogion* is therefore a fundamentally concerned with the fulfillment of religious desire in the possession of the being of God as the highest good.[128] Karl even emphasizes the communal nature of heavenly joy, which grounds the incomprehensible magnitude of heavenly joy in the perfect charity that is shared among the countless saints and angels.[129]

Karl's work is a monumental contribution to the understanding of Anselm's epistemology and anthroplogy, surpassing most treaments of his *Prayers and Meditations* and *Proslogion* in its depth of analysis. In particular, it is one of the few studies to take seriously Anselm's aim in the *Proslogion* to rise to the heavenly vision of God and the significance of chapters 24–26 as the achievement of this end. However, Karl's engagement with the *Proslogion* tends to orbit around his anthropological interests, particularly the interplay of human affect and reason in relation to the divine, and so the discussion frequently turns back to these concerns rather than textual considerations. Related to this, Karl places less emphasis on the topical development throughout the *Proslogion*, particularly in terms of the content of its middle portions. On the whole, while Karl's work is an invaluable account of the *Proslogion* as an expression of religious feeling and desire, it shows less interest in the content of the *Proslogion* that falls outside of the scope of this theme.

---

126. E.g., Karl, *Ratio und Affectus*, 790–92.
127. Karl, *Ratio und Affectus*, 735–36, 971–1006.
128. Karl, *Ratio und Affectus*, 972.
129. Karl, *Ratio und Affectus*, 990–92.

Furthermore, it runs the risk of being ignored in the English-speaking world—it was published too recently to tell whether this will be the case, but most of the other untranslated German, French, and Italian works on Anselm have had little impact on English-language interpretation of the *Proslogion*. More work needs to be done in the establishment of a holistic reading of the *Proslogion*, though Karl's insights will be useful to this end. Here we will interface with Karl throughout our engagement with the text of the *Proslogion*, particularly in chapter 4, where we offer a different sketch of the structure of the book than Karl, and also in chapter 5 throughout our commentary on *Proslogion* 24–26.

Conclusion: Toward a Holistic Reading

None of our comments are intended to detract from the real progress that has been made in the interpretation of the *Proslogion* amidst the "Anselm renaissance" beginning in the twentieth century. There is a vast difference between reading the *Proslogion* one hundred years ago versus reading it now on the heels of Schmitt's critical labors, Barth's theological employment of Anselm, the revival of interest in the ontological argument, Henry's analysis of Anselm's use of logic, Southern's biographical work, Evans's detailed concordance, Jaspers's thorough bibliography, the colossal contribution of the French scholars (not limited to Cattin and Gilbert), Logan's careful textual analysis, Sweeney's synthesizing interpretative work, and now Karl's study. The present study benefits from all this scholarship and seeks to follow in its overall pathway, particularly with respect to the work of Gilbert and Karl in approaching the *Proslogion* both as in its entirety and as a theological text.

Nonetheless, the logical development of the *Proslogion* leading into its concluding focus on heaven remains underexplored. Only Karl gives *Proslogion* 24–26 sizeable attention, and his interest is heavily toward the role of human reason and desire rather than

book's development; Cattin and Gilbert, in emphasizing the later portions of the book, place the emphasis on *Proslogion* 5–23 more than *Proslogion* 24–26 (especially Cattin). Gilbert emphasized the importance of *Proslogion* 13–22, especially the role of divine eternality in *Proslogion* 18–22; Cattin saw *Proslogion* 23 as the real climax of the book, with *Proslogion* 1 and *Proslogion* 24–26 as more background, introductory and concluding chapters. Now, it should be acknowledged that chapter 23 does represent an important turn in the book's overall development, with its introduction of the Trinity as the highest good for the soul. Nor should the recurring significance of divine eternality, as emphasized by Gilbert, be diminished. Nonetheless, these interpretations run the risk of making the same error as the (more common) isolation of *Proslogion* 2–4 in that they still do not end where Anselm ends. Anselm's terminating interest is not merely the identification of the Trinity as *unum bonum* in *Proslogion* 23 but the *application* of this reality to the human soul's deepest desire in the succeeding chapters. It is only here, in these final chapters of the book, that Anselm's yearning prayers from the early chapters of the *Proslogion* are finally resolved. The *Proslogion* is ultimately concerned with the divine nature (*Proslogion* 5–23) for the same reason it is concerned with divine existence (*Proslogion* 2–4): in order to participate in the divine beatitude (*Proslogion* 24–26, as the answer to *Proslogion* 1). In its most inner and driving interests, it is not a speculative exploration of God's being or attributes but, rather, a spiritual meditation on these themes as the ultimate human endeavor (in Gilbert's language, *le destin de l'homme*).[130]

---

130. Gilbert, *Le "Proslogion" de S. Anselme*, 243.

CHAPTER 3

The Purpose of the *Proslogion*

Excitatio and *Argumentum* in Chapters 1–4

> Anselm says, "I want to prove the existence of God. To that end I ask God to strengthen and help me"—but that is surely a much better proof of the existence of God, namely, the certainty that to prove it we need God's help. If we were able to prove the existence of God, without his help, that would be as if it were less certain that he were out there.
>
> —SØREN KIERKEGAARD

Sometime around 1086, Anselm wrote a letter to Hugh the Hermit, responding to Hugh's request for help in cultivating the happiness of heaven. After expressing his respect for Hugh as ultimately better qualified to answer this question, Anselm identified love as the central reality of heaven. The love between God and his people unites them together in one will, and the perfect happiness of heaven consists in this union of will.[1] To attain this love, we must empty our hearts of all other loves and "eagerly pursue heavenly things with prayers, conversations, and thoughts."[2] At the conclusion of the letter, he then wrote:

---

1. *Ep.* 112, Schmitt III 245:26–34.
2. *Ep.* 112, Schmitt III 246:62–63.

THE PURPOSE OF THE *PROSLOGION*

I have related these things to you briefly, dearest one, just as you asked; but your prudence will be able to bring forth many more things in their explanation than I have said. If, however, your holiness should desire to read something longer written by me about the fullness of eternal blessedness (*plenitudine beatitudinis aeternae*), you will be able to find this at the end of my little book which is called *Proslogion*, where I investigated fullness of joy [*pleno gaudio*].[3]

The fact that he directs Hugh to this passage at the end of the *Proslogion* suggests its significance to Anselm's doctrine of heaven. Nonetheless, we might inquire why Anselm's definitive teaching on the subject of heaven should come—of all places—at the end of the *Proslogion*. How does the *gaudium plenum* with which Anselm concludes the *Proslogion* relate to the earlier portions of the book and to Anselm's broader understanding of heaven as governed by love?

In this chapter we explore the purpose of Anselm's writing the *Proslogion*, against the backdrop we have painted in chapter 1 of Anselm's broader theological practice. We will argue that what is most intrinsic to Anselm's purpose in the *Proslogion* is his longing to be drawn up into that complete love for God that he commends to Hugh as the essence of the joy of heaven. Although the argument for God's existence in chapters 2–4 is an important part of the *Proslogion*, in relation to the entire *Proslogion* it is only the first step in a larger sweep of argument and prayer in which Anselm is ultimately concerned with *plenitudine beatitudinis aeternae*. Everything in the *Proslogion* plays a role in identifying God as the *gaudium plenum* for which the human soul longs—this and nothing else is its organizing purpose.

To attain a deeper understanding of Anselm's purpose in writing the *Proslogion*, we will first survey the historical circumstances

---

3. *Ep.* 112. Schmitt III 246:73–77. I have rendered *pleno gaudio* "fullness of joy," as opposed to, e.g., Fröhlich's "complete joy," in order to make the connection to *gaudium plenum* in *Proslogion* 26 visible (cf. Fröhlich, *The Letters of Saint Anselm of Canterbury*, vol. 1, 270).

that led to his writing it. This will involve particular attention to what Anselm describes as the purpose of the book in its *prooemium*, as well as the relationship between the *Proslogion* and the *Monologion*. Since Anselm considered the *Proslogion* to be drawn out of the earlier arguments of the *Monologion*, we cannot properly appraise the *Proslogion* without a consideration of this larger sweep of events in which the book came about. Second, we will analyze *Proslogion* 1, Anselm's important introductory chapter (longer than any of the 25 following chapters), giving careful attention to what Anselm himself establishes as his aims and method here at the start of the book. We will draw out three implications with respect to how the tension that drives *Proslogion* 1—Anselm's longing to see God but his inability to do so because of sin—bears upon the question of the book's purpose. Finally, we will explore *Proslogion* 2–4, suggesting that the particular species of "ontological argument(s)" we find in these chapters can only be accounted for in relation to the larger context of the book, particularly its spiritual and meditative qualities. We will conclude by drawing some implications for how the purpose of the *Proslogion* should compel us towards more holistic readings of the book.

The *Prooemium*: What Led Anselm to Write the *Proslogion*

The *prooemium* to the *Proslogion* was written after the work was completed, as an explanation of why it was written, and, particularly, how it came about in relation to the *Monologion*. Containing thus the benefit of hindsight, it is particularly important for shedding light on Anselm's own understanding of the purpose and nature of his work, particularly how it is related to the *Monologion*. Anselm opens the preface by explaining that since the *Monologion* was comprised of "an argument connected by the chaining together of many things" (*multorum concatenatione contextum argumentum*), after its publication he began to search for one argument (*unum argumentum*) by which he might establish the same claims as the *Monologion*. This explanation of purpose already establishes a close material relation between the *Monologion* and the *Proslogion*, which we will explore more below.

Anselm then delineates three distinct aims of his *unum argumentum*: "to prove that God truly is, that he is the highest good (*summum bonum*) needing no other and that which all things need for their being and well-being, and whatever else we believe about the divine substance."[4] Several observations of this important statement of purpose are in order. In the first place, in Anselm's context the verb "to prove"[5] does not strictly signify a process of rational justification, as in a syllogism, which moves from premises to conclusion—it is commonly used in a less technical way to simply mean to examine or judge.[6] Although Barth probably goes too far in limiting *probare* as the justification of certain presuppositions of Anselm's faith, he is right that in Anselm's own experience as well as in his stated method, *probare* follows rather than precedes *intelligere*.[7] Anselm's effort at *probare*, in other words, occurs within his already-established project of *fides quaerens intellectum*, not outside of it as its justification. Second, *Deus vere est*, both here and throughout the *Proslogion*, is better translated "God truly is" than "God really is" (as is reflected in most translations of the identical phrase in the title of chapter 2).[8] In Anselm's context, *vere est* was a technical term due to the influence of Augustine, who used *vere*

---

4. *P Prooemium*, Schmitt I 93:7–9.

5. Here as a future passive participle *probandum*.

6. We have already drawn attention to the significant influence of Boethius on Anselm's use of logic. For further discussion, see Marcia Colish, who suggests that there are four aspects of logic that Anselm probably derived from Boethius: paronyms (i.e., denominative naming), modal propositions, hypothetical syllogisms, and negative formulations (*Medieval Foundations of the Western Intellectual Tradition, 400–1400*, The Yale Intellectual History of the West [New Haven, Conn., and London: Yale University Press, 1997], 167.

7. Barth, *Anselm: Fides Quaerens Intellectum*, 14.

8. Cf. Hogg, who argues for "truly" rather than "really" based upon the 20 uses of the word through the *Proslogion* (*Anselm of Canterbury*, 91–92).

esse and its cognates hundreds of times in his writings to signify the nature of divine existence.[9] Translating *vere* in this phrase "truly" rather than "really" may initially seem like a subtle distinction, but it is important insofar as it throws the emphasis on the nature rather than the strict fact of God's existence. *Vere*, in other words, is not a mere intensification of *est* but a qualification of it: Anselm is not merely emphasizing God's existence here but describing it.

The second clause in Anselm's purpose statement confirms that Anselm's interests in the *Proslogion* are indeed broader than the mere fact of God's existence. Here he includes within the purview of the *unum argument* the fact that God "is the highest good needing no other and that which all things need for their being and well-being."[10] This is an assertion of God's unique self-sufficiency as well as of his instrumentality as the source of all other being. Anselm states this first negatively, in terms of the absence of God's need for anything else, and then positively, in terms of the need all other things have for God. Anselm's assertion in this second purpose clause that all other things depend upon God—not only in order to exist (*sint*) but also in order to exist well or be happy (*bene sint*) will take on greater significance as he proceeds throughout the *Proslogion*, in light of continual identification of God as the source of human happiness. It also reflects Anselm's emphasis on God as the answer to human happiness in *Monologion* 64–80—for instance, at the close of the book, where Anselm draws as a consequence of God's supreme greatness that "without him it goes well (*bene*) for nothing."[11] In Anselm's thinking, creaturely happiness is just as dependent upon God as creaturely existence, and thus throughout the *Proslogion* he will continually correlate his soul's desire for God and God's supreme greatness.

In identifying divine aseity as part of his purpose in the *Proslo-*

---

9. Frederick Van Fleteren, "Augustine's Influence on Anselm's *Proslogion*," in *Anselm: Aosta, Bec and Canterbury*, 59.

10. *P prooemium*, Schmitt I 93:8–9.

11. *M* 80, Schmitt I 87:6.

gion, Anselm associates it with his identification of God as the highest good: God as *nullo alio indigens* is drawn out of God as *summum bonum*. This connection is carried over throughout the rest of the book. In *Proslogion* 5, for instance, Anselm broadens and qualifies divine aseity specifically with reference to the doctrine of creation ex nihilo, calling God "the highest of all things (*summum omnium*), existing through yourself alone, who made everything else from nothing."[12] Anselm then moves on to assert the broader claim that God is whatever it is better to be than not to be, and, from this claim, all of the subsequent chapters unfold. He will use this same term, *summum bonum*, repeatedly in *Proslogion* 23–26 to identify the object for which the human soul is made—and frequently he will correlate the fact that all things depend on God with the fact that God alone is the happiness and well-being of all other creatures. For instance, the fact that God is the *summum bonum* will entail for Anselm in the book's later chapters that God is also "that in which all good is" (*in quo est omne bonum*)[13] and "the one good, in which all good things are" (*unum bonum, in quo sunt omnia bona*).[14] The association by which divine aseity and divine beatitude are interwoven in Anselm's mind goes some way in explaining why he draws upon Mary's language in Luke 10:42 at the conclusion of *Proslogion* 23 to communicate the practical implications of divine simplicity: for Anselm, the fact that God is *summum bonum* necessitates that he is the *unum necessarium* of the soul. In light of the implications that Anselm will draw from God's identity as the *summum bonum* later in the *Proslogion*, his emphasis on this theme in the book's stated purpose—together with his identification of God as the unique source of creaturely happiness (*bene sint*)—anticipates the appropriateness of heaven as the book's conclusion. Already we see implicit in Anselm's thinking a close connection between the *unum argumentum* and the *unum bonum*, between God's nature/existence

12. *P* 5, Schmitt I 104:12–13.
13. *P* 23, Schmitt I 117:21.
14. *P* 25, Schmitt I 118:16.

and the prayerful pursuit of the implications of those realities for human happiness and flourishing.

In a third and final clause, Anselm widens out the aim of his *unum argumentum* even further, including "whatever else we believe about the divine substance (*substantia*)."[15] While it would be an overly technical interpretation to press this clause so far as to conclude that the *Proslogion* is aiming at a comprehensive account of theology proper, it nonetheless adds a level of inclusiveness and flexibility to Anselm's purposes in the *Proslogion*. In some sense, Anselm seems to regard the argument he has arrived at in the *Proslogion* as a means by which to engage the entire doctrine of God that is affirmed by his faith. Apart from this third purpose clause, it would be difficult to understand the existence of the later chapters of the book, where he seems to be dealing with distinctly Christian and biblical aspects of the doctrine of God (such as the interrelations of the Father, Son, and Holy Spirit in *Proslogion* 23). On the other hand, the later developments in the *Proslogion* make more sense in light of the breadth of Anselm's purpose statement here—particularly in light of his desire to recapitulate the arguments in the *Monologion*, a book concerned with God's Triune essence and as such the source of human happiness.[16]

After establishing his aims in the *Proslogion* in this threefold purpose statement at the start of the *prooemium*, Anselm moves on to discuss the process by which he found this single, self-sufficient argument. It is noteworthy that Anselm arrived at the insight that led to the *Proslogion* only after a great deal of intellectual and existential struggle. He describes himself in a state of distraction and desperation, unable to move on to other ideas.[17] Eadmer describes further the loss of appetite that accompanied this struggle.[18] When Anselm does arrive upon his argument, it brings him

15. *P prooemium*, Schmitt I 93:9.
16. E.g., *M* 68–70, Schmitt I 78–81.
17. *P prooemium*, Schmitt I 93:10–19.
18. Eadmer, *Vita Sancti Anselmi* I:19, 30.

THE PURPOSE OF THE *PROSLOGION*

joy (*gaudium*), and part of his purpose in writing the book is to bring pleasure (*placiturum*) to the reader.[19] This deeply emotional struggle standing behind the writing of the *Proslogion* is difficult to account for if Anselm were simply advancing a proof of God's existence. On the other hand, if Anselm is concerned more specifically with God as the *summum bonum* of the human soul, one can more readily understand the struggle that brought it about, as well as the focus throughout the book on *gaudium*.[20] The entire *Proslogion* is animated with this experiential, joyful energy that stemmed from his profound experience during Matins and led Anselm to write the book—and part of his explicit purpose is to share the pleasure of this experience with the reader.

Eadmer's description of Anselm's aim in writing the *Proslogion* follows Anselm's, but emphasizes additionally the unity of the divine attributes in its final clause:

> Afterwards it came into his mind to try to prove by one single and short argument the things which are believed and preached about God, that he is eternal, unchangeable, omnipotent, omnipresent, incomprehensible, just, righteous, merciful, true, as well as truth, goodness, justice, and so on; and to show how all these qualities are united (*unum*) in him.[21]

Southern observes that "Eadmer's words at this point have almost the authority of autobiography, for there can be no doubt that Anselm was their source, and he probably read, and at first approved, what Eadmer had written."[22] What stands out in Eadmer's description of Anselm's aim in the *Proslogion* is not only the absence of any mention of a proof for God's existence but the particular twelve divine attributes he mentions, as well as his focus on the unity of these attributes in God's essence. Here the *unum argumentum*

---

19. *P prooemium*, Schmitt I 93:21.
20. Of all Anselm's commentators, Barth has drawn particular attention to the significance of *gaudium* for Anselm's project. See Barth, *Fides Quaerens Intellectum*, 15–22.
21. Eadmer, *Vita Sancti Anselmi* I:19, 29.
22. Southern, *Saint Anselm*, 116.

seems far more concerned with the nature of God's existence than the fact of his existence—in fact, from Eadmer's summary of Anselm's purpose in the *Proslogion*, one would not even discern that the book contains a proof of God's existence at all.

If the *unum argumentum* that Anselm derives cannot be limited to *Proslogion* 2–4, is it possible to delineate it more precisely? This is a long-standing debate, with many interpreters of Anselm seeing it as referring to Anselm's original formula *aliquid quo nihil maius cogitari possit*, while many others see it as also containing the conclusions that follow from this formula.[23] It is important to distinguish Anselm's term *argumentum* from a modern formal syllogism. In Anselm's context, *argumentum* was a less technical term than *argumentatio* and had a broader semantic range.[24] In Lewis and Short, for example, *argumentatio* refers to either (1) the process of adducing a proof or (2) the proof itself, while *argumentum* is a much more flexible term, containing meanings as broad as "the subject-matter of a poem or fictitious writing" or "the subject of artistic representation."[25] In the end, it is probably best not to identify the *unum argumentum* with some definite portion of Anselm's text but instead as an argument schema recurring throughout the book. Toivo Holopainen, for instance, interprets the *unum argumentum* as the "middle term" that joins together God and the other predicates derived from the formula throughout the book.[26] In light of the technical use of the term *argumentum* in Boethian logic, this is a compelling proposal.[27] We have already drawn attention to the influence of Boethian

---

23. See the helpful discussion in Sweeney, *Anselm of Canterbury and the Desire for the Word*, 147n164.

24. Gillian R. Evans, "Anselm's Life, Works, and Immediate Influence," in *The Cambridge Companion to Anselm*, 13. Cf. Evans, *Anselm and Talking about God*, 48.

25. Lewis and Short, *A Latin Dictionary*, 158–59.

26. Holopainen, Dialectic and Theology in the Eleventh Century, 133–45.

27. Jacob Archambault provides a helpful overview of the use of the term *argumentum* in Boethius and the potential influence on Anselm ("The Teaching of the *Trivium* at Bec and its Bearing upon the Anselmian Program of *fides quaerens intellectum*," paper presented at *Reading Anselm: Context and Criticism*, Boston, July 29th, 2015).

logic on Anselm. It is plausible that Boethius's theory of argumentation in *In Ciceronis Topica*, specifically its rule that the middle term in an argument could be considered itself an argument, enabled Anselm to refer to the divine name ("that than which nothing greater can be thought") as itself *unum argumentatum*.[28] However we precisely identify the *unum argumentum*, it cannot be seen as concluded within the first several chapters of the *Proslogion*, because the whole point of the argument is to recapitulate the connected chain of arguments in the *Monologion*, the vast majority of which (for instance, its sustained analysis of the Trinity) are not addressed by Anselm until the middle and later portions of the *Proslogion*.

Continuity and Crescendo: Reframing the Relation of *Monologion* and *Proslogion*

In order to understand the purpose of the *Proslogion*, it is necessary to consider its relation to the *Monologion*. Are the *Monologion* and *Proslogion* two phases of what is fundamentally one continuous effort, or do they represent two distinct projects? Issues of continuity/discontinuity between the two books have had a significant bearing on how the purpose of the *Proslogion* has been understood. Anselm Stolz's interpretation of the *Proslogion* as a work of mystical theology, for example, depended on his claim that it was a radically different work than the *Monologion*.[29] Gilbert's interpretation of the structure of the *Proslogion* drew much significance from his argument that two themes that are foundational in the *Monologion* are absent from the *Proslogion*, namely, the divine essence and the mind as its image.[30] In the other direction, those who detect in-

---

28. Holopainen, *Dialectic and Theology in the Eleventh Century*, 135–39.
29. Anselm Stolz, "Zur Theologie Anselms im *Proslogion*," 1–24. For a compelling case for continuity between the two works, arguing against the argument of Schufreider in favor of discontinuity, see Sweeney, *Anselm of Canterbury and the Desire for the Word*, 113–14.
30. Gilbert, *Le "Proslogion" de S. Anselme*, 18–29.

consistency or contradiction in Anselm's epistemology often operate on the basis of an assumed continuity between the two works (though the reasons for this continuity are not always drawn out). Furthermore, if the two works are interpreted as fundamentally representative of the same theological method, it is easier to read the *Proslogion* in relation to more recent ontological arguments. Charlesworth, for instance, is able to downplay the "'fideist' tendency" of *Proslogion* 1 by reading it in light of the *sola ratione* of *Monologion*.[31] Similarly, Brian Davies maintains (contra Barth) that the *Proslogion* contains arguments that can be characterized as "philosophical" on the basis of what he sees as a close connection between the *Proslogion* and *Monologion*.[32] In general, the emphasis among Anselm interpreters tends to fall towards reading the two works together.[33] Southern, for instance, so emphasizes their continuity that he can call the *Proslogion* an "appendix" to the *Monologion*.[34]

The relationship between these two works, however, may well be more complex than usually seen, embracing both continuity and discontinuity.[35] Careful attention to the tone, content, and (most

---

31. Charlesworth, *St. Anselm's "Proslogion,"* 54.

32. Davies, "Anselm and the Ontological Argument," in *The Cambridge Companion to Anselm*, 157–78, at 158.

33. The assertion by Hopkins is widely representative of most interpreters: "The characterization of faith and reason does not change from the *Monologion* to the *Proslogion*. It is true that the *Proslogion* does not explicitly mention proceeding *sola ratione* and that the *Monologion* nowhere advocates *crede ut intelligas*. Yet what could be clearer than the former exemplifies the suspending of authority just as the latter is at every point guided by the *Credo*?" (*A Companion to the Study of St. Anselm*, 62). Cf. Gilbert's discussion of the French literature on this point, Gilbert, *Le "Proslogion" de S. Anselme*, 17–19.

34. Southern, *Saint Anselm*, 125.

35. Toivo J. Holopainen is one of the few Anselm interpreters who embraces a more nuanced view of the relation of the two works, arguing that they share "a common objective and a common methodology," though they are written "from two different perspectives (impersonal monologue vs. devotional address)" ("The *Proslogion* in Relation to the *Monologion*," *The Heythrop Journal* 50 [2009], 590–602, at 597–98).

of all) stated purposes of each work shows that while the *Monologion* and *Proslogion* do fundamentally belong to one theological project, there is nevertheless a crescendo and amplification in the *Proslogion* that represents an advancement from the *Monologion* in both method and content. Both works fall under the rubric of *sola ratione* in that, as discussed in the first chapter, they both argue apart from the authority of Scripture—but the *Proslogion* shows more clearly than the *Monologion* the *relation* of this project to the earnest faith Anselm models, for example, in *Proslogion* 1 or his *Prayers and Meditations*. So the relation between the works cannot be reduced to either continuity or discontinuity, but is better characterized as a development and extension.

The evidence for a broad continuity between the two works is strong. Anselm himself associated the *Monologion* and the *Proslogion* together, as is evident from his statement in *On the Incarnation of the Word*, where he references "my two little works, namely, *Monologion* and *Proslogion*, which were made mainly for this purpose, that what we hold by faith concerning the divine nature and his persons, except the incarnation, could be proved by necessary reasons, without the authority of Scripture."[36] According to Anselm, therefore, the two works were bound together by both their mutual method and their mutual aim: both sought to establish certain truths by rational argumentation, apart from appeal to Scripture, and both concerned the divine nature and persons. That Anselm can refer to both works together as serving the same purpose suggests that they belong to the same broad overarching project. In addition, as observed in the last chapter, if one posits a tension between the *Monologion* and the *Proslogion* on the basis of their methodologies, one must posit the same tension within the *Cur Deus Homo*, which appeals to *sola ratione* as well as *credo ut intelligam*.[37]

Furthermore, as mentioned earlier, Anselm explains in the *prooemium* of the *Proslogion* that the book came about as a collaps-

36. *DIV* 6, Schmitt II 20:16–19.
37. Cf. Hopkins, *A Companion*, 63.

ing of the arguments of *Monologion* down into one argument. Once again this would seem to suggest that whatever differences may pertain to the two works, those differences cannot subsist in their overall purpose: Anselm states that he is simplifying and collapsing his arguments, not redirecting his focus.[38] This historical backdrop also helps explain the obvious similarities of style, length, and form between the two works. Furthermore, in much of its language and specific argumentation, the *Proslogion* picks up where the *Monologion* left off. A. Beckaert observes, for example, that even while the *Proslogion* transcends the *Monologion*, it presupposes the name of God which was arrived at previously in the *Monologion*.[39]

On the other hand, within this overarching unity there are important differences between the two works. The most obvious is the difference of genre: the *Proslogion* is a *prayer*, reminiscent of the style of Augustine's *Confessions*. Related to this shift of genre is a heightening of tone: both works have a meditative feel, but nothing in the calm reasoning of *Monologion* anticipates anything like the ecstatic delight that occasionally characterizes *Proslogion*.[40] One partial explanation for the shift of tone is that the *Monologion* was written in response to the requests of his fellow monks, while the *Proslogion* came at Anselm's own initiative. One gets the sense that in the *Monologion* Anselm is still working out his thoughts to some extent, while the briefer and more compact *Proslogion* gives the flavor of already having arrived at the crucial insights before the time of writing. But there is a deeper crescendo at play, beyond the compactness of expression and emotional quality of the *Proslogion*, and in order to understand it one must appreciate how Anselm's practices of prayer and theological contemplation were shaped by his monastic context.[41] In the *Proslogion* Anselm has not simply in-

---

38. Cattin, *La preuve de Dieu*, 136, draws attention to this point.
39. A. Beckaert, "A Platonic Justification for the Argument a Priori," in *The Many-Faced Argument*, 116.
40. Cf. Barth, *Anselm*: Fides Quaerens Intellectum, 84–85.
41. In her introduction to Anselm's *Prayers and Meditations*, Benedicta Ward provides a helpful summary of Anselm's monastic practice (27–82).

troduced a new style, but rather reverted to the heightened oratorical style of his *Prayers and Meditations*, which were written mostly between 1070 and 1080 (when both *Monologion* and *Proslogion* were also written). The *Proslogion* shares the same style and pattern as his *Prayers and Meditations*—withdrawal into solitude, self-examination, compunction, yearning for God, etc. (we will explore these features more in chapter 5). In a way, the *Proslogion* shares more in common with Anselm's *Prayers and Meditations* than it does with the *Monologion*. One can only understand the *Proslogion* as an expression of this monastic understanding of prayer—it is a work by a monk, for monks, and to assist monastic practices.[42] John Clayton even suggests that the Latin cadences of the *Proslogion* are crafted after the Psalms in order to more readily enable monks to use the book in silent meditation or out loud in communal devotion.[43]

Once again, the historical backdrop behind the *Proslogion* is an important piece for explaining its heightened tone. After Eadmer recounts Anselm's loss of interest in food, drink, sleep, and prayer, and his conclusion that his search for the *unum argumentum* must be a temptation from the devil, he presents Anselm's discovery of it as nothing short of a spiritual epiphany: "suddenly one night during matins the grace of God illumined his heart, the whole matter became clear in his mind, and a great joy and exultation filled his inmost being."[44] If the *Monologion* is the product of theological discussions among monks, the *Proslogion* is the product of a powerful spiritual experience during prayer—and this accounts, at least in part, for the crescendo of urgency and energy from the former to

---

42. Hogg, observing similarities of the interpretations of both Anselm Stolz and Benedicata Ward and noting that both have taken religious orders, suggests that it may not be coincidence that the general tenor of their works accords so well with that of the *Proslogion* (*Anselm of Canterbury*, 118).

43. John Clayton, "The Otherness of Anselm," in *The Otherness of God*, ed. Orrin F. Summerell, Studies in Religion and Culture (Charlottesville, Va.: University of Virginia Press, 1998), 20.

44. Eadmer, *Vita Sancti Anselmi* 1:19, 30.

the latter. The whole issue of the destruction of the wax tablets on which the argument was originally written, whatever other purposes this story may serve for Eadmer, only heightens the drama and energy that animate the book.[45] There is no comparable intrigue in the composition of the *Monologion*.

Furthermore, only a few commentators have noticed that the *Monologion* and *Proslogion* are each said in their respective prologues to be written *sub persona* or *in persona*—that is, from a particular and deliberately chosen role or character.[46] The word *persona* was originally used to refer to a mask or an actor in a play, and could still retain the sense of *character* or *role* in Anselm's day.[47] Thus, one way to understand Anselm's method in works like *Monologion* and *Proslogion* is as a sort of thought experiment or an exercise in theological imagination. In one sense, then, the author of each work is not Anselm proper but the particular *persona* that Anselm adopts to accomplish his purpose in each book. He may not have a sparring partner like Boso as he does in *Cur Deus Homo*, but he nevertheless is "in character"—that is, playing a role, from whose vantage point he hopes to see more of the divine essence. In the *Monologion*, Anselm identifies his "character" as "in the role (*in persona*) of someone investing things which he does not know by silent reasoning within himself."[48] In the *Proslogion*, his "character" is as one "under the role (*sub persona*) of someone trying to raise his mind to contemplating God and seeking to understand what he believes."[49] These two roles are significantly different, and when Anselm explains them in the prologue of *Proslogion*, his purpose is to distinguish them and thus illumine the differences between

---

45. Eadmer, *Vita Sancti Anselmi* 1:19, 30–31.

46. Sweeney is one of the few commentators who points this out (*Anselm of Canterbury and the Desire for the Word*, 116–17); Kapriev makes a similar but more limited point regarding Anselm's *sola ratione* (*Ipsa Vita et Veritas*, 26–27).

47. Lewis and Short, *A Latin Dictionary*, 1355–56. Cf. the discussion in Mackey, *Peregrinations of the Word*, 103.

48. *P prooemium*, Schmitt I 93:3–4.

49. *P prooemium*, Schmitt I 93:21–94:1.

the works. This makes it impossible to agree with Visser and Williams' claim that "the *Proslogion*'s being addressed to God is of no more consequence for our understanding of its arguments than the *Monologion*'s being addressed to oneself is of consequence for our understanding of its arguments."[50] If form and content could be neatly divorced, why does Anselm go to the trouble of distinguishing the *persona* of each book in the first place? In fact, why put the *Proslogion* in the form of prayer at all, rather than maintain the style of the *Monologion*? As Gene Fendt puts it, "if [Anselm's argument] is the rationalist's pure proof, Anselm has put it in the strangest and least well-fitting frame imaginable: a contemplative prayer."[51] Both the *Monologion* and *Proslogion* were written during the quiet morning hours reserved for *lectio* in the monastery at Bec, and both give evidence of carefulness and precision in their language and construction,[52] so differences of tone and authorial standpoint between them cannot be attributed to different writing circumstances. Anselm seems to have deliberately chosen two different "characters" or *personae* by which to write these two works, and it is worth exploring the differences.

The *persona* of the *Monologion* seems more self-referential ("silent reasoning within himself"), which helps explain why Anselm can title this work as a speech made to oneself (*soliloquium*). In contrast, he titles the *Proslogion* as a speech made to another (*alloquium*)—which as Eadmer explains, refers to both his address to self and his address to God throughout the book.[53] If the *persona* of *Proslogion* is "faith seeking understanding," that of *Monologion* could perhaps be labeled (seeking a parallel three-word summary), "ignorance investigating knowledge." Each word in this summary

---

50. Visser and Williams, *Anselm*, 74.

51. Gene Fendt, "The Relation of *Monologion* and *Proslogion*," *The Heythrop Journal* 46 (2005), 158.

52. Jean-Charles Nault, "The First Chapter of St. Anselm's *Proslogion*," in *A Man Born Out of Due Time*, ed. Dunstan Robidoux, OSB (N.Y.: Lantern, 2013), 34.

53. Eadmer, *Vita Sancti Anselmi* I:19, 31.

is important: *quaerentis* corresponds to the urgent, yearning tone of the *Proslogion*, while *investigantis* coheres better with the calmer, more contemplative mood reflected in the *Monologion*. Furthermore, *scientia* is a less explicitly spiritual goal than *intellectum*, which Anselm will elsewhere identify as "the intermediate between faith and vision."[54] Most important are the contrasting starting points of each *persona*: whereas Anselm writes the *Monologion* from the standpoint of ignorance (*nesciens*), the *Proslogion* is written specifically from the standpoint of faith, and his goal is the contemplation of God (*ad contemplandum Deum*) and an understanding (*intellectum*) concerning the things he *already* believes. This implies that whatever threshold the *persona* of the *Monologion* may seek to cross on the basis of reason, the *persona* of the *Proslogion* is at no time operating outside the boundaries of faith.

It is impossible to fully understand the purpose of the *Proslogion* without approaching the book in light of its own particular *persona*, particularly in the ways it is distinct from that of the *Monologion*. Before Anselm's commentators can drag out various "contradictory" statements in Anselm concerning his epistemology, for example, or filter the "fideistic tendencies" of the *Proslogion* through the grid of the method of the *Monologion*, the carefully crafted authorial standpoint of each work must be considered. Quotations from neither *Monologion* nor *Proslogion* are flatly identical with Anselm proper, although in the impassioned prayers of *Proslogion* (especially chapters 1 and 14), we occasionally get clearer glimpses into the soul and mind of the author behind the author, on his knees during Matins after another sleepless night and foodless day. If we allow the purpose of the *Proslogion* to be defined in relation to its *persona*, we might aptly summarize it in Anselm's own language: *ad contemplandum Deum*. In short, Anselm's goal is the beatific vision. Similarly, if we allow this definition of the purpose of the *Proslogion* to be further refined in relation to its original title, *fides quaerens intellec-*

---

54. CHD *Commendatio*, Schmitt II 40:10–11.

tum,⁵⁵ we can clarify that Anselm's desire to see God is everywhere pursued in the book specifically as an object of faith. In fact, *fides quaerens intellectum* is not merely a principle within the book, but it is so paradigmatic throughout the entire work that it can stand as its title. This explains how even in *Proslogion* 2, where Anselm seeks to establish God's existence, the God whose existence he seeks to prove he will first call *qui das fidei intellectum*.⁵⁶

Proslogion 1: Yearning for the Beatific Vision

Generally speaking, it is difficult to account for the purpose of a book without consideration of its beginning. Yet interpretations of the *Proslogion* have all too often neglected not only the latter bulk of the book (chapters 5–26) but also its introductory chapter. Nonetheless, it is significant to the interpretation of the *Proslogion* that Anselm does not begin his book with a proof for God but rather with a poignant expression of his sin and misery at being far away from God. Such a point of departure already implies that proving God exists is not all Anselm cares about, for establishing God's existence would not answer these emotional and spiritual expressions. Our exploration of *Proslogion* 1 will suggest that Anselm's purpose in this book is not so much to establish the existence of God as to arrive upon the sight and knowledge of God in an experience of joyful worship.⁵⁷

Proslogion 1 can be split roughly into 6 sections, corresponding to the six paragraph breaks in Schmitt's critical edition.⁵⁸ In the

55. *P prooemium*, Schmitt I 94:7.
56. *P* 2, Schmitt I 101:3.
57. It is worth observing that the conclusion of the *Monologion* has this same focus on worship and prayer. Anselm is concerned there to establish God's identity as the supreme essence specifically to draw out that he alone is the one whom all other natures should "lovingly worship and worshipfully love" (M 80, Schmitt I 87:10).
58. Interestingly, Anselm wrote in paragraphs, signifying them with a marking on the page. But it is not clear whether his own paragraph breaks can always be identified

first section, Anselm addresses himself, and then in the remaining five sections he then turns to address God. This second person address (*alloquium*) continues into *Proslogion* 2 and the rest of the work, interrupted only by occasional returns to self-examination and address (*soliloquium*)—for instance, in chapters 14 and 24. When it comes to the genre of the *Proslogion*, it is therefore accurate but not sufficient to say that it is prayer: rather, it is a very particular kind of meditative, introspective prayer, patterned after Augustine's *Confessions* and suited for the end of Anselm's quest for joy in God.[59] Anselm is not only speaking to God but speaking to himself *about* speaking to God: he is rousing himself into a kind of spiritual meditation and then examining himself along the way.

It is this deep yearning for joy and spiritual fullness that drives the entirety of *Proslogion* 1 and leaves the most profound impression from this opening paragraph. There is some uncertainty as to whether *homuncio*, the relatively rare term with which Anselm opens the *Proslogion*, refers narrowly to Anselm himself or more broadly to fallen humanity. While there is no reason why the term cannot also entail the latter by extension, the former is more likely here, given that Anselm will reference himself as a *contemptibilis homuncio* as part of his protest for his own unworthiness to defend the Christian faith at the start of *On the Incarnation of the Word*.[60] In other medieval theological literature, *homuncio* is often used as a term of self-deprecation.[61] It can connote insignificance or mor-

---

with Schmitt's, so it would not be wise to place much interpretative significance on the paragraph breaks. Instead, we use them simply for the sake of clarity and reference.

59. The influence of Augustine is everywhere in Anselm's thinking (for instance, his doctrine of God as the *summum bonum*), but there are particularly striking similarities of both tone and language between the beginning of *Proslogion* 1 and *Confessiones* I.i.1–6. As Van Fleteren shows, for instance, the exterior-interior movement is an Augustinian theme, and Psalm 26:8 is cited both in the *Confessiones* and elsewhere in Augustine's writings ("Augustine's Influence on Anselm's *Proslogion*," in *Anselm: Aosta, Bec and Canterbury*, 60). It is actually hard to find any major themes in *Proslogion* 1 that are unanticipated in the writings of Augustine.

60. *DIV* 1, Schmitt II 5:7.

61. Rabanus Maurus, for instance, will begin Book 2 of his *De Laudibus Sanctae*

tality, but here in *Proslogion* 1 its precise sense should probably be taken in light of Anselm's monastic vocation and in light of the rest of the chapter—particularly paragraphs 3–4, which concern human sin and its effects upon the knowledge of God. If this is right, then Anselm is a "little man" or "insignificant mortal" (*homuncio*) specifically because of the "grievous loss" (*grave damnum*) by which he and all other children of Eve have lost that for which they were created: the sight and knowledge of God.[62] *Homuncio* is used in the context of a lament for sin and folly in Augustine as well.[63] John of Fécamp (d. 1079), whose devotional writings bear many similarities to those of Anselm and likely influenced him, opened his *Confessio Theologica* with a reference to himself as a *homuncio* in the context of his lament of his "sins, vices, guilt, and negligences."[64]

Anselm will return to this term in *Proslogion* 25, where he chides the *homuncio* for wandering through many things to seek the "goods of your soul and your body" (*bona animae tuae et corporis tui*) rather than finding them in the *summum bonum*—an essentially moral error.[65] Anselm will likewise use *homuncio* in *Cur Deus Homo* in the sense of being sinful and needing redemption, where Boso refers to the *miser homuncio* who cannot escape the rational demands of justice.[66] This association of *homuncio* and vulnerability to divine justice also surfaces in his *Meditatio* 3, where Anselm uses the term in calling himself to leave the cruelties of those who crucified Christ to the justice of God.[67] In his *Prayers and Meditations*, the term *homuncio* is often used to denote Anselm's wretched

---

Crucis with reference to himself as a *vilissimus homuncio* (PL107 coll. 265A); Hincmar of Reims will refer to himself in his Epistle 4 as a *tantillus homuncio* in relation to the larger church (PL126 coll. 54B).

62. P 98:14–15, 99:6–7. Anselm uses a number of diminutives throughout this chapter: *aliquanticum, modicum*, etc.

63. Augustine, *Confessions* 1.16.26 (PL32 coll. 672); see also *City of God* II.7 (PL41 coll. 53), where the term occurs in his quotation of Terence.

64. Ward, *Prayers and Meditations*, 48. On John's influence on Anselm, see 47–50.

65. P 25, Schmitt I 118:15.

66. *CDH* I.24, Schmitt II 94:8–9.

67. *Med.* 3, Schmitt III 89:149.

state as a sinner and his need of divine grace. In his prayer to Peter, for instance, Anselm will refer to himself as a *pauperrimus et infimus homuncio* ("poorest and lowest little man"), beset with a long list of calamities which he contracted *de sordibus peccatorum suorum* ("from the filth of his sins").[68] Or in his Prayer by an Abbot to the Patron Saint of his Church, Anselm will refer to himself as *homuncio, vermis et putredo* ("little man, a worm and rottenness") because his many sins have made him unworthy of the office to which he has been called.[69] Finally, in his prayer to John, he will refer to himself as a *homuncio circumferens sarcinam peccatorum suorum* ("little man bearing around the burden of his sins"); hence, a man cut off from God and, indeed, an enemy of God (*inimicam Dei*).[70] In all these contexts, *homuncio* connotes sinfulness and guilt before God and, consequently, distance from God.

If *homuncio* also has a spiritual, moral thrust in *Proslogion* 1, denoting Anselm's sinfulness and consequent loss of fellowship with God, the remainder of the first paragraph of the *Proslogion* amplifies and extends this sense of spiritual need. The bulk of this paragraph consists of a series of parallel imperatives calling for flight from the cares and worries of life and retreat unto the inner, secret enjoyment of God, culminating in the quotation of Psalm 26/27:8.

Abice nunc onerosas curas, et postpone laboriosas distentiones tuas. Vaca aliquantulum deo, et requiesce aliquantulum in eo. Intra in cubiculum mentis tuae, exclude omnia praeter deum et quae te iuvent ad quaerendum eum, et clauso ostio quare eum. Dic nunc, totum cor meum, dic nunc deo: Quaero vultum tuum; vultum tuum, domine, requiro.[71]

---

68. *Or.* 9, Schmitt III 30:7–14.

69. *Or.* 17, Schmitt III 68:19–20. Ward renders more freely, "little man, a creeping and decaying thing." Ward, *The Prayers and Meditations of Saint Anselm with the "Proslogion,"* 208.

70. *Or.* 11, Schmitt III 43:34–39. The present active participle *circumferens*, better rendered "bearing around" or "carrying around," is once again translated quite freely as "weighed down" in Ward, *The Prayers and Meditations of Saint Anselm*, 159.

71. P1, Schmitt I 97:5–10.

Anselm's movement towards God here is depicted as a movement both from the external to the internal, as well as from activity to rest. His unhappy state is cast specifically in terms of "affairs" or "concerns" (*occupationes*) and "toils" (*laboriosas*), as well as "thoughts" (*cogitationibus*) and "cares" (*curas*). There is no specification as to what kinds of activities Anselm has in mind here, but the impression is of that specific kind of anxiety and unhappiness associated with worldly activity and work. This kind of retreat into solitude and reflection was commonly regarded in early medieval monastic piety as a necessary prerequisite to prayer, drawing from the instruction in John Cassian's *Conferences*.[72] Anselm then calls himself into the "chamber" (*cubiculum*) of his mind and stipulates that any distractions are to be "shut out" (*exclude*). Referencing Christ's call to secret prayer in Matthew 6:6, he then calls himself to "shut the door" (*clauso ostio*).[73] The urgent tone of this paragraph clears away any notion of meditation as a passive activity. One gets the sense of spiritual and mental straining upwards, as Anselm indeed describes his effort in the prologue as *contantis erigere mentem suam ad contemplandum deum* ("of one trying to raise his mind to the contemplation of God").

In fact, within paragraph 1 both the spatial (exterior/interior) and active (cares/rest) images are explicitly cast as ways of seeking God. Anselm calls himself not just to rest but to rest in God (*requiesce aliquantulum in eo*); he is not simply to go behind closed doors but to go there to seek God and shut out all else (*exclude omnia praeter deum*). In other words, to put it in terms of the chapter's title, the rousing of his mind (*excitatio mentis*) that Anselm seeks here is specifically to the end of seeking to contemplate God (*ad contemplandum deum*). This calling is then summed up at the end of the paragraph with the Psalm 26:8 quote: "I seek your face." Elsewhere in his writings, Anselm will use the term *cubiculum* to refer to the place of intimacy and fellowship with God. At the end of

---

72. See the discussion in Ward, *Prayers and Meditations*, 51–53.
73. V 1533.

Meditation on Human Redemption, for instance, he will pray, "admit me into the inner room of your love" (*admitte me intra cubiculum amoris tui*).⁷⁴ The images here of rest and interiority draw upon, in the first place, Anselm's high view of God as dwelling in *lucem inaccessibilem* ("inaccessible light"). As Schufreider observes, "the image of 'closing the door' behind one, of closing out, 'excluding' everything but God, implicitly invokes the radical distinction between the supreme being and all other beings we saw appear in all its metaphysical glory in the *Monologion*."⁷⁵ But Anselm's images also reflect a particular anthropology, especially his view of human reason as shaped by his monastic context. Anselm followed Augustine's correlation of the Trinity with the memory, understanding, and will, and therefore, for Anselm, "among the created things that we ordinarily encounter, the human mind bears the clearest traces of its creator."⁷⁶ In *Monologion* 67, Anselm asserts that the mind is the mirror and image of the Creator.⁷⁷ In *De Concordia*, Anselm will assert that the soul possesses and employs reason for its own purposes, just as the body possesses and employs its limbs and five senses for its purposes.⁷⁸ Here, his qualification of *cubiculum* ("inner chamber" or "closet") from Matthew 6:6 in the Vulgate with *mentis tuae* (your mind) reflects his view of rational meditation as an essentially spiritual activity. For Anselm, the *mens* is like a *cubiculum*: that special realm wherein lies the possibility of *ad contemplandum deum*. Hence, Anselm will cry out to God later in the *Proslogion*, "illumine the eye of my mind (*illumina oculum mentis meae*) so that it may see you."⁷⁹

It is difficult to exaggerate the importance of the opening paragraph of the *Proslogion* for establishing the tone and aims of the rest

---

74. *Med.* 3, Schmitt III 91:202–03.
75. Schufreider, *Confessions of a Rational Mystic*, 103.
76. William E. Mann, "Anselm on the Trinity," in *The Cambridge Companion to Anselm*, 273.
77. *M* 67, Schmitt I 77:26.
78. *DC* 3.11, Schmitt II 278:2–279:6.
79. *P* 18, Schmitt I 114:11–12.

of the book. Its images, drawing upon Anselm's tight correlation of the rational and spiritual, help the reader anticipate the combination of dense logic and spiritual yearning that will follow in the rest of the book. Its tone, bursting with the energy of a man writing with his *totum cor* ("whole heart"), invites the reader upward to share in Anselm's earnest pursuit. Most importantly, its content reveals the aim of that pursuit as specifically to seek the face of God (*vultum tuum, domine, requiro*). Gilbert draws attention to the repetition of the term *quaerere*, here used twice in quotation of Psalm 26/27, elsewhere throughout *Proslogion* 1 (paragraphs 2, 4, and 5).[80]

At the start of the second paragraph, the repetition of the introductory *eia nunc* prepares the reader for a fresh beginning, as Anselm transitions from addressing himself to now addressing God (*domine deus meus*).[81] The first paragraph thus seems to function as a kind of loosely set-apart introduction, in which Anselm rouses himself to the activity of seeking God's presence, while in the following five paragraphs (which flow more naturally from one to another) he then launches into his pursuit of God. But, as soon as he does so, he is arrested by the fact of his distance from God. He therefore begins with the supplication, "teach my heart where and how to see you, where and how to find you."[82] This petition reflects several concerns. First, Anselm's request for God to teach his heart (*doce cor meum*) reinforces his tight integration, contrary to many modern sensibilities, of the rational, the spiritual, and the emotional: for Anselm, the pursuit of God requires not merely retreat into the *mens* but instruction of the *cor*. Furthermore, in making this petition Anselm expresses his dependence upon God—doubly so by requesting help for both *where* God is to be sought and found, as well as for *how* to seek and find God (*ubi et quomodo* repeated twice). The combination of both *ubi* and *quomodo* in Anselm's expression of need communicates a sense of bewilderment,

---

80. Gilbert, *Le "Proslogion" de S. Anselme*, 39–40.
81. *P* 1, Schmitt I 98:1.
82. *P* 1, Schmitt I 98:1–2.

as though Anselm does not even know where to begin his search. Already here at the very start of the *Proslogion* we must feel that we are in a different solar system from that body of philosophical discussion associated with Descartes, Leibniz, Kant, etc. Can one even imagine the supplication "teach my heart how to seek you" at the start of any non-Anselmian articulation of an "ontological argument?"

As soon as Anselm makes this request, however, he is confronted by the paradox that God is both omnipresent yet impossible to find. To explain this contradiction Anselm introduces the language of I Timothy 6:16 that God dwells in *lux inaccessibilis*, an important term that will resurface throughout the *Proslogion*.[83] The usage of this term in Augustine makes it likely that it was also a technical term by Anselm's day.[84] Schufreider calls this term "standard fare in mystical theology," drawing attention particularly to its use in Pseudo-Dionysius.[85] Anselm will use the metaphor of light throughout chapter 14 to explain God's simultaneous distance and proximity, and in chapter 16 he turns to the question of whether *lux inaccessibilis* can be identified with the fact that God is greater than can be thought.

The bulk of paragraph 2 of *Proslogion* 1, as well as the rest of the chapter, is dominated by a tension inherent in Anselm's anthropology: Anselm was created to see God, but he cannot see God; he is a human being, but he is also fallen human being; he bears God's image, but that image has been distorted and twisted by sin. For Anselm, ultimate human happiness consists in the beatific vision, the unmediated sight of God that has been obstructed by sin.[86] Elsewhere, for instance, he will assert that the purpose of human nature

---

83. *P* 1, Schmitt I 98:4.
84. Van Fleteren, "Augustine's Influence on Anselm's *Proslogion*," in *Anselm: Aosta, Bec and Canterbury*, 61.
85. Schufreider, *Confessions of a Rational Mystic*, 105.
86. Anselm recounts his doctrine of original sin and of the fall of Adam more fully in *DCV* 1–2, Schmitt II 140–42.

is the enjoyment of eternal life in heaven[87] and will speak of heavenly life as the *species ad quam omnes anhelamus* ("sight for which we all long"), corresponding to our faith and understanding in this life.[88] To emphasize the agony and frustration of the loss of this vision, Anselm here employs four parallel constructions: (1) *anhelat videre te*; (2) *accedere ad te desiderat*; (3) *invenire te cupit*; (4) *quaerere te affectat*.[89] In each case, Anselm's wish is frustrated by God's distance (note the repetition of the term *inaccessibilis* with reference to God's *habitatio*) as well as by his own ignorance (*ignorat vultum tuum*). Anselm's language here emphasizes his close relationship to God— he declares, "you are my God, and you are my Lord" and acknowledges God's role in both creating and recreating him.[90] Yet Anselm also emphasizes his distance from God. He asserts twice, "I have never seen you" (*numquam te vidi*), and once, "I have not yet known you (*nondum novi te*).[91] This tension is then climactically asserted in the final, summative sentence of the paragraph: "for I was made for the purpose of seeing you, and I have not yet done that for which I was made."[92] This sentence provides a succinct summation of the burden that animates Anselm at the start of the *Proslogion* and that the rest of the book is intended to redress—Anselm has lost the *visio Dei*, and in so doing he has lost the very reason for his existence.

The third paragraph then stipulates the reason for God's distance, which is not merely a matter of God's infinitude or height but specifically the result of human sin. Brief, repetitive sentences, often introduced with declarative words like *O* or *heu*, heighten Anselm's tone even further.[93] Anselm is particularly burdened to express the totality of the loss that was incurred at humanity's fall into sin: "that without which nothing is happy has gone, and that

---

87. *CDH praefatio*, Schmitt II 42:15–16.
88. *CDH Commendatio*, Schmitt II 40:12.
89. *P* 1, Schmitt I 98:9–12.
90. *P* 1, Schmitt I 98:12–14.
91. *P* 1, Schmitt I 98:7, 13, 14.
92. *P* 1, Schmitt I 98:14–15.
93. E.g., *P* 1, Schmitt 1 98:17–18, 22–23.

THE PURPOSE OF THE *PROSLOGION*

which by itself is nothing but misery has remained."[94] To communicate the comprehensiveness of this contrast between un-fallen Adam and fallen humanity now, Anselm once again turns to repetition and to metaphor: "he belched with fullness, we sigh with hunger. He overflowed, we go begging. He happily had possessions and miserably deserted them, we unhappily lack them and miserably desire them, and alas, we remain empty."[95] Having expressed his doctrine of the fall through the metaphors of food/hunger and prosperity/poverty, he then turns to several further metaphors (specifically: light/darkness, life/death, sight/blindness, home/exile) in the forms of brief interrogative questions, designed to communicate both the folly of sin (why?) and the extent of its loss (whence?). These metaphors are frequently accompanied by adjectives of lament, expressing the transition from happiness (*felix*) and joy (*iucunditas*) to unhappiness (*infelix*), bitterness (*amaritude*), and dread (*horror*).[96] Importantly, Anselm identifies the cause of all this misery as the loss of the beatific vision for which humanity was created, that is, the transition *a visione dei in caecitatem nostram* ("from the vision of God into our blindness").[97] The intensity of the paragraph climaxes in the final sentence with the threefold repetition of *gravis* and with *totum* placed in a concluding emphatic position: *grave damnum, gravis dolor, grave totum* ("burdensome loss, burdensome sorrow, completely burdensome").[98]

---

94. P 1, Schmitt 1 98:19–20.

95. *P* 1, Schmitt I 98:23–25. It seems to me that the force of the contrast Anselm draws as the consequence of sin can be retained best here by leaving his language in its original abstractness and flexibility: for instance, rendering *ille abundabat* simply as "he abounded," rather than "he had everything he needed" (as does Williams, *Anselm: Basic Writings*, 80). Nonetheless, in the third sentence I have supplied an implied direct object ("possessions") to try to make the sentence more sensible in English. Charlesworth's rendering of *ructabat* as "he groaned" is lexically unwarranted and arguably obscures Anselm's meaning (*St. Anselm's "Proslogion,"* 113). The word means "to belch, eructate" (Lewis and Short, *A Latin Dictionary*, 1602).

96. P 1, Schmitt I 98:25–99:6.

97. P 1, Schmitt I 99:4–5.

98. P 1, Schmitt I 99:7.

This *grave damnum* is the transition that he believes to have occurred at the human fall, and, as paragraph 4 makes clear, Anselm's present unhappiness and blindness of God is the result of being one of the unfortunate children of Eve. This fourth paragraph serves to apply the doctrines of humanity and sin propounded in the previous one specifically to Anselm in the context of his quest for God. Anselm has roused himself into the *cubiculum mentis* for the purpose of *ad contemplandum deum*, but he is confronted by the fact that sin has rendered his spiritual desires impossible and is thus in a state of existential and spiritual crisis. A heightened tone is maintained in this paragraph once again through repetition, this time in the form of brief, staccato questions and through further emphasis on the totality of the contrast between his desires and his actual state (this time focused in terms of happiness vs. misery). This paragraph, even more so than the rest of the chapter, is dense with biblical allusions and quotations.

The lengthy paragraph 5 also opens with a dense string of biblical references, as Anselm delves into a series of earnest appeals that God would help his wretched condition. If paragraphs 3–4 establish sin as the problem obstructing Anselm's fellowship with God, paragraph 5 makes it plain that Anselm believes divine aid and favor can indeed remedy this problem. Anselm's series of requests recapitulate his earlier metaphors for the fall (particularly food/hunger) but also introduces two new, ancillary metaphors: sweetness/bitterness and wealth/poverty.[99] Once again, the profound sense of tension in Anselm's situation as a sinner is accented by these rapid juxtapositions. He was created to see God: he has never seen God: and thus his entire existence is dominated by contradiction and misery. In the concluding series of petitions in this paragraph, perhaps the point of climax in this chapter, Anselm asks that God would enable him to know him despite the vast distant caused by sin: "let me look up at your light, whether it be from afar or from

---

99. *P* 1, Schmitt I 99:22–23, 100:2–3.

the depths. Teach me to seek you, and reveal yourself to me as I seek; for I cannot seek you if you do not teach me how, nor find you unless you show yourself."[100] These petitions follow on the heels of quotations of Psalm 38:4 (37:5) and 69:15 (68:16), in which Anselm is concerned about the weight and burden of his sins and petitions God for salvation from them. The biblical background for Anselm's plea here, combined with the fact that Anselm nowhere asks for God's distance to be removed, but instead asks to see God "from afar or from the depths," further suggests that it is specifically sin that has caused Anselm's distance from God. Hence the petitions of *Proslogion* 1 are essentially a prayer for spiritual cleansing and deliverance. We grasp something of Anselm's desperate plight in his plea: *evolve me, exonera me, ne urgeat puteus earum os suum super me* ("extricate me, unburden me, lest their [my sins'] pit close its mouth over me").[101]

This paragraph reaches a crescendo in an expression of need that will enable Anselm to transition into his famous epistemological principle in paragraph 6.

Doce me quaerere te, et ostende te quaerenti; quia nec quaerere te possum nisi tu doceas, nec invenire nisi te ostendas. Quaeram te desiderando, desiderem quaerendo. Inveniam amando, amem inveniendo.[102]

Anselm brings the paragraph to climactic conclusion with two chiasms here (a literary device that Anselm will use regularly throughout the *Proslogion*): "let me seek you in desiring you, let me desire you in seeking you. Let me find you in loving you, let me love you in finding you."[103] Here the purpose of the chiasms seems to be to accent the comprehensiveness of Anselm's pursuit of God: he desires to attain God in every possible way that a fallen human being can (again, with both *mens* and *cor*). What emerges most forcefully

---

100. *P* 1, Schmitt I 100:8–10.
101. *P* 1, Schmitt I 100:7.
102. *P* 1, Schmitt I 100:8–11.
103. *P* 1, Schmitt I 100:10–11.

from this quoted section, however, is Anselm's absolute dependency upon God in order to know God. Before his well-known articulation of *fides quaerens intellectum* in the next paragraph, Anselm can already say, "I cannot seek you unless you teach me how, nor find you unless you show yourself."[104] In other words, it is not enough for God to merely teach Anselm how to seek him (*doce me quaerere te*); he must reveal himself to Anselm within that process of Anselm's seeking (*et ostende te quaerenti*).[105] Anselm seems to believe that God must, so to speak, both show him the path on which to walk as well as meet him along the pathway. The dual nature of Anselm's sense of need here recalls his earlier dual questions of *ubi* and *quomodo* with reference to *lux inaccessibilis*, underscoring again the depth of his dependence on divine grace and condescension. Anselm's need for God is as comprehensive as his desire for God.

In paragraph 6, an important new theological concept is introduced: the *imago Dei*.[106] This doctrine is the occasion for Anselm's gratitude, because it enables him to think of God, love God, and know God (*ut tui memor te cogitem, te amem*).[107] Yet it is also a source of lament for Anselm, because the divine image in him is so damaged and darkened by sin that he must be reformed and recreated for it to carry out its proper function.[108] Anselm therefore knows that he cannot fully attain to the knowledge of God, but he longs to see as much of God as he can, and so he once again petitions God for help.[109] The function of Anselm's reference to the *imago Dei*, therefore, seems to be to accent and provide further theological explanation for the contradiction that Anselm has found to dominate existence: he exists to see God, yet he cannot see God. He was made in God's image, yet that image is marred and twisted because of sin.

104. *P* 1, Schmitt I 100:9–10.
105. *P* 1, Schmitt I 100:8–9.
106. *P* 1, Schmitt I 100:12–13.
107. *P* 1, Schmitt I 100:13.
108. *P* 1, Schmitt I 100:13–15.
109. *P* 1, Schmitt I 100:15–17.

THE PURPOSE OF THE *PROSLOGION*

It is in this context, then—the wretchedness of the loss of the *visio Dei* due to sin and the deep yearning to recover it as a result of the *imago Dei* abiding within him—that Anselm introduces his famous formula: "for I do not seek to understand in order to believe, but I believe in order to understand. For I believe this also, that unless I believe, I shall not understand."[110] This second sentence (often sliced off in quotation) is from Isaiah 7:9, and, as observed in the first chapter, recurs at pivotal points both *On the Incarnation of the Word* and *Cur Deus Homo* in his explication of his understanding of the knowledge of God.[111] It is almost certain that Anselm derives this formula from St. Augustine, given that he uncharacteristically quotes a non-Vulgate version of Isaiah 7:9 and given Augustine's frequent use of this text to establish the priority and necessity of faith for understanding.[112] It is difficult to exaggerate the importance of this assertion, although it has at times been disconnected from Anselm's argument in the following chapters. In the first place, it is located at a pivotal intersection of the book: it occurs at the climax of this significant, introductory chapter, functioning as the resolution into which all the mounting tension culminates and immediately preceding his famous proof for God's existence. Furthermore, it flatly contradicts all those rationalistic interpretations of Anselm's thought and purpose in the *Proslogion* that insist he leaves room for the possibility of knowing God apart from faith. Anselm not only insists, "I do not seek to understand in order that I may believe," he also leaves a good deal of room for that which he simply *cannot*

---

110. *P* 1, Schmitt I 100:18–19.

111. *DIV* 1, Schmitt II 7:11–12, *CDH Commendatio*, Schmitt II, 40:8.

112. For instance, *De Trinitate* XV.2.2, where Augustine argues (strikingly similar to *Proslogion* 1) that God should always be sought even though he is incomprehensible. Anselm's language (*nisi credidero, non intelligam*) follows Augustine's (*nisi credideritis, non intellegetis*) except for the change from second person to first person (a natural change, given the first person throughout Anselm's prayer) while the Vulgate's language (*si non credideritis non permanebitis*) employs different vocabulary, most notably the change from *intellegetis* to *permanebitis*, which alters the sense of the phrase. Cf. the discussion in Logan, *Reading Anselm's "Proslogion,"* 91.

understand, claiming, "my understanding (*intellectum*) is in no way equal to your height."[113] Furthermore, Anselm seeks to understand what his heart *already* believes and loves (*veritatem tuam, quam credit et amat cor meum*); his understanding in no way establishes or even enhances his love but only elucidates and clarifies its object. These final sentences of chapter 1, then, join together with the *quaerentis intelligere quod credit* of the *Prooemium* to clarify that Anselm is not so much concerned with establishing God's existence in the *Proslogion* as he is with understanding what his faith already articulates about God. In fact, given the doctrines of sin, humanity, and happiness that Anselm has introduced throughout chapter 1, his aim seems to be nothing short of reestablishing the beatific vision for which he was created and for which his soul now longs.

What *Proslogion* 1 Reveals about the Purpose of the Book

What conclusions, then, can we draw from *Proslogion* 1 with respect to Anselm's purpose in the book? First, this chapter establishes the spiritual and aesthetic dimensions of the book: Anselm is concerned not merely with proving God intellectually but with meditating upon God as the remedy to his sinful misery and as the object of his deepest longings. Hence Anselm's *fides* is *quaerens gaudium* as much as it is *quaerens intellectum*, and as such it is a matter of *cor* as much as *mens*. The words *ad contemplandum deum* in the title of chapter 1 recall Anselm's stated *persona* in the *prooemium*, while the words *excitatio mentis* in the title anticipate the chapter's meditative feel. Apart from this call for rousing oneself to meditation, apart from the earnest requests for cleansing and illumination in this chapter, it is difficult to account for the rest of the book—not to mention the fact that Anselm can regard the entire book as a recapitulation of the many-chained arguments of *Monologion*.

113. *P* 1, Schmitt I 100:16.

Second, *Proslogion* 1 establishes that Anselm's method is *fides quaerens intellectum*. This principle is formally introduced at the close of the chapter, but it is operative implicitly throughout the chapter and indeed throughout the rest of the book (e.g., the first six words of *Proslogion* 2). We will misunderstand the *Proslogion* if we read the later philosophical discussion concerning the "ontological argument" back into it, forgetting that we are dealing with the text of an eleventh-century monk for whom philosophy, logic, theology, meditation, and Scripture were all harmonious tools in a larger effort directed at prayer and worship. In essence, the *Proslogion* is the product of a monastery, written to aid meditation on the divine essence. Any effort at bringing the *Proslogion* into dialogue with the later Western philosophical tradition must first appreciate this original context and the method of procedure expressed at the end of *Proslogion* 1.

Finally, *Proslogion* 1 establishes that Anselm's aim in the *Proslogion* is nothing less than the beatific vision. Whatever else follows in *Proslogion* 2–26 must redress the problems that Anselm articulates in chapter 1. That is why it is crucial to engage Anselm's doctrine of sin in order to understand the *Proslogion* (which involves his doctrine of creation, specifically the *imago Dei*). Any interpretation of the *Proslogion* that fails to account for Anselm's misery at the loss of the *visio Dei*, or his pursuit of *gaudium* in its rediscovery, has essentially eviscerated it from its original horizon of concerns. *Proslogion* 2–26 must be about the vision of God, not the mere existence of God, or Anselm has written *Proslogion* 1 in vain.

In an effort at breaking down the essential elements of the purpose of the *Proslogion*, we might summarize our conclusions in this threefold schema:

1. The *essence* of the *Proslogion*: *excitatio mentis ad contemplandum deum*
2. The *method* of the *Proslogion*: *fides quaerens intellectum*
3. The *object* of the *Proslogion*: *gaudium in visio dei*

That is to say: in the *Proslogion* a believing monk seeks the joy of the beatific vision by means of meditation on the divine essence.

Given this purpose, interpretations of the *Proslogion* that engage only chapters 2–3 of this work, or even only chapters 2–23, fall short of the whole *point* which these chapters serve. It is important for Anselm, of course, to prove what kind of being God is, and that certainly includes his existence and "necessary existence." But this same argument drives him on, not only to God's attributes and nature in chapters 5–24, but all the way to his doctrine of heaven in chapters 24–26. If our interpretation of the *Proslogion* does not enable us to explain why the book does not terminate with Anselm's identification of the Trinity as the *summum bonum* in chapter 23, we have likely failed to read the *Proslogion* whole. It is only in the anticipation of the soul's infinite joy in the vision of God in heaven that Anselm's purpose, as established by his own expressions in chapter 1, is actually realized. The movement of the whole book, in other words, is most basically a movement from misery to joy. It goes from "burdensome loss, burdensome sorrow, completely burdensome" (chapter 1) to "what great joy is there where so great a good is present!" (chapter 25). Only with *Proslogion* 1 in view can the book's logical arc from misery to ecstasy be visible.

Proslogion 2–4: More than an Ontological Argument

We can gain further insight into the purpose of the *Proslogion* by exploring the particular features that distinguish Anselm's proof(s) for God's existence in chapters 2–4. The term "ontological argument" as a heading for these chapters is somewhat misleading, and many of the unique qualities of Anselm's argument(s) have been overlooked in relation to those qualities shared by other kinds of "ontological argument." In fact, just as we have been suggesting that the later chapters of the *Proslogion* have been neglected, so some features of *Proslogion* 2–4 have received greater attention than others. In other words, when a focus on the so-called "ontological argument" governs the reading of the *Proslogion*, this involves not only an overfocus on *Proslogion* 2–4 to the neglect of the surrounding material but also certain kinds of prioritization and selectivity within *Proslogion* 2–4.

Already from the first sentence of *Proslogion* 2, it is evident that Anselm's concerns are stretched outside of the realm a generic theism: "Therefore, Lord, you who grant to faith understanding, grant to me that, insofar as you know it is useful, I may understand that you are just as we believe (*sicut credimus*), and that you are that which we believe."[114] It is evident that Anselm is interested here in the existence of a particular God, the God of his faith, and—what is more—the unique *kind* of existence he has. The chapter title is "that God truly exists" (as established above, "truly" is a better rendering of *vere* than "really") and *sit* here (and *es* throughout the chapter) could be just as easily translated is/are rather than exist/ exists. If Anselm were interested only or primarily in the fact of God's existence here in *Proslogion* 2, rather than the nature of God's existence, it is a strange request to make that God would "grant to me that, insofar as you know it is useful, that I may understand that you exist." Anselm's request is articulated here in a prayer (which presupposes the existence of the object of prayer), as a knowledge that must be *given* by God ("grant that," *da mihi*). Furthermore, Anselm qualifies this request with *quantum scis expidere* ("insofar as you know it is useful"). It is not easy to conceive how knowledge of the mere fact of God's existence could be more or less useful to Anselm, while, on the other hand, the particular quality and character of God's existence can be more readily understood as only useful or comprehensible in certain ways and, to a certain extent, as a gift of divine condescension for which Anselm must petition. Such a request recalls the immediately prior petition at the end of *Proslogion* 1, where Anselm identifies God's "height" and "truth" as only

---

114. P 2, Schmitt I 101:3–4.

partially graspable to his *intelligere*: "I do not try, Lord, to penetrate your height, because my understanding is in no way comparable to that. But I desire to understand your truth a little, that my heart believes and loves."[115] It would seem a crass equivocation that sought to identify God's "height" and "truth" here as his mere existence.

Furthermore, the specific request Anselm makes is not merely to know that God exists but that God exists *sicut credimus* ("just as we believe")—a phrase then further qualified with the clause *et hoc es quod credimus* ("and that you are what we believe"). These qualifying phrases are often interpreted as functioning in a parenthetical way here, as qualifiers of *es*, which is the real interest of Anselm's request. Arthur McGill's position is similar to this, where *sicut credimus* is taken parenthetically, while *et hoc es quod credimus* is then taken as a description of God's nature, with the result that Anselm is making the traditional distinction between God's existence and nature.[116] In this interpretation, the emphasis falls upon God's existence, which could be brought out with this paraphrase: "grant to me ... to understand that you exist (just as we do, in fact, believe you exist)." On the other hand, it is possible to read *both* of these qualifying phrases adverbially, as included within the purview of Anselm's request. In this interpretation, the emphasis in the first clause would fall upon *sicut* rather than *es*. This could be brought out in this kind of paraphrase: "grant me ... to understand that you are what we believe you are."

It seems superior on several grounds to take *sicut credimus* adverbially rather than parenthetically. To begin with, in the case of McGill's interpretation, the first qualifying phrase seems superfluous—one might ask why Anselm need bother to include the words *sicut credimus* in the first place. Grammatically, an adverbial interpretation of *sicut credimus* allows it to stand in parallel placement with *et hoc es quod credimus*, with *quia* functioning to introduce

---

115. *P* 1, Schmitt I 100:15–18.
116. Arthur C. McGill, "Anselm: *Proslogion*," in *The Many-Faced Argument*, 4n7.

both clauses and demarcating them both as objects of *intelligam*.[117] Furthermore, as stated earlier, the request occurs in the form of a prayer, a particular kind of prayer that reflects a deep awareness of the need for dependence upon God for knowledge of God (*da mihi*). If God's existence were Anselm's dominant interest, this kind of prayer would seem more natural once the argument has established that God indeed exists as the object of prayer in the first place. However, it is worth pointing out that *even if* one takes *sicut credimus* parenthetically, *Proslogion* 2 is still concerned with more than the mere fact of God's existence, because Anselm includes the additional clause *et hoc es quod credimus* as within the purview of his request.

A focus on the nature of God's existence in *Proslogion* 2, as articulated by his faith, becomes all the more plausible when we recall from the *prooemium* that Anselm's stated purpose includes *quaecumque de divina credimus substantia*. Such a wide horizon of interests makes it only expected for Anselm to seek *intellectum* concerning the nature of this God's existence. In this sense, *Proslogion* 2 is comparable to *Monologion* 28, titled "that this spirit exists simply, and created things do not exist compared to him."[118] Such a broader focus on the nature of God's unique existence is also to be expected in books designed to facilitate meditation on the divine essence, which is how Anselm articulates the purpose of the *Monologion* and *Proslogion*, not only in their own prefaces but also later in his career. For instance, in *On the Incarnation of the Word*, Anselm defines the primary purpose of both books (*quae ad hoc maxime facta sunt*, "which were made mainly for this") as proving not God's existence but his nature (*de divina natura et eius personis*, "the divine nature and persons").[119] In his private correspondence, Anselm will more explicitly identify the *Monologion* as a *De Trinitate*.[120]

---

117. This is the third usage listed by Lewis and Short, *A Latin Dictionary*, 1511.
118. *M* 28, Schmitt I 45:24.
119. *DIV* 6, Schmitt II 20:17–19.
120. As observed by Marcia L. Colish, *The Mirror of Language: A Study in the*

Just as in the first sentence of *Proslogion* 2 Anselm is not praying to a generic *deus* but to the *domine* of his faith, so the famous divine name introduced in the second sentence of *Proslogion* 2, *aliquid quo nihil maius cogitari possit* ("that than which nothing greater can be conceived"), is articulated specifically as an article of faith: *credimus te esse* ("we believe you to be").[121] Here Anselm is not operating on the basis of some abstract philosophical principle that could arise from a neutral standpoint. He is exploring a particular article of his faith, in a manner compelled by his faith, and this article of faith already includes within it all that will follow in *Proslogion* 2–26, as a seed contains all that will blossom into a tree. In other words, before Anselm uses the formula *aliquid quo nihil maius cogitari possit* as the means by which to establish the existence of God, he situates this formula in his faith. Of course, this kind of argumentative movement, in which *intelligere* is sought by and within *fides*, should have been expected in light of the procedure Anselm has outlined in *Proslogion* 1. Nonetheless, it is also evident from a careful reading of these first two sentences of *Proslogion* 2.

It is only after these first two sentences that Anselm proceeds more specifically to the question God's existence, in the much analyzed passage initiated in sentence 3: "or can it be that a thing of such nature cannot exist?"[122] Anselm is indeed interested in a proof for God's existence at this point, but as we shall see it is a very particular kind of proof. To help elucidate his argument, Anselm introduces the quotation of the fool from Psalm 13:1/52:1 that "there is no God." Augustine will quote the same text in his *Enarrationes in Psalmos* (though using the term *imprudens* instead of *inspiens*), claiming that there are men who deny the existence of God but that those who do not believe say so in their hearts because they

---

Medieval Theory of Knowledge, rev. ed. (Lincoln: University of Nebraska Press, 1983), 90. The parallels between *Monologion* and Augustine's classic text are frequently observed.

121. P 2, Schmitt I 101:4–5.
122. P 2, Schmitt I 101:5–7.

dare not say it openly.[123] Elsewhere in his writings, Anselm will contrast the fool with the orthodox Christian who accepts "sacred authority," identifying the fool as one who arrogantly rejects what he cannot understand.[124] Despite Anselm's medieval context, it is unlikely that he was unaware of the real denial of God's existence as a philosophical position.[125] Two of Anselm's own disciples (Rodulphus and Gilbert Crispin) would later write dialogues in which they address those who believe in nothing but what they can see with their eyes.[126] Eileen Sweeney observes that another common approach in Anselm's time, from Cassiodorus to Peter the Chanter, was to identify the fool of the Psalms passage as the Jew who does not confess Christ's deity.[127]

Nonetheless, Anselm's use of the term *insipiens* must be defined both in relation to his monastic vocation and to its specific function in *Proslogion* 2. As a Benedictine monk, Anselm would have recited the fool's denial of God at least twice a week, since it occurs at the start of both Psalms 13 (14) and 52 (53), and the *Rule of St. Benedict* suggests chanting the Psalms once per week at a minimum (and Lanfranc may have required much more than this). Thus, as John Clayton puts it, Anselm thus "would have lived with the fool and reflected on his foolishness every week of his life."[128] It is not unnatural that Anselm would draw upon such a concept deeply ingrained into his prayer life as a sort of *persona* by which to elucidate his conception of God (just as he uses dialogue form in so many other writings).

Strictly speaking, then, the fool is neither an atheist nor a theist, nor a person at all, but rather an intellectual construct of Anselm

123. Cf. Logan, *Reading Anselm's "Proslogion,"* 93.
124. *Resp.* 8, Schmitt 137:28–138:3; *CDH* 1:25, Schmitt II 95:18–20; *DIV* 6, Schmitt II 21:1–3.
125. On this point, cf. the balanced analysis of Colish, *The Mirror of Language*, 85.
126. See the discussion in Charlesworth, *St. Anselm's "Proslogion,"* 57.
127. Eileen Sweeney, *Anselm of Canterbury and the Desire for the Word*, 113.
128. John Clayton, "The Otherness of Anselm," in *The Otherness of God*, ed. Orrin F. Summerell, 24.

THE PURPOSE OF THE *PROSLOGION*

the monk. Were this construct to be fully instantiated in any actual person, it would doubtless entail an atheist—but it is also possible to conceive of the fool as manifested more subtly in any impulse of the heart against the practical reality of God in various spheres of life, including the fallen heart of the believer seeking to meditate upon God's essence.[129] Thus the *function* of the fool in the *Proslogion*, as Colish puts it, is as "a hypothetical straw man rather than an organized contemporary threat to the Christian faith."[130] In other words, for Anselm the fool represents not so much an opponent to the believer but a tool by which the believer explores his faith, and God's theoretical non-existence in these chapters arises not as an external threat to Anselm's project of *fides quaerens intellectum* but within that project, as one stage of the pursuit of the *visio dei*.

Furthermore, Anselm's aims in relation to the fool are considerably less ambitious than those of modern "apologetics." In *Cur Deus Homo* Anselm seeks to "refute the foolishness of unbelievers and break down their obstinacy," and in *On the Incarnation of the Word* he seeks to "curb the presumption" of those who arrogantly reject what they cannot understand. Similarly, in the *Proslogion* Anselm is not seeking to bring the fool to faith so much as to elucidate the implications of his denial of God.[131] How could Anselm seek to bring the fool to *intellectum* by means of his argument and apart from *fides*, in light of the methodology outlined in *Proslogion* 1—to say nothing of his insistence elsewhere on the necessity of the cleansing of the heart, enlightening the eyes, and living in childlike obedience, according to the Spirit?[132]

To be clear, Anselm's interest in *Proslogion* 2 cannot be *less* than divine existence. If Anselm has no interest in proving that God ex-

---

129. Cf. Sweeney, *Anselm of Canterbury and the Desire for the Word*, 111n4: "the 'fool' in Anselm's argument is not so much an atheist but the atheist or at least agnostic within the believer."
130. Colish, *The Mirror of Language*, 86.
131. Cf. *CDH* Schmitt II 39:3–4, *DIV* I, Schmitt II 6:5–10.
132. *DIV* I, Schmitt II 8:7–19.

ists, as in the tradition of Stolz's interpretation, it is curious to find Anselm thanking God at the end of *Proslogion* 4 that his argument has proven *tu esse*.[133] One is also not well positioned to explain why Anselm seeks to illumine the nature of God's existence in relation to the claim of the fool or how his distinction throughout *Proslogion* 2 between existence *in intellectu* or *in re* functions. In other words, the fact that there is much more than an argument for God's existence in *Proslogion* 2–4 need not entail a denial of the presence of that kind of argument as well, as though *esse* and *vere esse* were at odds with one another. But for Anselm, the fact of God's existence and the nature of God's existence were not independent data that could be treated in isolation. Ironically, the denial of an argument for God's existence here seems to result from the same modern tendency to split apart God's nature and existence, as though one could imagine the prayerful pursuit *intelligere* in *Proslogion* 2 as interested in God's existence but not the *nature* of that existence (or vice versa).

The movement from *Proslogion* 2 to *Proslogion* 3 is commonly held to be a movement from God's existence to God's necessary existence, thus revealing two distinct arguments for God's existence in the *Proslogion*.[134] This way of construing the relationship between *Proslogion* 2–3, while helpfully illuminating some of the differences between the two chapters and furthering sensitivity to the nuances of Anselm's text, nonetheless still falls far short of amounting to an adequate description of these chapters. In the first place, such a schema tends to obscure the organic continuity that connects *Proslogion* 2–3 in the single flow of thought toward chapter 4.[135] For Anselm, the argument of chapter 3 is already entailed

---

133. *P* 4, Schmitt I 104:6.

134. This interpretation was advanced by Hartshorne and Malcolm in the 1960's as a means of reviving the ontological argument and has become a standard schema for interpreting the relationship between these two chapters since that time. See Norman Malcolm, "Anselm's Ontological Arguments," 41–62, and Charles Hartshorne, *The Logic of Perfection*.

135. Mackey refers to the argument of *Proslogion* 3 as an "intensification" of the

in the divine name recounted in chapter 2, and the argument of chapter 2 is actually incomplete without the argument of chapter 3, since its aim is to show *quod Deus vere est*, and it is not until chapter 3 that this conclusion is actually reached. The earliest manuscripts of the *Proslogion* did not contain chapter divisions in the text—the chapter titles were listed at the beginning, and then the transition from one chapter to another was indicated by Anselm with a number in the margin of the text.[136] So originally the text ran continuously from chapter 2 to chapter 3, and the *quod* that begins *Proslogion* 3 refers specifically back to the *aliquid* in the last sentence of *Proslogion* 2, referring to "that than which nothing greater can be thought."[137] Having demonstrated the existence of a being than which nothing greater can be thought in chapter 2, Anselm now restates this conclusion to derive further implications concerning the nature of this being's existence (*sic vere est ut*), only then connecting this being with the God of his faith. Thus *Proslogion* 2 and *Proslogion* 3 represent not two distinct arguments so much as two phases of one longer argument schema (which, additionally, is not yet completed within chapter 3).[138]

Furthermore, the label "necessary existence" is not strictly accurate for what concerns Anselm in *Proslogion* 3, despite its common usage.[139] This is a later philosophical category of thought and terminology that is incorrectly projected back onto Anselm, the eleventh-century monk. Anselm never actually refers to the necessary existence of God in *Proslogion* 3, although it may well be

---

argument of *Proslogion* 2 ("Peregrinations of the Word," 83). This is one helpful way of construing the organic connection between the two arguments, without diminishing the development that takes place from the first to the second.

136. Logan, *Reading Anselm's "Proslogion,"* 88; Schufreider, *Confessions of a Rational Mystic*, 114, 148, 165.

137. Logan, *Reading Anselm's "Proslogion,"* 95.

138. For further discussion of the relation of *Proslogion* 2 and 3, as well as the relation of both to *Monologion* 28, see Schufreider, *Confessions of a Rational Mystic*, 156–68.

139. Barth's title for *Proslogion* 3 is superior: "the special existence of God" (*Anselm: Fides Quaerens Intellectum*, 132).

an implication of what Anselm does speak of here, which may be more accurately summarized as the unthinkableness of the nonexistence of God. This is what he refers to in the chapter title (*quod non possit cogitari non esse*), and this is what he then returns to as his established conclusion at the ending of the argument of the first paragraph in the chapter (*ut nec cogitari possit non esse*).[140] The distinction between these labels is important: the label "necessary existence" usually refers to entities that could not *not* exist[141]—not to entities that could not be *thought* not to exist, which is what concerns Anselm. Furthermore, when Anselm states the kind of existence he has in view here in positive terms, he speaks of God's "true" existence: God exists "so truly" (*sic vere*, used twice) that he therefore cannot be thought not to exist.[142] That "true existence" is a broader category of thought than "necessary existence" seems entailed by the fact that Anselm will draw as its consequence both that God possesses existence most "greatly" (*maxime*) and that God possesses existence in a way that is different than all other things: *solus igitur verissime omnium, et ideo maxime omnium habes esse* ("you alone therefore, exist of all things most truly, and therefore you possess existence of all things most greatly").[143] We may say that Anselm is concerned not just with God's necessary existence, therefore, but with his true existence, his great existence, and therefore his absolutely unique existence of all other existing things. Indeed, Anselm emphasizes that existence is God's *possession* rather than an external reality in which he participates (*habes esse*).

All this is entailed in Anselm's argument thus far: which is a

---

140. *P* 3, Schmitt I 102:5, 103:1–2.

141. Cf. Barry Miller, "Making Sense of 'Necessary Existence'," *American Philosophical Quarterly* 11, no. 1 (Jan 1974): 47–54.

142. Logan suggests translating *sic vere* "truly in such a way" rather than "so truly" or "truly to such an extent," in order to avoid importing Neo-platonic categories onto the phrase (*Reading Anselm's "Proslogion*," 95). "So truly" seems to me to reflect sufficient ambiguity so as to avoid the same danger, while perhaps remaining a little less clumsy.

143. *P* 3, Schmitt I 103:8–9.

good deal more than God's existence, so much so that if a mere divine proof were all that were drawn from the text thus far, it would actually obscure Anselm's argument. For Anselm's whole point is that God exists in a way that is so ontologically distinct from everything else that God is *not* like other existing things. As Barth puts it, "God exists—if he does exist—in the unique manner that befits him as the only One who ultimately really exists."[144] How could Anselm emphasize in the *Monologion* such a stark contrast between divine existence and all other forms of existence that he can assert, "created things do not exist compared to him"[145]—only to then to return to a proof of generic existence in the *Proslogion*? Such a proof would not concern the God to whom Anselm prays but would necessarily involve some other entity. Therefore, to see nothing more than a proof of divine existence in *Proslogion* 2–3 is not merely to fall short of Anselm's aims but actually to be at cross-purposes with them. A God who has *esse* but not *vere esse*, a God who is merely an object within reality (*tu esse*) rather than the ground of reality (*habes esse*), a God who is merely the instantiation of a species within a larger genus—such a God is neither *aliquid quo nihil maius cogitari possit* nor the God whose *habitatio* is *lux inaccessibilis* and is thus not the God whose sight is the fulfillment of all of Anselm's longings.

Common interpretations of *Proslogion* 3 typically fail to make visible the twofold division of this chapter. In the first paragraph, Anselm argues for the incomprehensibility of the nonexistence of God. In the second paragraph, Anselm identifies the "God" (*deus*) whose nonexistence is incomprehensible with the "Lord" (*domine*) in whom he has been trusting and to whom he has been pleading, further expounding upon the nature of his existence: *et hoc es tu*.[146] Importantly, at this point the transition to third person that was initiated in the third sentence of *Proslogion* 2 reverts back to the second person personal address of prayer that characterizes the entire

---

144. Barth, *Anselm: Fides Quaerens Intellectum*, 98.
145. *M* 28, Schmitt I 45:24.
146. *P* 3, Schmitt I 103:3.

work. It is therefore at this point—halfway through chapter 3, not at the start of chapter 3—that a substantive transition occurs. It is not the transition of the introduction of a new argument, however, but the transition of a reverting back to prayer, the transition of identification—for at this point Anselm identifies *aliquid quo nihil maius cogitari possit* as his *deus* and *domine*. It is significant that Anselm only makes this identification after he has proven *both* that God truly exists and that God cannot be thought not to exist, for evidently both of these axioms are important before he can connect the dots between what he has proven and what he believes in, between *aliqua talis natura* ("some such nature") and *domine deus noster* ("Lord our God"). This understanding of the flow of *Proslogion* 2–3 further underscores Anselm's concern with the nature of God's existence. Furthermore, that Anselm continues in this section to be motivated and directed by the concerns of his faith is evident from the fact that God's role as creator and judge is axiomatic in Anselm's argumentation: "for if some mind was able to think of something better than you, the creature would rise above the creator, and judge concerning the creator, which is completely absurd."[147] Were Anselm operating outside of the domain of *fides quaerens intellectum* at any point here, he could hardly introduce such essentially Christian doctrines as creation and judgment to advance his argument without some kind of justification for them.

Anselm's concern with the incomprehensibility of God's nonexistence in chapter 3 explains a fact that seems difficult to account for under many readings of the book, namely, the existence of *Proslogion* 4. If Anselm were narrowly interested in an ontological argument for God's existence, this chapter would seem quite superfluous. But given Anselm's larger interests concerning the nature and uniqueness of God's existence, the logical flow from chapter 3 to chapter 4 becomes sensible and even necessary: if it is indeed unthinkable that God should not exist, it is only natural to inquire how the fool can

---

147. *P* 3, Schmitt I 103:4–6.

deny his existence in the first place. After responding to this dilemma by positing a distinction between two different kinds of "thinking a thought" with respect to signification, Anselm concludes:

> Thanks be to you, good Lord, thanks be to you, because what I first believed through your grace, now I thus understand through your illumination, so that even if I did not want to believe that you exist, I could not fail to understand it.[148]

It is evident from this summary conclusion that Anselm does not perceive his argument to have produced any kind of transition from unfaith to faith but rather from faith to understanding (as we would expect from his concluding formula in *Proslogion* 1). Furthermore, as his faith is the product of God's grace (*te donante*), so his understanding is the product of God's illumination (*te illuminante*). This is a term that is used elsewhere in Anselm's writings in reference to spiritual eyes being illumined through obeying God's commandments, where it stands parallel to having the heart cleansed by faith.[149] The fact that Anselm concludes this chapter by giving thanks to God for his illumination once again underscores his interest not just in a generic proof of Divinity but with a particular kind of knowledge of God—a knowledge that results from faith and furthers him along in his desire to see God.

Conclusion: Why the Purpose of the *Proslogion* Encourages a Holistic Reading

The purpose of the *Proslogion* established in this chapter necessitates reading this book in a more holistic way than it is usually read. If the *Proslogion* most basically consists of Anselm's worshipful pursuit of the beatific vision rather than most basically consisting of an "ontological argument," then we must embrace it as a work of twenty-six chapters; we must resist the temptation to slice off those "philosoph-

---

148. *P* 4, Schmitt I 104:5–7.
149. *DIV* I, Schmitt II 8:8–9.

ical" elements of the book from the monastic, meditative thrust with which they are interwoven; we must submit to the discipline of tracing out that logical arc of thought that begins with the *grave damnum* of *Proslogion* 1 and ends with the *gaudium plenum* of *Proslogion* 26. From the first word of the book—*homuncio*—to the final words of the book—*deus benedictus in saecula amen*—Anselm has not simply established the existence of God: he has traversed that entire span from human sin and misery to redemption and beatitude; and his argument for God's existence is the same argument (*unum argumentum*) that enables him to make this entire journey. The same insight by which he has seen that God exists most truly is what has enabled him to see that God is also the *summum bonum* of the human soul and, further, "whatever else we believe about the divine substance." All this is included within the *purpose* of the *Proslogion*.

But before Anselm arrives upon his doctrine of the soul's joy in heaven in *Proslogion* 24–26, he will first explore a whole range of reflections concerning God's nature and attributes in *Proslogion* 5–23. If we take it as axiomatic that Anselm was not wasting space in the *Proslogion* and that we should read the book according to his own intentions rather than later philosophical discussion, then these chapters are worth exploring, and we should not regard their whole range of topics as irrelevant to Anselm's purposes in the book. Instead, all these meditations on theology proper—from the problem of divine justice and mercy in *Proslogion* 9–10, through the nature of the *lux inaccessibilis* in *Proslogion* 16, to the interrelation of simplicity and Trinity in *Proslogion* 23—must be relevant to Anselm's pursuit of the *visio Dei* for which his soul yearns. Therefore, in our next chapter, before we explore the doctrine of heaven in *Proslogion* 23–26, we will trace out, as best we are able, the logical flow of thought by which Anselm progresses to that point in *Proslogion* 5–22. Once we have grasped the structure of the book, we will then be positioned to explore how heaven is a fitting resolution its earlier themes, just as the view from the peak of a mountain brings fitting resolution to the long walk upward.

CHAPTER 4

The Structure of the *Proslogion*

Spirals Upward from Chapter 5 to Chapter 22

> A profound book answers a problem less than
> it poses a question more vividly and more
> accurately.
>
> —PAUL GILBERT

In a recent article, Dom Jean-Charles Nault has objected to the isolation of *Proslogion* 2–4 in relation to the rest of the work:

Very often one can reduce the *Proslogion* just to chapters 2 to 4, which one is accustomed to call the "ontological argument." Certainly, those three chapters are essential, but the *Proslogion* is not limited to establishing a proof of the existence of God. In proposing a continuous reading of this text under the perspective of prayer, one can rediscover the underlying dynamism of the whole work.[1]

Nault also references that the book concludes with the themes of joy and heaven, suggesting that these themes appropriately follow from its argument for God. As he put it, "the quest for God opens out into joy."[2] But in the space of

---

1. Nault, "The First Chapter of St. Anselm's *Proslogion*," 35.
2. Nault, "The First Chapter of St. Anselm's *Proslogion*," 40.

his eight-page article he does not explore these intriguing observations. Here we attempt our own "continuous reading" of the *Proslogion*, particularly focused on chapters 5–22, seeking to explore what kind of "underlying dynamism" characterizes the work's structure and flow of thought.

There is a natural pause at the end of *Proslogion* 4, because at this point Anselm stops to thank God that what he formerly believed by God's grace, now he understands by God's illumination:

Gratias tibi, bone domine, gratias tibi, quia quod prius credidi te donante, iam sic intelligo te illuminante, ut si te esse nolim credere, non possim non intelligere.[3]

Anselm clearly understands himself to have crossed some kind of threshold from the beginning of *Proslogion* 2 to his current state here at the end of *Proslogion* 4: there is a transition from *prius* to *iam*, from belief (*credidi*) to understanding (*intelligo*), from God's giving (*te donante*) to God's illumination (*te illuminante*). But what exactly is the threshold Anselm has crossed? Many interpreters of the *Proslogion* see the *unum argumentum* as coming to a close here, and the frequent impression is that the real labor of the *Proslogion* is over, so that chapters 5–26 are really a kind of appendix or afterword to the real substance of the book (just as chapter 1 is often seen as a kind of "warm up" to chapters 2–4). Thus, for Gillian R. Evans, *Proslogion* 2–4 contain the *unum argumentum*, while *Proslogion* 5–26 evidence the "implications of his *argumentum*."[4]

But Anselm himself identifies the particular illumination he has received in *Proslogion* 2–4 as the undeniability of God's existence (*ut si te esse nolim credere, non possim non intelligere*)—which is evidently not the exclusive interest of the *unum argumentum*, as outlined in the book's *prooemium*. As we have observed, the *unum argumentum* of the *Proslogion* is designed to recapitulate the "many-chained" arguments of the *Monologion*, and it aims to establish not

3. P 4, Schmitt I 104:5–7.
4. G. R. Evans, *Saint Anselm of Canterbury*, 53.

merely that God exists but that he exists as the *summum bonum* and thus as the greatest human joy.[5] Hence Anselm picks up immediately in *Proslogion* 5 with the same divine formula produced by his *unum argumentum* to explore what else can be proved about God: "what therefore are you, Lord God, than whom nothing greater can be thought?"[6] The energy with which Anselm pursues this question throughout *Proslogion* 5–26 indeed gives the impression of an extension and continuation of the central and animating concerns of the book, rather than mere implications or consequences of those concerns. So, if we approach these chapters in search of an "underlying dynamism" that binds them together, what do we find?

At first glance, Anselm's topical arrangement in *Proslogion* 5–26 may seem a bit haphazard. We might wonder by what rubric, for instance, divine eternity is given such emphasis (chapters 13, 18, 19, 20, 21), while other divine attributes (say, divine omniscience) seem to be out of view. The recurrent role given to divine simplicity (chapters 12, 18, 22, and especially 23) might appear a bit clumsy or repetitive. Several chapters might appear altogether random, like *Proslogion* 21, "whether this is 'the age of the age' or 'the ages of the ages.'" Nonetheless, in this chapter we will suggest that the structure of the later chapters of the *Proslogion* is not haphazard but rather deliberate and incremental. Anselm composed the *Proslogion* with a great deal of care and precision, and, if we follow the logical transitions carefully, we will be able to detect a guiding thread throughout these chapters—one that is, in fact, not unrelated to the proof of God's existence in chapters 2–4.[7] That is to say, the *unum argumentum* that Anselm pursues in the book's early chapters places him on a certain trajectory, and each subsequent

---

5. *P prooemium*, Schmitt I 93:7–9.
6. *P* 5, Schmitt I 104:11.
7. As we observed in the last chapter, the chapter titles were not included in the body of Anselm's original text but were instead listed at the front of the book and then indicated by a number in the margin. This means that the text is more continuous and fluid than sometimes realized, even while the chapter breaks are hermeneutically significant and original to Anselm.

part of the book plays an important role in helping him arrive at the goal of this trajectory.

Specifically, we will suggest three distinct "spiraling" movements in the *Proslogion* as Anselm ascends upward toward the beatific vision. In this schema, the book is divided roughly into two halves, and three sections from the latter half pick up on themes of the earlier half even while they also transcend them.[8] First, we will observe various aspects of *Proslogion* 14 that seem to both draw upon and simultaneously transcend *Proslogion* 1. Both of these important "prayer chapters" have been overlooked in the study of the *Proslogion*, although they are programmatically significant for Anselm, slicing the book into two 13-chapter halves.[9] Anselm's emphasis on divine hiddenness and incomprehensibility in *Proslogion* 14 is an important step *en route* to the beatific vision and leads him into the second "spiral," his identification of the *lux inaccessibilis* as divine hiddenness in chapters 15–17. Just as *Proslogion* 14 recapitulates and simultaneously transcends *Proslogion* 1, so Anselm's conception of God as "greater than can be thought" (*maius quam cogitari possit*) draws on the language of his earlier divine formula in *Proslogion* 2–4, while it also surpasses it. It is essential to the interpretation of the *Proslogion* that Anselm does not arrive at the insight of chapter 15 (an essential contribution to his doctrine of God) within his proof of God's existence but only after the further theological elaboration on divine attributes in chapters 5–13 and

8. The image of "spirals" in the structure of the *Proslogion* is similar to Gilbert's image of "rings" (*anneaux*), but Gilbert seems to conceive of the progression of the *Proslogion* in terms of rings primarily to highlight its incremental nature, whereby each section follows from the previous one and succeeds into the next one; by "spirals" I mean to indicate, in addition to this, distinct repetitions of earlier material in the later chapters. Cf. Gilbert, *Le "Proslogion" de S. Anselme*, 143. Elsewhere Gilbert will speak of "repetition" as a motif in the development of the *Proslogion*, in the Kierkegaardian sense of the term (197).

9. In addition to Stolz and Cattin, Henri de Lubac also draws attention to the significance of *Proslogion* 14. Henri de Lubac, "'Seigneur, je cherche ton visage': Sur le chapitre xiv du Proslogion de saint Anselme," in *Archives de Philosophie* 39 (1976): 201–25.

the prayer of chapter 14. Not yet by chapter 14, let alone by chapter 4, have the prayers of *Proslogion* 1 been answered.

Finally, we will argue that chapters 18–22 represent a spiraling upward from chapters 6–13 with respect to God's attributes, moving from "lower" to "higher" or "hidden" attributes.[10] To construct a metaphor: in *Proslogion* 6–13, Anselm is surveying the mountain that rises up in front of him; in *Proslogion* 18–22, he is gazing through squinted eyes to the sun above and beyond the mountain, which is ultimately beyond his vision. Chapters 18–22 thus bear a similar relationship to chapters 6–13, as chapters 15–17 do to chapters 2–4, and chapter 14 does to chapter 1: they draw from the earlier material as well as transcend it. While the focus of chapters 6–13, for instance, is on solving apparent contradictions in the divine attributes by the divine formula ("that than which nothing greater can be thought"), chapters 18–22 use Anselm's new formula ("that which is greater than can be thought") to emphasize the unity and wholeness of God's nature. That is to say, *Proslogion* 6–13 is concerned with the harmony of the divine attributes; *Proslogion* 18–22 is concerned with the simplicity and uniqueness of the divine essence. This is a meaningful progression, in light of the expressed aims of *Proslogion* 1, because Anselm's ultimate purpose is to establish God as the highest good of the human soul. A God with merely harmonious attributes is not yet the *omne et unum et totum et solum bonum* for which Anselm's soul yearns.[11]

This identification of the Trinity as *unum bonum* is made in *Proslogion* 23, which leads Anselm into his vision of heaven in *Proslogion* 24–26. It is possible to divide each thirteen-chapter half of the book into further chiastic 4- and 9-chapter sections, resulting in a

---

10. The term "attributes" is not intrinsic to Anselm and may not be the most accurate term for describing Anselm's interests in these chapters, but nonetheless we will use the traditional terminology for the sake of clarity; the terms "lower" and "higher" are my own attempt to differentiate those more definite and more revealed attributes of God from those more intrinsically related to his essence and incomprehensibility.

11. P 23, Schmitt I 117:21–22: "the complete, one, total, and only good."

4–9–9–4 sequence. In this schema, the first four chapters introduce the beatific vision as the intent of the book, while in the last four Anselm anticipates the realization of this intention. The middle sections of the book then represent the ascent upward into the doctrine of God, with the first 9 chapters (*Proslogion* 5–13) focusing more on "lower" divine attributes and the second 9 chapters (*Proslogion* 14–22) focusing more on "higher" divine attributes. *Proslogion* 23, then, initiates the final section of the book, where Anselm identifies God as the *unum bonum* of the human soul; in *Proslogion* 24–26 he then applies this conclusion to his soul's hunger for God. One might summarize the overall chapter progression in two phases, like this:

	first iteration	*spiraling up*
Prayer	1	14
Divine formula	2–4	15–17
Divine attributes	5–13	18–22

The logical progression we detect in *Proslogion* 5–22 is not intended to exclude the possibility of occasional diversions or "rabbit trails" in Anselm's text or to locate every instance of symmetry or progression as a conscious intention on Anselm's part. Strictly speaking, "flow of thought" might be superior to "structure" as a label for this chapter. Nonetheless, Anselm does not randomly stumble into his vision of heaven in *Proslogion* 24–26. There is an undeniable and purposeful trajectory throughout the book, and each of the spiraling movements upward plays an important role in getting him to this point. To explore this, we will walk through *Proslogion* 5–22, looking for indications as to how Anselm understands his argument to develop and the major turning points in the progression of thought. Since we are dealing with such a large amount of text, we cannot be exhaustive but must restrict our focus to some of the more important passages and broader patterns. Before tracing through the chapters chronologically, however, we will engage with several recent German and French works as entry points into the structure and nature of the chapters of the *Proslogion*.

Gilbert and Karl on the Structure of the *Proslogion*

Paul Gilbert's approach to the structure of the *Proslogion* draws attention to its parallels with the *Monologion*:

	Monologion	Proslogion
existence de Dieu	1–2	2–4
essence de Dieu	13–28	5–22
Trinité	29–63	23
anthropologie	64–78	24–26[12]

Later, Gilbert divides the section *essence de Dieu* into two further subsections: *Proslogion* 5–12, which deals with the essential divine attributes as given in Scripture; and *Proslogion* 13–22, which Gilbert places under the rubric of divine eternity.[13] Gilbert continues his comparison of the structure of the *Monologion* and *Proslogion* into these smaller sections of the book—for instance, he argues that *Proslogion* 5–11 roughly correspond to *Monologion* 15 and must be read in light of it.[14] In his shorter writings as well, Gilbert also treats *Proslogion* 5–11 as a unit in relation to *Monologion* 15, while *Proslogion* 5–22 is considered in relation to *Monologion* 13–28.[15]

The fourfold structure that Gilbert detects in the *Proslogion* is in many respects an accurate reflection of the flow of topics in the *Proslogion*, and the comparison to the structure of the *Monologion* makes it a compelling proposal for consideration. One of the strengths of his proposal is that it highlights the *progression* of thought in the *Proslogion* from God to human faith. This certainly surpasses those proposals that break down the *Proslogion* simply in terms of a back-and-forth alternation between prayer exercises and intellectual inquiry, without a clear conception of the logical

---

12. Gilbert, *Le "Proslogion" de S. Anselme*, 16.
13. Gilbert, *Le "Proslogion" de S. Anselme*, 111.
14. Gilbert, *Le "Proslogion" de S. Anselme*. 121.
15. Gilbert, "Justice et miséricorde dans le *Proslogion* de saint Anselme," 227–37.

development from earlier sections to later ones.[16] Nonetheless, while Gilbert's schema works as a general description of the flow of topics in the book, his chapter breaks and the more general breakdown into four sections present several challenges. First, slicing *existence de Dieu* and *essence de Dieu* into two separate categories raises troubles. As we have seen in chapter 3, Anselm does not regard God's existence and God's essence as issues that can be treated in separation, and *Proslogion* 2–4 concerns the latter as well as the former. Moreover, it is not at all clear that *Monologion* 1–2 should be placed under the category *existence de Dieu* rather than *essence de Dieu*, since Anselm's focus there is specifically with God's identity as the supreme source of all good. The absence of a strict proof of divine existence in the *Monologion* recalls our comments in the last chapter concerning the differences between the two books and limits the extent to which the comparison between them should function as a controlling hermeneutic for their structure.

Second, Gilbert does not situate *Proslogion* 1 or *Monologion* 79–80 in relation to his schema. It is difficult to imagine these monumentally important sections, the one introducing Anselm's goals at the beginning of the text and the other encapsulating them at the end, with each representing an emotional peak within their respective contexts, as irrelevant to their structures. If they are included, they further complicate the comparison of the structure of the two books. *Proslogion* 1 is especially disruptive to this comparison. Third, it seems a bit forced to place *Monologion* 64–78 under the rubric *anthropologie*, particularly to the extent that *anthropologie* is also the label for *Proslogion* 24–26. *Monologion* 64–78 are more concerned with individual human faith and rationality, whereas *Proslogion* 24–26 are more explicitly focused on the communal joy of heaven. These two sections seem parallel to one another only in a very general and somewhat superficial way.

Fourth, the disproportionate amount of text that Anselm gives

---

16. Cf., e.g., Adams, "Anselm on Faith and Reason," in *The Cambridge Companion to Anselm*, 36.

to the Trinity in the *Monologion* versus the *Proslogion* raises suspicions about whether *Proslogion* 23 merits a place as its own unit.[17] Perhaps Anselm, in condensing the "many-chained" arguments of the *Monologion*, has really collapsed thirty-four chapters into sixteen lines. But the disparity of length also might suggest that the *Proslogion*'s treatment of the Trinity is better understood as distinct from, rather than a distillation of, that of the *Monologion*.[18] Fifth, clumping a section as large as *Proslogion* 5–22 together as a unit, particularly in relation to the size of the other units, runs the risk of minimizing important transitions that occur within this unit. The climactic and recapitulative prayers of *Proslogion* 14 and 18, for instance, appear to occupy too little significance in this interpretation—though, to be fair, Gilbert does note the fact that these chapters return to the form of prayer initiated in *Proslogion* 1.[19] The fact that Gilbert divides *Proslogion* 5–22 into two sections at times (for instance, in the larger structure of his book) mitigates but does not eliminate this concern, because even when treating the subsections within these chapters, Gilbert insists that "chapters 5 to 22 constitute a homogeneous whole (*ensemble homogène*)."[20]

Sixth, Gilbert's fourfold division of the *Proslogion* runs the risk of obscuring the organic and incremental development of the book. Anselm does not end by simply moving from *Dieu* to *anthropologie*, but from *la grandeur de Dieu* to *la joie d'anthropologie*. In other words, Anselm ends by *applying* what his argument has established about God to human joy, bringing resolution to the petitions of *Proslogion* 1. From this angle, the *Proslogion* does not have four

---

17. Gilbert recognizes this disproportion (*Le "Proslogion" de S. Anselme*, 203).
18. So Evans provides a detailed comparative analysis of the *Monologion* and the *Proslogion*, arguing that the treatment of the Trinity in the former has no direct parallel in the latter (*Anselm and Talking about God*, 59–60). Instead, the *Proslogion*, with only the briefest exception in chapter 23, confines its focus to the attributes of God's substance (such as omnipotence, immutability), rather than Trinitarian relations.
19. Gilbert, *Le "Proslogion" de S. Anselme*, 147.
20. Gilbert, *Le "Proslogion" de S. Anselme*, 146.

topics but one; it is a book about God as the object of all human longing, and the entire text represents the unpacking of this single theme. Any breakdown of its chapters must reflect this overarching unity.

Siegried Karl's depiction of the structure of the *Proslogion* is shaped not by a comparison to the *Monologion* but rather by exploration of the relation of reason and religious affection throughout the work. As we have noted, Karl approaches the *Proslogion* fundamentally as a model for how human rationality and affection relate in the contemplative ascent to the knowledge of God.[21] He speaks much of the beatific vision (*beseligenden Anschauung Gottes*) as the fulfillment of all human desire, and much of his work is spent exploring the various *functions* of human affect in rising to the knowledge of God. For Karl, the book's structure of alternating philosophical reflection and prayerful contemplation is an important component of its deeper dualism of *ratio* and *affectus*. He sees the structure of the *Proslogion* as deliberately structured "from step to step" (*von Stufe zu Stufe*), highlighting five steps in particular:

1. The prayer of chapter 1, which analyzes the human condition.

2. The first mode of knowledge (knowledge *per intelligentiam*), which for Karl consists of the unfolding of the divine formula *aliquid quo nihil maius cogitari possit* and proceeds in two movements: chapters 2–4, which provide insight into the rational necessity of the existence and essence of God; and chapters 5–23, which provide insight into the nature of God in light of his necessary existence.

3. The second mode of knowledge (knowledge *per affectum*), which for Karl is predicated upon the goodness and mercy of God and results in a more experiential relation to God—he uses words like *experientielle* and *affektive* and *emotional* and *innere* to refer to this human capacity in relation to the divine. He draws attention to its presence particularly in chapters 6–12, with the central prayer coming in chapter 9 concerning the consistency of the justice and mercy of God.

---

21. Karl, *Ratio und Affect*, 723.

4. The painfully felt lack of experiencing of God's nearness in chapters 14–18, which compels Anselm to seek the inner healing of God's forgiveness and presence.

5. The perfect joy of the eschatological joy and knowledge of God, which fulfills all human desire and affection. This joy is not able to be grasped in life, although it is the object our continual striving and our highest good.[22]

Karl's breakdown has many features to commend it. Its analysis emphasizes and makes visible the dual nature of Anselm's writing involving both rational and spiritual qualities. It situates chapters 2–4 in relation to the larger structure of the book, and it draws some attention to the development throughout the *Proslogion*—especially noting the importance of divine mercy in chapter 9, Anselm's unmet desires of chapters 18, and the heavenly vision of chapters 24–26.

At the same time, Karl's vision of the structure of the *Proslogion* may be sharpened and/or extended in certain ways. First, he says precious little about the development throughout chapters 5–23. Chapters 6–12 and 14–18 are considered as units, but they are not situated in the larger flow of thought, leaving chapters 5, 13, and 19–23 overshadowed. Related to this, the distinction between knowledge *per intelligentiam* and knowledge *per affectum* is difficult to maintain within the chapters Karl has placed them—partly because he does not trace *per intelligentiam* through chapters 5–23, and partly because *per affectum* does not seem to be limited to chapters 6–12 but recurs throughout chapters 1, 14, 18, and elsewhere. Similarly, Karl shows less interest in the development from the earlier portions of the *Proslogion* to the later—for instance, how Anselm's anguish of God's distance in *Proslogion* 14–18 builds from that of *Proslogion* 1 or how the heavenly joy of *Proslogion* 24–26 brings resolution to the themes of *Proslogion* 1, 14, 18, etc. On the whole, Karl's engagement with the *Proslogion* is filled with useful and penetrating insights about its various parts, but he is less focused on drawing them together into a

22. Karl, *Ratio und Affectus*, 735–36.

coherent, intuitive account of the whole book. What most deeply characterizes the movement of the *Proslogion* is not the interplay of *ratio* and *affectus* but the arrival upon that vision of heavenly joy that Anselm's *ratio* and *affectus* are deployed to achieve.

Cattin on the Chapters of the *Proslogion*

Because the chapter divisions and titles in the *Proslogion* are original to Anselm, it may be helpful to consider the nature of Anselm's chapters before attempting to sketch their flow from one to another. Why does Anselm write the *Proslogion* with chapters at all? And is there any consistency in how each chapter is designed and structured?

Yves Cattin has provided an insightful treatment of both the nature and structure of the chapters of the *Proslogion*. Cattin detects several distinct kinds of chapters in the *Proslogion*, based on the beginning of the title of the chapter. Cattin sees each chapter giving the appearance of a deliberate answering of certain questions. He offers the following general summary:

- 11 chapters begin with *Quod*: 2, 3, 5, 7, 16–20, 21, and 23
- 9 chapters begin with *Quomodo*: 4, 6–11, 13, 14
- 2 chapters begin with *An*: 21, 26
- 1 chapter begins with *Quae et quanta*: 25
- 1 chapter begins with *Quale et quantum*: 24.[23]

Cattin observes, following the suggestion of Schmitt, that the Latin word *an* is often an indicator of where Anselm begins to answer in each chapter the issue proposed by the title.[24] Further, he suggests that the conclusion of each individual chapter follows from the answer provided after the *an* and is more or less a reprise of the answer given at that point.[25] Thus Cattin detects four essential stages to each chapter:

23. Cattin, *La preuve de Dieu*, 19.
24. Cattin, *La preuve de Dieu*, 27–28.
25. Cattin, *La preuve de Dieu*, 30.

1. The title.
2. The *status quaestionis*, where Anselm states the problem, often beginning with *quod* or *quomodo*. This is in objective prose and personal form.
3. The solution of the question, which comprises the essence of the chapter. It is always in objective prose and most of the time in impersonal form.
4. The conclusion, which reprises and sums up the response. This is in objective prose and often in personal form.[26]

Cattin's insights are useful, though there are exceptions to some of the patterns he detects. For instance, as we observed earlier, it is not clear why, in his summary of the first word of each chapter, Cattin has passed over the important term *coniectatio* in *Proslogion* 24, listing instead the next words, *Quale et quantum*. One also notes the absence of *Proslogion* 1 from his list. If we include *Proslogion* 1 and use the actual first word of the title of *Proslogion* 24, the words *excitatio* and *coniectatio* must be added—and these nouns seem to stand out against the other articles and conjunctions that start the chapters, slightly skewing the apparent symmetry of Cattin's outline.

More basically, it is not always convincing that that *introductory word* in each title demarcates a distinct kind of chapter. For example, *Proslogion* 2–3 and *Proslogion* 4 function quite similarly, with a connected chain of thought, despite the former starting with *quod* and the latter with *quomodo*. Or is it really plausible to associate *Proslogion* 23 with *Proslogion* 7 or *Proslogion* 16 on the basis of their shared introductory *quod*? Perhaps Cattin simply intends to designate the nature of the argument of each chapter (proving *whether* something is, or *how* it is, etc.)—but this is such a benign conclusion that it is difficult to see how it helps us interpret the book, and again, some chapters appear not to function as an argument establishing a conclusion, but as an *excitatio* or *coniectatio*. It is helpful to reflect upon Anselm's chapter titles, but we should resist overly schematizing them.

---

26. Cattin, *La preuve de Dieu*, 32–33.

With respect to Cattin's summary of the structure of each chapter, his suggestion of a fourfold sequence is an illuminating but somewhat inconsistent heuristic by which to read the *Proslogion*. Some chapters are simply too brief to be able to know where to identify a *status quaestionis* or conclusion (e.g., *Proslogion* 12 or *Proslogion* 15). The Latin word *an* is often missing where it would be expected. Some chapters seem to contain *more* than the four sections Cattin observes—for instance, the first paragraph of *Proslogion* 6 seems to introduce the divine attributes that will be treated in *Proslogion* 7 and 8, as well as those introduced in the second paragraph of *Proslogion* 6 (with *Proslogion* 9–11 subsequently arising out of the resolution achieved in *Proslogion* 8). There is a danger here of flattening out differences in the nature and function of each chapter. As a general rule, Cattin's fourfold schematization works well with the more logical, deductive chapters (think "objective prose")— say, *Proslogion* 2–4, or 6–11, or 19, or 22—but tends to break down with respect to the more "allocutive" and/or "poetic" chapters (Cattin's terms)—as well as the shorter chapters.

Despite these qualifications, Cattin's insights are valuable to reflect upon insofar as they reflect some of the frequent (if not universal) features of Anselm's writing and organization, thus alerting us to read the *Proslogion* with greater sensitivity and awareness. Even where it is not clear exactly what utility Cattin's insights carry in terms of the interpretation of the book, they attest to the careful precision with which the *Proslogion* was written. Furthermore, Cattin's emphasis on the chapter titles draws attention to one feature of the structure of the *Proslogion* that is highly relevant to our study of the book—namely, the uniqueness of *Proslogion* 1 and 24 from the surrounding material. *Proslogion* 1 seems to make particular use of meditation; *Proslogion* 24, of imagination. In *Proslogion* 1 Anselm stirs up his mind; in *Proslogion* 24 he stretches his mind outwards. Both efforts are somewhat unparalleled in the rest of the book. We will return to this point concerning the importance of *Proslogion* 24, including the way it draws upon earlier material in the book, in the next chapter.

Proslogion 5: Divine Supremacy as a Lever

Many interpreters find chapter 5 to be a key lever within the book. In Gilbert's approach surveyed above, for instance, *Proslogion* 5 initiates the longest section of the book, continuing through *Proslogion* 22, with *Proslogion* 5–11 as the first distinct unit within this section. The instinct to detect a distinct line of argumentation in *Proslogion* 5–11 has much data to support it. In the concluding prayer of 11, for instance, Anselm summarizes all that he has established in this section of the book: "therefore you are truly perceptive, omnipotent, merciful, and impassible, just as you are living, wise, good, blessed, eternal, and whatever it is better to be than not to be."[27] The first four adjectives with which Anselm describes God here (perceptive, omnipotent, merciful, and impassible) correspond to the conclusions Anselm has arrived at throughout *Proslogion* 6–11. Then, Anselm connects these conclusions with the larger principle of divine supremacy he has established in *Proslogion* 5 (whatever it is better to be than not to be). This concluding, recapitulative prayer is reminiscent of the closing prayer of *Proslogion* 4, making it plausible to conceive that Anselm has reached some kind of closure at the end of *Proslogion* 11.

Nonetheless, it is also possible to read *Proslogion* 5 as a trigger or lever for Anselm's flow of thought even beyond *Proslogion* 11. In the opening sentence of the chapter, Anselm asks "what therefore are you, Lord God, than which nothing greater can be thought?"[28] Anselm is thus unpacking what the divine formula means for the nature of God. On the basis of this formula, Anselm has established that God exists and that he exists in an absolutely supreme way as God. Now Anselm wants to deduce what else can be proven about God on the basis of the same formula. This general strategy is by no means exhausted within *Proslogion* 5–11, and many of the specific themes of *Proslogion* 5 will recur throughout the book. *Proslogion* 5

27. *P* 11, Schmitt I 110:1–3.
28. *P* 5, Schmitt 1 104:11.

is therefore a pivotal transition chapter within the flow of the book: it functions as a kind of gateway through which the divine formula passes from proving God's existence to proving God's nature, so that the *unum argumentum* that has established "that God truly exists" can further widen out to establish "whatever else we believe about the divine being." It is as though Anselm has found a ship with which to sail out of the harbor: and having done so, he now uses the same ship to enter into the open sea.

There are fundamentally three axioms that Anselm wants to draw out from the divine formula in *Proslogion* 5: (1) God alone exists per se; (2) God makes all other things from nothing; (3) God is whatever it is better to be than not to be. All three of these are asserted as the topics of the chapter in the chapter title, with (1) and (2) standing in close relation to each other—and it is these two that are then asserted in the second sentence of the chapter, as Anselm's first answer to his opening question. Borrowing from the language of Visser and Williams, we will call (1)—that God alone exists through himself—*divine aseity*; and the second half of (2)—that all other things exist through God—*divine ultimacy*.[29] Both divine aseity and divine ultimacy correspond to much of the material in the early chapters of the *Monologion*, where Anselm has unpacked them at much greater length, and both will feature prominently throughout the rest of the *Proslogion*—for instance, Anselm will return to them to move forward in the first sentence of *Proslogion* 12: "but certainly whatever you are, you are, not through another, but through yourself."[30]

We will coin our own term for (3)—"God is whatever it is better to be than not to be"—*divine supremacy*. This principle is drawn out in sentences 4–6 of *Proslogion* 5 as a further consequence of the divine formula, as well as a further consequence of divine aseity and ultimacy. Anselm's conception of what makes one thing better (*melius*) than another has Platonic overtones, as is often observed,

29. Visser and Williams, *Anselm*, 96.
30. P 12, Schmitt I 110:6.

but the specific assertion that *melius* (better) is tantamount to *maior* (greater) can be more directly traced to Augustine's *De Trinitate* 6.8, where Augustine makes this argument, noting physical mass as an exception.[31] More immediately, divine supremacy draws from Anselm's longer discussion in *Monologion* 15, and, as Gilbert notes, it will continue to function in the later portions of the book, albeit more subtly.[32] In *Proslogion* 5–11, specifically, it is a continual reference point for his further elaboration on the doctrine of God: Anselm has arrived upon it as a consequence of his divine formula, and he will continue to get a lot of mileage from it as he moves forward. For instance, in *Proslogion* 9, Anselm will draw his assertion that God is kind to the wicked as a consequence of the fact that "you would be less good, if you were not kind to the wicked."[33] Or, in *Proslogion* 11, Anselm will apply the logic of the divine formula to divine justice: "it is certainly just that you are so just that you cannot be thought to be more just."[34] Or, in *Proslogion* 13, Anselm will use divine supremacy to establish that God is not confined to any place or time.[35] Thus, in the sweep of the whole *Proslogion*, God's kindness, justice, and omnipresence are as much a consequence of the *unum argumentum* as his existence.

Proslogion 6–13: The "Lower" Divine Attributes

Having established divine supremacy at the conclusion of *Proslogion* 5, Anselm then turns to use this principle to sort out several apparent contradictions in the divine attributes. The first sentence of *Proslogion* 6 signals the specific issues Anselm has in mind: "but since it is better to be perceptive (*sensibilem*), omnipotent, merciful, and impassible than not to be: how are you perceptive, if

---

31. Cf. Logan, *Reading Anselm's "Proslogion,"* 98.
32. Gilbert, *Le "Proslogion" de S. Anselme*, 192.
33. *P* 9, Schmitt I 107:4–5.
34. *P* 11, Schmitt 109:11.
35. *P* 13, Schmitt 110:13–14.

you are not a body; or omnipotent, if you cannot do all things; or merciful and at the same time impassible?"[36] These topics are then borne out in the following chapters: how God can be perceptive despite the fact that he is not a body in *Proslogion* 6, divine omnipotence in *Proslogion* 7, and divine mercy and impassibility in *Proslogion* 8. But why does Anselm choose these specific topics? It appears that Anselm perceives a tension, or apparent contradiction, in each of them, and he wants to use the divine formula that he has already arrived upon (in conjunction with divine supremacy) to resolve the tension. The resolution of the problem of divine mercy and impassibility in *Proslogion* 8 will then lead Anselm on to the expansion and refinement of these themes in *Proslogion* 9–11, where he deals with divine justice and mercy.

It should be stated that in seeking to resolve these apparent contradictions, Anselm does not intend his answers to remove mystery regarding the divine nature. He will frequently admit his inability to understand God fully, and at one point in *Proslogion* 9 he even petitions God for help in understanding what he is saying: "help me, just and merciful God, whose light I seek, help me to understand what I am saying."[37] Even at the finale of his argument in *Proslogion* 11, he will insist that the ultimate reason why God spares some and punishes others is enshrouded in mystery, impenetrable by any human reasoning.[38] So the intellectual resolution Anselm seeks is not comprehensive but specific to each of the issues he raises. Nor is Anselm's discussion kept in the impersonal and abstract, for he cannot help himself but ask God to experience the realities with which he is concerned. Thus, while seeking to show that God's mercy is just, he will not hesitate to pause and pray, "let that mercy come upon me, which proceeds from such great wealth of yours. Let it flow over me, what flows forth from you."[39] It is

36. *P* 6, Schmitt I 104:20–22.
37. *P* 9, Schmitt I 108:8–9.
38. *P* 11, Schmitt I 109:22–24.
39. *P* 9, Schmitt I 107:27–108:2.

as if the more emotional and prayerful qualities of the *Proslogion* cannot help but keep breaking in even among what Cattin calls the "objective prose" sections.

It is not surprising that the first issue Anselm addresses in *Proslogion* 6 concerns that God is not a body, since at the end of *Monologion* 15 he has made the same transition from "God is whatever it is better to be than not to be" to the conclusion that God is not a body.[40] Anselm ultimately solves this problem in the second paragraph of *Proslogion* 6 by positing that perception is simply a kind of knowledge and that God therefore has perception in a manner appropriate to his knowledge. This kind of logical move is similar to that made in *Proslogion* 7–8, where Anselm is burdened to show that those very things that seem to be a limitation on God's power or knowledge are actually an expression of its perfection. In other words, for each "contradiction" Anselm tackles in *Proslogion* 6–8, the goal is not merely to establish that resolution is possible but that the resolution results in manifesting some new aspect of God's greatness and beauty. This is another way that *Proslogion* 6–8 represents the extension of the divine formula unpacked in *Proslogion* 2–4.

If Anselm's subtle and careful use of logic is evident in *Proslogion* 6, *Proslogion* 7 exhibits his grammatical and linguistic skills. Here he argues that the apparent contradiction between divine omnipotence and God's inability to do many things is ultimately a matter of language. For Anselm, God would be less powerful if he were able to be corrupted, to lie, or to cause what is true to be false, since these things are not beneficial and should not be done, and are they are therefore ultimately expressions of weakness. The only reason something like lying appears as an "ability" (*potentia*) is because of the language by which we express it. According to Henry, this chapter represents a *prise de position* of Peter Damian's argument in *De Divina Omnipototentia* 7 that if God could change the past,

---

40. *M* 15, Schmitt I 29:21–33.

his omnipotence would be limited.[41] Anselm's concern seems to be to protect divine omnipotence from any external limitation—as Leftow puts it, "even metaphysical necessities do not constitute an external boundary on the power of Anselm's God."[42] So Anselm will conclude that God is "thenceforth more truly omnipotent" as a result of his supposed inability to do these things.[43] Then, in *Proslogion* 8, Anselm seeks to resolve the apparent tension between divine mercy and impassibility by positing a distinction between God's mercy in relation to us and his mercy in relation to himself. This distinction between God-as-he-is-himself and God-as-he-is-to-us seems once again concerned to protect God's transcendence over creaturely imperfection.

Proslogion 6–8 exhibit a careful and deliberate progression of thought. In the first paragraph of each chapter Anselm will ask questions in order to introduce the new dilemma. He will say, in effect, Lord, how can you be x (some article of faith) in light of the fact that you are also y (some other article of faith)? The most frequent introduction to each section is *sed quomodo es*? Anselm then employs the axioms of *Proslogion* 5 to resolve the dilemma and demonstrate God's surpassing greatness as a result of the resolution. It is important to see the deliberate and incremental nature of the movement from one chapter to another here. In the first place, Anselm's questions should be taken as sincere expressions of uncertainty, not merely abstract proposals. The occasional anguish and uncertainty in his expressions indicate that he is genuinely burdened that *fides* issues forth into *intellectum*. Furthermore, progress can be detected throughout the chapters by considering the particular doctrines Anselm regards as needing resolution in the first place. Why is there is no discussion of, say, divine omniscience in

---

41. Desmond P. Henry, *The Logic of Saint Anselm* (Oxford: Clarendon Press, 1967), 151.

42. Leftow, "Anselm's perfect-being theology," in *The Cambridge Companion to Anselm*, 132–65, at 151.

43. *P* 7, Schmitt I 106:1.

these chapters? Is this not within the purview of "whatever else we believe about the divine essence?" It seems that Anselm is especially concerned with the apparent tensions or contradictions in the doctrine of God, which he must sort out in order to justify his claim of divine supremacy in *Proslogion* 5. To the extent that various divine attributes such as omniscience do not fit into this trajectory, Anselm has no reason to go there (although one might infer it from Anselm's discussion of God's knowledge as perfect in *Proslogion* 6). In other words, the *Proslogion* is not a comprehensive work; its movements are those of a direct journey to a desired destination, not a thorough scouting or surveying of the land.

Proslogion 9–11 are an important early crescendo within the book, following closely on the heels of *Proslogion* 8, and they are bound together through their mutual interest in the relation of divine justice and mercy. The length of these chapters, particularly *Proslogion* 9, testifies to Anselm's thoroughgoing concern with divine righteousness and human sin, topics that we have seen Anselm wrestling with throughout *Proslogion* 1 and that indeed exercise Anselm continually throughout his other writings.[44] It is interesting that the question of universalism never even arises for him in seeking to emphasize the maximal goodness of divine mercy. Rather, Anselm seems more eager to demonstrate God's consistency in relation to himself, and he continues to stress the difficulty of human understanding of the relation of God's various attributes.

The transition from *Proslogion* 6–8 to *Proslogion* 9–11 can be characterized by a slight redirection and further specification of focus, but far more striking is the elevation of tone and emotion that is evident from the former to the latter. Perhaps the height of the crescendo comes in the third paragraph of *Proslogion* 9, where Anselm bursts forth into exclamation: "O mercy, from what rich

---

44. The most obvious example is *Cur Deus Homo*, but throughout his writings Anselm is concerned with the problem that sin creates with respect to divine justice. His *Prayers and Meditations* perhaps reflect the most emotional expression of these themes.

sweetness and sweet richness you flow forth to us! O immensity of the goodness of God, with what affection should you be loved by sinners!"[45] The remainder of this lengthy paragraph maintains this heightened tone as Anselm marvels at the overflowing nature of God's mercy and begs that he might experience it. This paragraph also initiates Anselm's basic answer to the apparent tension between divine justice and mercy, which is the topic that concerns him throughout the chapter and on into *Proslogion* 10–11. God's mercy and justice are harmonious, Anselm argues, because his mercy flows out of his goodness, and there is no goodness apart from justice. Therefore, God is merciful precisely because he is just.[46]

Divine goodness receives a strong emphasis in *Proslogion* 9. Not only is it the mediating link by which Anselm controls the relation of divine justice and mercy, but it seems to be the particular doctrine that elicits the strongest emotional cries throughout the chapter. He emphasizes the ineffability and incomprehensibility of divine goodness, speaking of it as a river whose stream we can discern but whose source or spring remains hidden from us.[47] Anselm seems to regard divine goodness as more hidden and intrinsic to the divine essence than both mercy and justice. It is striking, for instance, that before Anselm identifies the *lux inaccessibilis* as divine incomprehensibility in *Proslogion* 16, he pauses here in *Proslogion* 9 to speculate whether the *lux inaccessibilis* is not, in fact, divine goodness.[48] The energy with which Anselm pursues the doctrine of divine goodness in this chapter—as the deeper, hidden root that manifests itself as both mercy and justice to human beings—recalls his emphasis in the *prooemium* on creaturely dependence on God for happiness (*bene sint*) and suggests that he is touching on issues that strike at the nerve of his interests throughout the book. It is always when those aspects of the divine nature most related to hu-

---

45. *P* 9, Schmitt I 107:22–23.
46. *P* 9, Schmitt 108:2–9.
47. *P* 9, Schmitt 107:14–16.
48. *P* 9, Schmitt I 107:4–5.

man happiness come into view that the tone of the book heightens.

The transition from *Proslogion* 9 to *Proslogion* 10 is subtle, and there is much overlap between the two chapters, but the difference can be summed up in this way: in *Proslogion* 9, Anselm is concerned with the justice of divine mercy; in *Proslogion* 10, he is concerned with the selectiveness of divine punishment. Having established that God is just to spare the wicked, Anselm stipulates that it is also just to punish them, and he therefore wonders how both can be true. To answer this question, Anselm picks up on the distinction he has already drawn in *Proslogion* 8 between God in relation to himself and God in relation to us.[49] Anselm argues that God is just, not because his action accords with human merit, but because it is consistent with (once again) divine goodness. The similarity of argumentation at this point signals continuity not only with *Proslogion* 9, but more generally with *Proslogion* 6–8. One way to construe the relationship between these sections is to see *Proslogion* 9–11 as a further foray into—and explication of—the answer arrived at in *Proslogion* 8 regarding the problem of divine justice and mercy. Both sections seek to resolve apparent contradictions in the divine nature by appealing to divine goodness; while *Proslogion* 6–8 rather quickly covers three particular doctrines, and then *Proslogion* 9–11 hones in on one of them with greater detail, complexity, and emotion.

Having established in *Proslogion* 10 that God is just in relation to himself both to punish the wicked and also to spare them, Anselm now reasserts this conclusion in *Proslogion* 11 with reference to Psalm 24/25:10 and 144/145:17. *Proslogion* 11 is similar to *Proslogion* 21 in that it likely represents the application of an arrived-upon principle to some disputed issue (often related to the interpretation of Scripture) in Anselm's day. The emphasis in this chapter seems to fall on the comprehensiveness of divine justice: God is just in *all* that he does, such that no inconsistency is possible for him. A strong doctrine of election seems to issue forth as a consequence,

---

49. P 10, Schmitt I 110:1–2.

and Anselm asserts the harmony of the divine will and divine justice: "only what you will is just, and only what you do not will is not just."[50] The presence of a recapitulative summary at the end of *Proslogion* 11 not only indicates a structural break between *Proslogion* 11 and 12, as we observed earlier, but confirms that he does not regard *Proslogion* 9–11 as a diversion or rabbit trail. It is as a consequence of the chain of argumentation ending in *Proslogion* 11, not *Proslogion* 8, that Anselm asserts, "therefore you are truly perceiving, omnipotent, merciful, and impassible."[51] In other words, what Anselm has been seeking to establish throughout *Proslogion* 9–11 is not a deviation from the larger context and flow of thought, but it is in fact directly related to these four stated attributes he has been problematizing in *Proslogion* 6–8, particularly *misericors et impassibilis* in *Proslogion* 8.

Whereas Anselm is problematizing throughout *Proslogion* 6–11 (*sed quomodo es?*), in *Proslogion* 12–13 he moves on to assert more definite conclusions (*sed certe es*). The transition, broadly speaking, is from how God's attributes function in relation to each other to how they function in relation to his essence; or, more basically, from what God is (*quod*) to how God is (*quomodo*). But, significantly, *Proslogion* 12–13 draw as much from *Proslogion* 5 as *Proslogion* 6–11 do. Anselm has established the harmony of a number of divine attributes on the basis of divine supremacy in *Proslogion* 5; now he must further harmonize these various attributes with the divine aseity and ultimacy of *Proslogion* 5. God not only embraces all goodness but does so in an absolutely unique way as its source.

Though brief, *Proslogion* 12 is extremely significant in the structure of the book because Anselm will refer back to the doctrine of divine simplicity established in it repeatedly in the rest of the *Proslogion* (chapters 18, 19, 21, and 23). *Proslogion* 12 is thus comparable to *Proslogion* 5 as a transitional or "gateway" chapter—both chapters establish certain axioms that are then utilized for lever-

50. P 11, Schmitt I 109:18–19.
51. P 11, Schmitt 110:1.

age in further exploration into the divine essence. But *Proslogion* 12 also draws directly upon *Proslogion* 5, for it asserts divine simplicity as a consequence of divine aseity, which was established there. If God exists per se, Anselm reasons, then God must be the very life by which he lives, the very justice by which he is just, etc.[52] Thus, whereas previously Anselm has been considering the harmony of God's various attributes to each other, he now draws them into complete unity by identifying them with the divine essence. This signals the beginning of Anselm's ascent from the "lower" to the "higher" planes of his doctrine of God, as he presses into those qualities that are closer and more intrinsic to the divine essence.

Divine simplicity was also drawn from divine aseity in *Monologion* 16–18, where both doctrines issued forth in the doctrine of divine eternity, as they do also now in *Proslogion* 13. But *Proslogion* 13 is also concerned to establish that God is "unbounded" (*incircumscriptus*)—and more strictly, how God *alone* is both eternal and unbounded, even though we speak of other spirits in this way. In other words, *Proslogion* 13 does not simply introduce two more divine attributes (eternality and unboundedness) to be stacked on to and treated like the previous attributes of *Proslogion* 6–11. Rather, the whole goal in treating these attributes is different, as is the reason for their selection: in *Proslogion* 6–11, Anselm was burdened by the *harmony* of divine attributes; in *Proslogion* 13, he is burdened by the *uniqueness* of divine attributes. There he asked, how is God both ___? Now he is asking, how is God *alone* ___? Nonetheless, *Proslogion* 12–13 stand broadly in closer relation to *Proslogion* 5–11 than to *Proslogion* 14–22, because *Proslogion* 14–16 initiate an even more radical turn in the flow of the book.

---

52. P 12, Schmitt I 110:6–8.

Proslogion 14: Still Ascending toward the Beatific Vision

The first sentence of *Proslogion* 14 signals a pause from Anselm's ascent upward into the divine attributes as he now turns inward to discern what progress has been made thus far with respect to his original desire: "have you found, my soul, what you were seeking?"[53] Here Anselm returns, for the first time, to the self-address that characterized the book's opening paragraph. This, combined with the focus throughout this chapter on his soul's hunger for the *visio Dei*, seems to point backwards to the prayers of *Proslogion* 1. As a whole, this chapter can be conceived in relation to the rest of the *Proslogion* as kind of midpoint self-evaluation with respect to the book's progress. Anselm has been engaged in the pursuit of God, but now he pauses to look back over his shoulder and note what progress has been made (note the imperfect tense of *quaerebas Deum*).[54]

In the next sentence, Anselm summarizes what he has thus far discovered in his pursuit of God. "You were seeking God, and you have found that he is the highest of all things, than which nothing better can be thought; and that he is life itself, light, wisdom, goodness, eternal happiness and happy eternity; and that he is everywhere and always."[55] When seeking to ascertain the nature and structure of a book, it is significant to discover a passage in which the author summarizes what they believe has been established so far within it. So Anselm's self-interpretation here cannot be overlooked: it provides a kind of hermeneutical window into the first half of the book. Several observations are in order regarding this important sentence. First, Anselm demarcates the book's conclu-

---

53. *P* 14, Schmitt I 111:8.
54. The placement of *Proslogion* 14 halfway through the book is not observed by many English commentators but is more common in the French and German literature. Corbin, for instance, calls *Proslogion* 14–15 the "geometric center" (*le centre géométrique*) of the book (*Anselme*, 163).
55. *P* 14, Schmitt I 111:8–11.

sions within three movements here (each separated by a semicolon and fresh introductory *et hoc esse*): (1) the divine formula and God's identity consequently as *summum omnium*; (2) divine attributes like wisdom or goodness; and (3) divine omnipresence and eternality. These three sections seem to correspond to *Proslogion* 2–4, 6–11, and 13, respectively. What is most striking about this conceptual organization is the absence of an emphasis on God's existence in the first of these summaries. When it comes to his own self-interpretation of what he has accomplished, Anselm apparently does not consider it worth mentioning that he has proved God's existence; rather, he summarizes the book's early chapters as establishing God's *identity* as the *summum omnium*. This makes it plausible to see the nature of God's existence rather than the fact of God's existence as most relevant to the larger flow of the book.

Second, Anselm substitutes *melius* for *maior* in the divine formula here. This suggests that Anselm perceives little difference between the two concepts, and he reinforces the essentially Platonic undertones in his conception of greatness. But it also indicates a close association between the divine formula of *Proslogion* 2–4 and the principle of divine supremacy in *Proslogion* 5, thereby hinting at the larger *purpose* that divine formula is playing in the larger flow of the book. Anselm is not interested in a maximally great deity just to assert his existence, as in a Cartesian proof; rather, such a God is important for him because it can function as the *summum bonum* that he will come to identify as his *summum gaudium*. In other words, Anselm seeks the greatest being because he seeks the highest good: *quo nihil maior cogitari potest* is interesting to him because it can equally yield *quo nihil melius cogitari potest*.

Third, many of the qualities ascribed to God here are not formally covered within the earlier chapters but rather are implicit in the axioms he has established—*sapientiam* and *vitam* are listed only in the summarizing sentence at the end of *Proslogion* 11, for instance, and *lucem* has not previously occurred except with reference to the *inaccessibilis lux* motif. Evidently Anselm believes that

Proslogion 1–13 has established more than the strict topics covered in those chapters; he seems more interested in the overall approach to God that he has discovered than the explicit facts about God that this approach happens to have uncovered thus far. Once again, this tilts our expectations forward to see where his approach to God will ultimately lead throughout the entire flow of the book.

Finally, the inclusion of a reference to God as eternal happiness and happy eternity in Anselm's characteristic chiastic expression (*aeternam beatitudinem et beatam aeternitatem*) recalls Anselm's interest in God as fulfillment of human desire. One thinks of the inclusion of the words *bene sint* in the *prooemium*, as well as the eagerness of the expressions of desire in *Proslogion* 1 and 9. Especially because there has been no explicit mention of *aetemam beatitudinem et beatam aeternitatem* in *Proslogion* 5–13, but it is nonetheless stated as a consequence of what has been established there, the inclusion of this phrase suggests that God's role as the object of human happiness is never far away from the various movements of the *Proslogion*. All throughout, Anselm seems to have been pursuing axioms that will enable him to draw these conclusions, even when those conclusions are not actually stated.

Nonetheless, for all the progress he believes he has made, Anselm does not yet perceive of himself as actually attaining to the kind of vision of God he desires. In fact, in the remaining sentences of this paragraph, Anselm expresses uncertainty as to whether his pursuit has arrived upon the knowledge of God at all. On the one hand, he cannot conceive that the object of his pursuit is anything *less* than God; whom else could this be, whom he has understood with such "certain truth and true certainty?"[56] On the other hand, if he has found God, he is perplexed as to why he does not perceive God: "Why does my soul not perceive (*sensit*) you, Lord God, if it has found you?"[57] The perplexity with which Anselm poses this question confirms that he has never been interested in merely establishing God's existence, or

56. P 14, Schmitt I 111:13.
57. P 14, Schmitt I 111:14–15.

even establishing all his attributes—rather, he has been interested in these aims only to the greater end of his soul's perception (*sensit*) of God. That is why all that he has established, including God's identity as *aeternam beatitudinem et beatam aeternitatem*, only leaves him in a state of further angst if it does not result in the soul's vision of God. This reinforces the essentially spiritual purpose of the book, as established in the last chapter. Anselm does not simply want clarity but joy; he is seeking not just knowledge but food. In fact, the anguish of *Proslogion* 14 is even greater than that of *Proslogion* 1—all that Anselm has proven has only exacerbated his angst because it has not yet issued forth into the purpose of that proving.

In the second paragraph, Anselm restates his uncertainties through the framework of the *light* and *truth* motifs, which will recur throughout *Proslogion* 14 and beyond. The emphasis of this paragraph and the next is on divine incomprehensibility, which represents the primary point of this first spiral upward from *Proslogion* 1. If Anselm has proven anything in *Proslogion* 1–13, it is that God is utterly beyond his understanding and experience. Anselm has broken through the ceiling and climbed up to a higher floor, only to discover innumerable ceilings and floors still further; he has reached that ledge on the mountain at which he thought he could view the peak, only to find that peak rising up still higher before him. The ascent towards the beatific vision, it turns out, involves this kind of paradoxical focus on God's incomprehensibility and hiddenness (it will recur in all three spiraling movements). Evidently, Anselm can only attain God after having discovered that God is utterly beyond his every device.

In the third and final paragraph of *Proslogion* 14, Anselm redoubles his requests from *Proslogion* 1 that God would assist him in his journey toward the beatific vision. This paragraph initiates a transition from looking backward at what he has already accomplished to looking forward to what is still ahead, from addressing his own soul to again addressing God directly. This again suggests an intentionality and care in the placement of *Proslogion* 14, for it is appropriate to look both backward and forward at the midpoint

THE STRUCTURE OF THE *PROSLOGION*

of a book. But Anselm does not know how to move forward at this point, and he must petition God to show him what else is necessary on the journey toward the beatific vision: "Lord my God, my Creator and Redeemer (*formator et reformator meus*), say to my longing soul what else you are, other than what it has seen, that it might clearly see what it desires to see."[58] Once again the similarities with *Proslogion* 1 are palpable: the covenantal, personal forms of address to God, the intensity of longing to see God, the almost bewildered sense of need for God's help in the process, and the explicit reference to *seeing* God (the beatific vision) as his aim. Once again, such a request makes it clear that Anselm does not consider himself to have attained this vision yet.

The following sentences express Anselm's sense of exile from the *visio Dei*, as a consequence of both God's splendor as well as his own infirmity. Anselm expresses the anguish of his distance from God with brief repetitions, employing three different images: light/darkness, smallness/immensity, want/fullness.[59] Both the rhetorical device of brief repetition as well as the explicit imagery employed by that device here is, once again, reminiscent of *Proslogion* 1. Each sentence serves to reinforce the desperation and longing that Anselm feels as a result of his condition.

In the final five sentences of *Proslogion* 14, Anselm turns from a focus on his own condition to marvel at the divine essence he longs to see, returning to the *lux* and *veritas* motifs of paragraph 2.

Quam ampla est illa veritas, in qua est omne quod verum est, et extra quam non nisi nihil et falsum est! Quam immensa est, quae uno intuitu videt quaecumque facta sunt, et a quo et per quem quomodo de nihilo facta sunt! Quid puritatis, quid simplicitatis, quid certitudinis et splendoris ibi est! Certe plus quam a creatura valeat intelligi.

The repeated exclamation points highlight a crescendo of tone at this point, as does the vivid language, as do the introductory terms

---

58. *P* 14, Schmitt I, 111:22–24
59. *P* 14, Schmitt I 112:2–5.

THE STRUCTURE OF THE *PROSLOGION*

of measurement (*quanta ... quam ... quid*) by which Anselm expresses his astonishment at God's immeasurable immensity. Just as the self-address at the start of *Proslogion* 14 recalls that of *Proslogion* 1, now the argumentative strategy here at the end of *Proslogion* 14 anticipates that of *Proslogion* 24, where the greatness of the divine source is discerned from the greatness of created objects. But the comparisons of Creator and created things in *Proslogion* 14 and *Proslogion* 24 serve different purposes and move in different directions: there the focus will fall on the supreme joy and desirability of God, as a result of the joy and goodness of created things; here the focus is the immeasurable greatness and vastness of God and its resulting exclusive relation to truth.

The first sentence of this section not only reflects Anselm's spiritual view of the role of reason, as discussed previously, but also intermingles the *lux* and *veritas* imagery together: "for how great is that light (*lux*), from which shines (*micat*) every true thing (*verum*) that enlightens (*lucet*) the rational mind (*rationali menti*)."[60] Implicit in this assertion is the notion that all truth is from God and is perceived only through his illumination—a notion that is only further sharpened by the following reference to "that truth, in which is everything that is true, and outside of which is nothing except nothingness and what is false."[61] Anselm then affirms the simplicity with which God sees all other things and their creaturely nature as existing through him and created *de nihilo*.[62] His concluding sentences then seem to devolve into simple expressions of astonishment: "what purity, what simplicity, what certainty and splendor are there!"[63] But the four nouns he piles up here are quite striking in their correlation of divine transcendence with human *knowledge* (of all things): Anselm

---

60. *P* 14, Schmitt I 112:5–6.
61. *P* 14, Schmitt I 112:6–8. The identification of God and truth will also serve as axiomatic for Anselm through his treatise *De Veritate*, where the student opens the whole book, "since we believe that God is truth." See *DV* 1, Schmitt I 176:4.
62. *P* 14, Schmitt I 112:8–9.
63. *P* 14, Schmitt I 112:9–10.

speaks not merely of splendor but of certainty in connection with the divine essence. In other words, for Anselm, God's very height and distance as the supreme light and truth are correlated to his central role in human knowledge, which can only proceed by participating in (God's) truth and light. Somewhat paradoxically, then, divine incomprehensibility, even as it baffles and staggers Anselm with his distance from God, simultaneously shoots him forward towards the beatific vision (or we might say, *spirals* him upward). The purpose of the spiraling nature of the *Proslogion* is thus not simply dramatic or stylistic but corresponds to the book's goal of ascending upward towards the beatific vision.

This helps account for the somewhat surprising use of abstract, third-person descriptors of God such as *illud* and *ibi* in these sentences (as opposed to Anselm's typical covenantal, direct address). This language (*illud/ibi*) seems to identify a new target for Anselm's pursuit in the subsequent chapters. It is as though divine incomprehensibility, this supremely transcendent *veritas* and *lux*, sets Anselm on a new pathway by which to approach God at the same time as it asserts his inability to attain God. Anselm's final and concluding assertion—"certainly it is greater than a creature can understand"[64]—coming as does on the heels of Anselm's expression of its purity and certainty, reinforces the paradoxically constructive role of divine incomprehensibility. Somehow God is both beyond knowledge and, at the same time, certainty itself.

This final sentence then leads Anselm directly into the title of *Proslogion* 15.

Proslogion 15–17: The *Lux Inaccessibilis* Identified

Proslogion 15 signals the beginning of the second great spiral upward in the *Proslogion*, as Anselm heightens his definition of God from "that than which nothing greater can be thought" (the origi-

---

64. P 14, Schmitt I 112:10–11.

nal divine formula) to "that which is greater than can be thought" (which we will call divine incomprehensibility). That Anselm does not perceive these two assertions to be contradictory or in tension with one another is evident from that the fact that the second is drawn out as a consequence of the first. The similarity to *Proslogion* 2 in Anselm's argumentation here is striking: "for since it is possible to think that something of this kind exists: if you are not this very thing, it is possible to think of something greater than you, which is impossible."[65] Thus divine incomprehensibility draws upon the divine formula even as it spirals up from it. One might say that implicit in the divine formula already are those principles by which it will eventually be surpassed and expanded. Therefore, although *Proslogion* 15 introduces a new axiom in Anselm's thinking about God, moving the book forward in new directions, it still functions within an overarching unity in the larger flow of the *unum argumentum*.[66]

It is significant, however, that it takes Anselm roughly ten chapters to get from "that than which nothing greater can be thought" to "that which is greater than can be thought." This latter formula, which we will refer to as divine incomprehensibility, comes at this point in the book because it marks the spiral upward from the "lower" divine perfections that are drawn from God's *unrivalled* goodness and aseity to the "higher" divine perfections that are drawn from God's *surpassing* goodness and incomprehensibility. Like *Proslogion* 5, *Proslogion* 15 acts as a lever or trigger for what will follow, and huge chunks of what follows have divine incomprehensibility as their dominant theme (*Proslogion* 16, 17, and the first half of 18). It is striking, in the larger progression of the *Proslogion*, that Anselm begins with God's more visible qualities and then moves

---

65. *P* 15, Schmitt I 112:15–17.
66. We must therefore interpret the arguments of *Proslogion* 2 and 3 in light of these later developments. In fact, the existence of *Proslogion* 15 contradicts a common critique of *Proslogion* 2 that Anselm is simply conjuring up God's existence from his own mental conception of God. In fact, he denies there is any such conception of God.

onto his more hidden qualities, rather than the other way around. One might expect God's hiddenness to be reduced, not increased, as Anselm comes to understand God more accurately. As Sweeney observes, there is a real progress throughout the *Proslogion*, but it is a paradoxical kind of progression in that Anselm "progresses to a sense of God as beyond his grasp and concludes not in the satiation of desire but in its increase."[67] Somehow in the very bewilderment that Anselm continually falls back upon, he is moving forward toward joy and certainty.

In *Proslogion* 16, Anselm finally identifies divine incomprehensibility as the *lux inaccessibilis* about which he has written so much.[68] Anselm is overwhelmed here by his inability to look upon the *lux inaccessibilis*, even while he recognizes that everything he sees is seen only by its light.[69] He compares it to the sun, which shines too brightly to be looked at, but illumines everything else: "The eye of my soul (*oculus animae*) cannot bear to grasp it for very long."[70] Once again Anselm uses the light and truth motifs interchangeably here—*summa et inaccessibilis lux* is in apposition with *tota et beata veritas*—suggesting that both are adequate images for divine incomprehensibility.[71] As in *Proslogion* 1 and 14, Anselm stacks up images in short succession to emphasize the extent of his soul's bewilderment before God's *lux* and *veritas*: *reverberatur fulgore, vincitur amplitudine, obruitur immensitate, confunditur capacitate* ("it is repelled by its brightness, conquered by its fullness, overwhelmed by its immensity, confounded by its capacity").[72]

In the final few sentences of this chapter, divine incomprehensibility takes on an active rather than passive role as Anselm becomes exercised not only by how little he knows of God but by how much

---

67. Sweeney, *Anselm of Canterbury and the Desire for the Word*, 169.
68. P 16, Schmitt I 112:20–22.
69. P 16, Schmitt I 112:22–24.
70. P 16, Schmitt I 112:25.
71. P 16, Schmitt I 112:27.
72. P 16, Schmitt I 12:25–27.

THE STRUCTURE OF THE *PROSLOGION*

God knows of him even *while* he knows so little of God: "how far you are from me, who is yet so near to you!"[73] In other words, it is not mere distance that separates Anselm and God, as though they were equally cut off from each other. The blindness and inability are totally on Anselm's part: he is infinitely unable to see, yet infinitely seen himself. He concludes:

Ubique es tota praesens, et non te video. In te moveor et in te sum, et ad te non possum accedere. Intra me et circa me es, et non te sentio. ("You are everywhere wholly present, and I do not see you. In you I move and in you I have my being, and I am not able to draw near to you. You are within me and around me, and I do not feel you.")[74]

Divine incomprehensibility thus leaves Anselm with a paradox: God is both infinitely distant and intimately near, both all around him and yet completely inaccessible.

Proslogion 17 follows on the heels of *Proslogion* 16 in further lamenting the hiddenness of the beauty of the divine essence. Here, for the first time, Anselm links God's *lux* with his happiness: "still, Lord, you are hidden from my soul in your light and happiness (*in luce et beatitudine tua*), and for that reason it still dwells in its darkness and misery (*in tenebris et miseria*)."[75] This bringing together of God's light and happiness here (with the corresponding link of Anselm's darkness and misery) reinforces that the purpose of the *lux inaccessibilis* motif throughout the *Proslogion* is not merely that God is hidden but that God is hidden specifically from the possibility of *visio Dei*. Divine incomprehensibility, in other words, is not an abstract idea for Anselm but a concern on which his whole happiness rests.

Anselm then describes God's hiddenness in terms of the five human senses, not the senses of the body but of the soul: "for it looks around, and it does not see your beauty. It listens, and it does

---

73. *P* 16, Schmitt I 112:27–113:1.
74. *P* 16, Schmitt I 113:3–4.
75. *P* 17, Schmitt 113:8–9.

THE STRUCTURE OF THE *PROSLOGION*

not hear your harmony. It smells, and it does not perceive your fragrance. It tastes, and it does not know your flavor. It touches, and it does not sense your smoothness."[76] Anselm's reference to the five physical senses in the spiritual realm here is significant on several different levels. First of all, it widens out and gives texture to his doctrine of the *visio Dei*: Anselm apparently believes that the human soul has, as well as its own kind of vision, its own kind of ears and taste buds and so forth; and he can speak, not only of God's beauty, but of his taste/flavor (*sapor*) and fragrance (*odor*) and smoothness/softness (*lenitas*). Hence the pursuit of the *visio Dei* occupies his entire being.

But the next sentence reveals that Anselm's language here is not merely a function of his anthropology or doctrine of the soul but, more deeply, of his view of God: "for you have these things, Lord God, in your own ineffable way; and you have given them to the things created by you in their own perceptible way."[77] The parallel placement here of *tuo ineffabili modo* and *suo sensibili modo* here recalls the correlation that Anselm has drawn between the Creator and created things at the end of *Proslogion* 14 and anticipates the same correlation in *Proslogion* 24. This sentence clarifies that for all Anselm's emphasis on divine incomprehensibility, he is still working within an analogical rather than strictly equivocal view of the relationship of God and creation. Thus, right in the middle of his bemoaning God's hiddenness, he will interpret physical, perceptible qualities like smoothness or harmony as expressions of something analogous in the divine essence (*habes enim haec*). For Anselm, what creaturely beauty has in a *sensibili modo*, God has in an *ineffabili modo*. Therefore, God is both beyond comprehension and yet truly revealed in our physical senses.

The overall emphasis of *Proslogion* 17 on divine beauty and hiddenness reflects the upward trajectory of the book. Whereas in *Proslogion* 6–11, Anselm had in view divine attributes, here his focus in

76. P 17, Schmitt 113:9–13.
77. P 17, Schmitt 113:12–14.

on God's essence; whereas there he was burdened by apparent contradictions in God, here Anselm's anguish is over God's distance and ineffability. But in the final sentence of *Proslogion* 17, a shift of focus occurs as Anselm specifies the cause of God's hiddenness as the "longstanding languor of sin" (*vetusto languore peccati*).[78] As Gilbert notes, the reference to sin at the end of *Proslogion* 17 is relatively unique since *Proslogion* 1;[79] even in *Proslogion* 14, when Anselm laments his distance from God, he has attributed it to his *brevitas* (smallness) and *angustia* (narrowness) rather than his *peccatum*.[80] The reintroduction of sin here prepares Anselm for the third great prayer within the *Proslogion*, that of *Proslogion* 18, which will both draw from and transcend the earlier prayers of *Proslogion* 1 and 14.

This strong assertion of divine incomprehensibility in *Proslogion* 15–17 is an important step in the larger flow of the *Proslogion*. If we miss this spiral upward, we miss the whole point of the book (much in the way we miss the point of a novel if we stop reading halfway or two-thirds through it). Anselm has proved the existence and supreme existence of "that than which nothing greater can be conceived" (*Proslogion* 2–4), having established its identity as the *summum omnium* (*Proslogion* 5), with the consequent attributes appropriate to such an entity (*Proslogion* 6–13). But all this has only exacerbated his originating anguish (*Proslogion* 1), for he remains no closer to his goal of finding the *visio Dei* (*Proslogion* 14). Therefore, by means of the same divine formula, Anselm ratchets up his conception of God to "that which is greater than can be conceived" (*Proslogion* 15–17). Paradoxically, Anselm will now find that God's very invisibility and distance is the key forward as he progresses toward the beatific vision.

---

78. *P* 17, Schmitt 113.
79. Gilbert, *Le "Proslogion" de S. Anselme*, 155.
80. *P* 14, Schmitt I 112:4.

Proslogion 18–22: The "Higher" Divine Attributes

Anselm has paused to marvel at God's incomprehensibility in *Proslogion* 14, established it in terms of the divine formula in *Proslogion* 15, identified it with the *lux inaccessibilis* in *Proslogion* 16, and lamented its persistent hiddenness in *Proslogion* 17. Now divine incomprehensibility leads Anselm into a deeper focus on those "higher" divine attributes concerned with God's absolute wholeness and uniqueness. Gilbert is right to emphasize that eternity is a recurrent theme in the later chapters of the *Proslogion* (throughout chapters 13, 18–21), as well as that it surrounds the new divine formula in *Proslogion* 15.[81] In a way, a focus on divine eternity is not surprising at this juncture of the *Proslogion*, since it played a key role at a similar place in *Monologion* (throughout chapters 18–24), just before its exploration of the Trinity. But for Gilbert, the importance of eternity is bound up with his view of the significance of the new divine formula that Anselm introduces in *Proslogion* 15. In his interpretation, *Proslogion* 15 represents the "axis" (*l'axe*) of the *Proslogion*, the hinge around which *Proslogion* 13–21 are organized in a chiastic sequence:[82]

13: incirconscriptibiblé et éternité
14: voir et ne pas voir
15: quiddam maius quam cogitari possit
16–17: lumière ineffable
18–21: tout dans l'éternal

Gilbert's interpretation helpfully captures the upward trajectory of Anselm's thought from the divine attributes in *Proslogion* 5–11 to these more ineffable qualities of divine existence in the middle and later chapters. One wonders, however, if his focus on the introduction of divine eternity in *Proslogion* 13 and the new divine formula in *Proslogion* 15 to some extent enshrouds the transitional

81. Gilbert, *Le "Proslogion" de S. Anselme*, 143.
82. Gilbert, *Le "Proslogion" de S. Anselme*, 148.

significance of *Proslogion* 14. In the first place, it is not clear why *Proslogion* 13 should be regarded as the introduction of a new section, rather than a mere continuation of Anselm's treatment of how God relates to and instantiates his properties in *Proslogion* 12. Furthermore, it is only in light of the self-examination and petition in *Proslogion* 14 that one can see the *need* for the new divine formula, because this prayer concludes with the recognition that God's light and truth are "more than can be understood by a creature."[83] This is often not evident in Gilbert's focus on *Proslogion* 15. On the other hand, Gilbert does note similarities between the tone and form of *Proslogion* 14 and those of *Proslogion* 1, and he does see it as an important threshold in the larger context of the second half of the book. At one point, for instance, he claims that *Proslogion* 14–17 come just after the geographic center (*le center géographique*) of the book, highlighting the significance of the transition from *Proslogion* 13 to 14.[84] The strength of Gilbert's interpretation is his emphasis on *Proslogion* 18–22, particularly in relation to *Proslogion* 13 and 15. But divine eternity for Anselm is, as we will see, simply one more rung on the ladder upward toward the beatific vision.

The first paragraph of *Proslogion* 18 represents the third great prayer in the book, after *Proslogion* 1 and 14. As in *Proslogion* 14, Anselm here returns to the opening petitions of *Proslogion* 1 and laments his inability to fulfill his desires on account of sin. Anselm begins: "and again, behold confusion, again, behold mourning and grief stand in the way of one seeking joy and happiness."[85] The introductory words here "and again, behold confusion" (*et iterum ecce turbatio*) are a reference to Jeremiah 14:19 and recall Anselm's lament in *Proslogion* 1, "I have sought good things, and behold, confusion" (*quaesivi bona, et ecce turbatio*).[86] The word *iterum* suggests that Anselm is consciously referring back to *Proslogion* 1, and

83. *P* 14, Schmitt I 112:10–11.
84. Gilbert, *Le "Proslogion" de S. Anselme*, 154.
85. *P* 18, Schmitt I 113:18.
86. *P* 1, Schmitt I 99:10.

several other biblical references and phrases are also drawn from *Proslogion* 1 (e.g., the quotation of Psalm 26/25:1). The style is also consistent with *Proslogion* 1—repetition, anguish, dense biblical quotation, imagery (hunger/fullness, light/darkness), etc. It is evident that Anselm has not yet extricated himself out of the darkness of *Proslogion* 1—if anything, he has regressed, or at least he has seen more clearly just how *inaccessibilis* the *lux* is.

And yet, even as *Proslogion* 18 admits Anselm's continual frustration of desire, it also evidences a further spiraling up from the earlier themes, for here Anselm seems to indicate that there is a sense in which God is seen precisely in being not seen. As Schufreider puts it, "the claim that we cannot see the totality of God in one single simultaneous intuition is not just regarded as a revelation of his absolute unity but as evidence of his incomprehensibility."[87] Thus in a real sense Anselm has made progress from *Proslogion* 1 to *Proslogion* 14 and *Proslogion* 18, for the very impotence and frustration that he arrives at in *Proslogion* 18 represents a real insight into the divine nature, and a necessary one, on his pathway to the beatific vision. Cattin identifies three distinct upward movements from *Proslogion* 1 to *Proslogion* 18, and his insights are worth drawing out because they also highlight how the petitions of *Proslogion* 18 transcend those of *Proslogion* 1.

First, where *Proslogion* 1 laments the impossibility of searching for God when human beings have never seen him, *Proslogion* 18 draws out the affliction and distress that the loss of the sight of God causes.[88] Although *Proslogion* 1 laments the loss of the *visio Dei* as well, Cattin is right that there is a sense of amplification in the lament of *Proslogion* 18. Second, where *Proslogion* 1 invokes the fall of Adam and its consequences to account for the impossibility of the search for God, *Proslogion* 18 invokes Anselm's personal fall into sin and consequent helplessness.[89] In other words, Anselm seems

---

87. Schufreider, *Confessions of a Rational Mystic*, 215.
88. Cattin, "La prière de S Anselme dans le *Proslogion*," 377.
89. Cattin, "La prière de S Anselme dans le *Proslogion*," 377.

to regard himself as having personally recapitulated Adam's error, even amidst his efforts at seeking God. Anselm traces his own fallenness back to Adam's original sin and the universal state of humanity.[90] But the emphasis is on his *own* "fall." He draws together Psalm 51:5/50:7 ("I fell before my mother conceived me")[91] with the light/darkness imagery—referencing not only his fall into sin and darkness from birth but how that sin and darkness now entangles his current efforts: "I attempted to rise to the light of God, but I fell back into my darkness. Indeed, not only did I fall into it, I find that I am enveloped in it."[92] Thus Anselm traces his current theological difficulties back to his doctrine of original sin—he is trying to ascend upward to the beatific vision, but keeps "falling" back down into the darkness, recapitulating the original error of Adam.

Third, Cattin underscores that where *Proslogion* 1 called for divine help in searching for God, *Proslogion* 18 issues a new call for new help to persevere in this same search. Anselm's language here once again reflects that his ultimate aim in the *Proslogion* is the beatific vision: "cleanse, heal, sharpen, illumine the eye of my soul, that I might look upon you. Let my soul gather its strength, and with all its understanding again strain unto you, Lord."[93] Cattin draws attention to the similar vocabulary of these petitions in *Proslogion* 1 and *Proslogion* 18. He emphasizes that their difference is a matter both of their placement in the book and that *Proslogion* 18 depicts the consequences of sin more severely and more personally to Anselm in the midst of his current efforts.[94] That Anselm would see his need for divine illumination and cleansing even here in *Proslogion* 18 reflects the fact that he is still "spiraling" upward and has not yet reached his destination.

At the start of the second paragraph, Anselm asks, "what are

90. *P* 18, Schmitt I 114:5–8.
91. *P* 18, Schmitt I 114:3–4.
92. *P* 18, Schmitt I 114:2–3.
93. *P* 18, Schmitt I 114:11–13.
94. Cattin, "La prière de S Anselme dans le *Proslogion*," 377.

you, Lord, what are you, what shall my heart understand you to be?"[95] The fact that Anselm would return to this question at this stage in the book (again drawing from language in *Proslogion* 1 verbatim) deepens the sense that, for all Anselm has discovered thus far in the *Proslogion*, he is still fundamentally on the journey upward—he does not yet consider himself to even know what God is, let alone to have found him. This second paragraph of *Proslogion* 18 moves at a calmer, more deliberate pace than the first. Anselm's overall effort at this point is to tease out divine simplicity in terms of eternity. First, drawing from the earlier summaries in *Proslogion* 5 and 11, he identifies his conclusions about God's nature and attributes: "surely you are life, you are wisdom, you are truth, you are goodness, you are happiness, you are eternity, you are every true good (*omne verum bonum*)."[96] But Anselm is troubled by the fact that these are many things and that he cannot see them all in "one simultaneous view" (*uno simul intuitu*); therefore, he cannot delight in them all at once.[97] In an effort at perceiving God's beauty all at once, Anselm thus stipulates that since each of these attributes of God is all of what God is, therefore God cannot be broken up, even in the understanding.[98] Once again, Anselm establishes this assertion on the basis of the divine formula: if God could be broken up into parts, he would not be *quo nihil melius cogitari potest*.[99] In *Proslogion* 18, then, the purpose of divine simplicity is not theoretical but bound up with the beatific vision: Anselm is seeking some way for his soul to see God *uno simul intuitu*. In the final few sentences of *Proslogion* 18, Anselm then draws out divine eternity as a consequence of divine simplicity, with the result that God exists "as a whole everywhere" (*ubique totus*) and God's eternity exists "as a whole always" (*tota ... semper*).[100]

---

95. *P* 18, Schmitt I 114:14.
96. *P* 18, Schmitt I 114:14–16.
97. *P* 18, Schmitt I 114:17.
98. *P* 18, Schmitt I 114:18–21.
99. *P* 18, Schmitt I 114:21–22.
100. *P* 18, Schmitt I 115:3–4.

THE STRUCTURE OF THE PROSLOGION

In characterizing the transition from *Proslogion* 6–13 to *Proslogion* 18–22, we have used the language of "lower" to "higher" divine attributes. This could be taken to imply that Anselm is concerned with a different set of attributes in each section. This is largely true, but it is important to see elements of continuity from one section to the next—for instance, the interrelation of divine simplicity and eternity in *Proslogion* 18 draws from the earlier movement from *Proslogion* 12 to 13. Once again, however, there is a transcending or spiraling upward from the earlier section to the later one, for the kind of divine eternity in view in *Proslogion* 18–21 is really a different kind of eternity than in view in *Proslogion* 13. In *Proslogion* 13, Anselm defines God's eternity by stating that God does not cease to exist, just as he did not begin to exist.[101] But in *Proslogion* 18–22, Anselm ties up divine eternity with divine simplicity, using it to delineate God's transcendence over, and penetration of, all other things. Thus in the beginning of *Proslogion* 20 Anselm will draw as a consequence of divine eternity, "therefore you fill and encircle all things, and are before and beyond all things."[102] It is evident that Anselm is using the term "eternity" in a deeper way than it is often used in theological writing—he is more interested in the fullness and quality of God's existence than its mere duration. In these chapters, God is never simply *semper* but always *tota semper*.

In *Proslogion* 19, Anselm pauses to address a potential snag in his doctrine of divine eternality: how God can be *tota semper* if the past, present, and future are all different things?[103] To solve this Anselm posits that God is outside time altogether, likely drawing from Boethius's definition of eternity as God's "whole, simultaneous, and perfect possession of unending life" (*interminabilis vitae tota simul et perfecta possessio*).[104] Thus it is not that God *was* yes-

---

101. *P* 13, Schmitt I 110:17–18.
102. *P* 20, Schmitt I 115:18.
103. *P* 19, Schmitt I 115:7–9.
104. Boethius, *De Consolatione Philosophiae* 5.6.4, ed. Claudio Moreschini, Bibliotheca Teubneriana (Munich/Leipzig: K.G. Saur, 2000). In the same way,

terday and *will be* tomorrow but, rather, yesterday and tomorrow God simply *is*. In fact, it is not even quite accurate to say this, for God does not exist in yesterday or today or tomorrow at all but "simply" (*simpliciter*) and "outside all time" (*extra omne tempus*).[105] As it did for Boethius, therefore, eternity has therefore more of an active thrust for Anselm than a passive one: it is not that God is in all times and places but that all times and places are in God. "For nothing contains you, but you contain all things."[106]

In *Proslogion* 20, as in *Proslogion* 13, Anselm wants to distinguish God's eternality from that of other "eternal things" (*aeterna*), that is, those created things that will have no end (*finem non habebunt*). It is not enough for God to be endless; he is must be absolutely unique, absolutely "beyond" (*ultra*) all other endless things. Anselm gives three reasons for the utter uniqueness of God's eternity in the second paragraph of *Proslogion* 20. First, other eternal things can in no way exist without God, whereas God would not exist any less if they returned to nothingness.[107] Second, they can be thought to end and thus they do have an end in some sense, whereas God cannot even be thought to end.[108] Third, they do not yet possess the part of their eternity that is yet to come, whereas the future is always present to God.[109] Thus, because other *aeterna* are contingent, can be thought to end, and do not yet possess the future, there are at least three senses in which God is "beyond" them.

In *Proslogion* 21, Anselm pauses to make an application of his doctrine of divine eternity to a particular question of biblical interpretation relevant to his own context, namely, why scriptural language for divine eternity is both in the singular (*saeculum saeculi*) and the plural (*saecula saeculorum*). Both of these phrases were com-

---

Boethius will define divine omnipresence not that God is present in every place but that every place is present to him (*Opuscula Sacra* I 4:225–38).

105. P 19, Schmitt I 115:11–13.
106. P 19, Schmitt I 115:15.
107. P 20, Schmitt I 115:21–23.
108. P 20, Schmitt I 115:23–26.
109. P 20, Schmitt I 115:26–116:3.

mon in the Bible and liturgy of Anselm's day and are often translated as "forever and ever" or "world without end."[110] According to Logan, the phrase *saeculum saeculi* occurs twenty-eight times in the Psalms and twice elsewhere; the phrase *saecula saeculorum* occurs thirteen times in Revelation and twelve times elsewhere.[111] So here Anselm is asking which phrase more properly refers to God's eternality. To answer this question, Anselm suggests that just as a *saeculum temporum* contains all temporal things, so God's eternity contains *saecula temporum*.[112] Therefore, God's eternity is both an "age" (*saeculum*) with respect to its "indivisible unity" (*indivisibilem unitatem*) as well as "ages" (*saecula*) with respect to its "boundless greatness" (*interminabilem immensitatem*).[113] Thus, for Anselm, both phrases are permissible to refer to divine eternity and are useful in different ways. Anselm concludes by reasserting that although all things are in God, God has no spatial extension, so there is no middle or half or part in him.[114] This sudden reversion back to divine simplicity here at the end of the chapter testifies once again to the close interplay between divine simplicity and eternity in these chapters.

In the larger thrust of *Proslogion* 18–22, divine eternality and simplicity have been bound up with the absolute uniqueness of God. That is why Anselm has been concerned to assert that God is *tota semper* in *Proslogion* 18 and to distinguish his eternity from that of other beings in *Proslogion* 20 on the basis of God's aseity and necessary existence. Now in *Proslogion* 22, divine uniqueness comes directly into the forefront as Anselm distinguishes divine existence from all other kinds of existence in several further ways. He begins by asserting, "you alone, therefore, Lord, are what you are and who you are."[115] This is an assertion, not merely of God's

---

110. Cf. Williams, *Anselm: Basic Writings*, 93.
111. Logan, *Reading Anselm's "Proslogion,"* 109.
112. *P* 21, Schmitt I 116:6–8.
113. *P* 21, Schmitt I 116:8–9.
114. *P* 21, Schmitt I 116:10–12.
115. *P* 22, Schmitt I 116:15.

unique nature, but of God's unique manner of instantiating that nature. In other words, Anselm does not say, "you alone, therefore, are the Lord"; rather, he says, "you alone, therefore, Lord, are what you are and who you are." His uniqueness is not just that alone he is God but that *as God* he alone *is*. In other words, it is not merely content of divine existence, as it were, but its manner, that separates it from all existence.

In the remainder of the first paragraph of *Proslogion* 22, Anselm demarcates seven ways that all created existence differs from divine existence, concerning qualities like composition, changeableness, contingency, and so forth.[116] Whatever possesses these qualities, Anselm argues, does not exist "strictly and absolutely" (*proprie et absolute*).[117] God, by contrast, has a fundamental grasp of his own existence. "But you are what you are, since whatever you are at any time and in any way, you are wholly and always that."[118] In the second paragraph, Anselm therefore stipulates that God alone exists "strictly and simply" (*proprie et simpliciter*) because he alone has no past or future but only a present, and he alone cannot be thought not to exist.[119] Anselm then concludes by reasserting a number of divine attributes that have been established throughout the *Proslogion* (including *lux* and *beatitudo*), then summarizing God's existence as the *unum et summum bonum* who is completely self-sufficient but whom all things need for their being and well-being (*bene sint*).[120] Thus, the final sentence of *Proslogion* 22, significantly, returns to the purpose statement of the book's *prooemium*. This is an important structural indicator, as is the list of divine attributes that is also recapitulated here. Anselm seems to be drawing to some kind of a close here at the end of *Proslogion* 22.

---

116. *P* 22, Schmitt 116:15–19.
117. *P* 22, Schmitt 116:19–20.
118. *P* 22, Schmitt 116:20–21.
119. *P* 22, Schmitt 116:22–4. Cf. Williams, who translates this more loosely contextually as, "in a strict and unqualified sense" (*Anselm: Basic Writings*, 93).
120. *P* 22, Schmitt 116:24–117:2.

Robert Herrera sees *Proslogion* 22 as a kind of bridge chapter between Anselm's focus on divine unity in *Proslogion* 18–21 and his focus on divine goodness in *Proslogion* 23–25.[121] This is a helpful way to construe the overall spiral upward in these chapters, but *Proslogion* 22 should also be seen as more than a transition. It makes its own contribution in the ascent of the *Proslogion* by revealing the whole point that divine eternity and wholeness have been serving over the last several chapters. Just as Anselm utilized divine simplicity in connection to his movement toward the beatific vision, in order to see God *uno simul intuitu* rather than piecemeal, so divine eternity has functioned to help him arrive at divine uniqueness and goodness here at the end of *Proslogion* 22, where God is finally said to be *unum et summum bonum*. In other words, the *purpose* of the spiraling up in *Proslogion* 18–22 is to transcend higher into the doctrine of God. Anselm is ascending upward towards the beatific vision, which concerns the beauty of the divine essence—thus, he cannot remain in simply harmonizing God's attributes, bemoaning his incomprehensibility, or marveling at his wholeness. He must quickly pass through these stages to get to the whole point for which they serve: to identify God alone as the unique object of his soul's longing, the *unum et summum bonum*. Everything else is driving toward this great end.

Conclusion: Looking Back, Looking Ahead

Anselm has come a long way from the beginning of *Proslogion* 5 to the ending of *Proslogion* 22. He began by asserting God's identity as *summum omnium* and then drawing various attributes as a

---

121. Herrera, *Anselm's "Proslogion,"* 27. In Herrera's view, *Proslogion* 5–26 is split into three sections: divine attributes (chapters 5–13), the quest for experience (chapters 14–19), and the adumbration of beatitude (chapters 20–26). See Herrera, *Anselm's "Proslogion,"* 25–28. Later, drawing from the work of Paul Evdokimov, Herrera emphasizes the structural significance of *Proslogion* 14, noting the incremental movement in the following chapters (especially 16–18) from theoretical knowledge to experiential joy (*Anselm's "Proslogion,"* 75–76).

consequence; he ends by reasserting various divine attributes, then drawing as a consequence God's role as *unum et summum bonum*.

- *Proslogion* 5: "What are you other than that which is the highest of all things (*summum omnium*) who, existing alone through yourself, made all other things from nothing? ... You are therefore just, truthful, happy."[122]

- *Proslogion* 22: "And you are life and light and wisdom and happiness and eternity and many good things of this kind, and yet you are nothing other than the one and highest good (*unum et summum bonum*), altogether sufficient for yourself (*tu tibi omnino sufficiens*), lacking nothing, while all things need for their being and well-being (*ut sint, et ut bene sint*)."[123]

Along the way, Anselm has established several regulating axioms regarding the divine nature, from divine supremacy to divine simplicity; he has harmonized various divine attributes; and he has ascended upward into divine incomprehensibility, eternity, and uniqueness.

Nonetheless, for all this progress, the prayers of *Proslogion* 1 have not yet been answered but have only been reiterated with greater urgency and anguish in *Proslogion* 14 and 18. Thus, the basic point of the *Proslogion*—to see God—remains unfulfilled. Now, in the final stage of the book, Anselm is finally able to identify the *summum bonum* with the Trinity articulated by his faith (*Proslogion* 23), and thus as the object of his soul's longing (*Proslogion* 24–26).

---

122. *P* 5, Schmitt I 104:11–15.
123. *P* 22, Schmitt I 116:24–117:12.

CHAPTER 5

The Climax of the *Proslogion*

The *Visio Dei* in Chapters 23–26

> Anselm's concept of heaven and the saints was a
> central theme throughout his life from childhood
> to death.
>
> —BENEDICTA WARD

In a 1973 paper delivered to the Anselm Society at St. Augustine's College, Canterbury, Benedicta Ward drew attention to the relationship between Anselm's theological output and his monastic vocation. Toward the end, she suggested that "the *Proslogion* may hold the intricacies of philosophical argument in the celebrated chapters about the existence of God; but the whole prayer is basically a prolonged example of how to think about God as Trinity in order to love and attain to him."[1] Conceiving of the *Proslogion* as, at its core, an example of thinking about God to the end of loving God and attaining God—this is a good encapsulation of the heart of our argument thus far. The problem, however, is that by *Proslogion* 22 Anselm has done much of the "thinking"—even much of the "loving"—but yet little yet of the "attaining."

---

1. Ward, *Anselm of Canterbury: A Monastic Scholar*, 18.

THE CLIMAX OF THE PROSLOGION

If the driving question of our last chapter concerned Anselm's logical flow of thought up to *Proslogion* 23, the driving question of this chapter is how the book's final chapters provide a fitting conclusion to that flow of thought and bring resolution to the purpose of the book as a whole. As we will see, in *Proslogion* 23 Anselm identifies the Trinity as the *summum bonum* he has been exploring throughout the book, then further identifies this Trinity as the *unum necessarium* of human happiness. This identification marks an important milestone in his ascent upward into the doctrine of God, but it does not conclude the book. Instead, Anselm progresses further into a vision of the soul's *enjoyment* of the Trinity as the *summum bonum* in heaven in *Proslogion* 24–26. This final section bears many of the literary features of the earlier prayers of *Proslogion* 1, 14, 18, marking perhaps the highest crescendo of tone and energy in the book (particularly in *Proslogion* 25).

Why should Anselm conclude his book in this way? Too often interpretations of the significance of the *Proslogion* have been formed apart from a careful consideration of these final chapters. In fact, where the concluding chapters of the *Proslogion* have been engaged at all, they are often regarded as a mere appendix or epilogue to the real substance of Anselm's work—and even those interpreters who seek to trace the thread of Anselm's argument throughout the entire *Proslogion* tend to break off the book's final chapters as unrelated to its flow of thought. Mackey, for instance, opens his engagement with the later chapters of the *Proslogion* by asserting that "the *Proslogium* proof does not end with chapter 4. The *Proslogium* proof is the *Proslogium*, and neither its logic nor its import is clear until the argument is seen in this larger view."[2] Nonetheless, he ultimately reduces the Trinitarian reflection of *Proslogion* 23 and the heavenly aspirations of *Proslogion* 24–26 to a "denouement of sorts," locating *Proslogion* 22 instead as the real "climactic moment of the *Proslogium*."[3] As a result, *Proslogion* 23–26 merit virtually no

2. Mackey, *Peregrinations of the Word*, 93.
3. Mackey, *Peregrinations of the Word*, 99.

THE CLIMAX OF THE *PROSLOGION*

comment in his analysis of the *Proslogion* proof.⁴ Similarly, Herrera calls *Proslogion* 25–26 a "rather lengthy excursus" that directs Anselm's thought in a new direction.⁵

We suggest, however, that *Proslogion* 23–26 are essential to the meaning of the book as a whole. In fact, in light of Anselm's expressed purpose in the earlier prayers of *Proslogion* 1 and elsewhere, as we have noted particularly in chapter 3, it is only natural that he would conclude with a meditation on the soul's joy in the *visio Dei* in heaven. Without this section, the book would be incomplete, because his passionate prayers would be unanswered—God's greatness might be established by his argument but it would have no personal *consequence* for Anselm's state of anguish. To use Ward's categories, Anselm would have "loved" but not "attained." Thus he would have prayed in vain in *Proslogion* 1, "my heart is bitter from its desolation, sweeten it with your consolation."⁶ Nothing in the middle chapters of the *Proslogion* has answered this prayer—even in *Proslogion* 18, Anselm is still praying, "once again, behold mourning and grief stand in the way of one seeking joy and happiness."⁷ Only after his long journey upward into the doctrine of God, only after the *unum argumentum* has propelled Anselm up through the *lux inaccessibilis* into the Father and the Son and the Spirit as the *unum necessarium* of the human soul, only finally in *Proslogion* 26 can Anselm at last pray, "I have found a joy that is full, and more than full."⁸ At long last, Anselm has passed (to use Ward's terms again) from "thinking" and "loving" into "attaining."

Here we offer a brief account of how *Proslogion* 23–26 bring resolution to the book. First, we situate the doctrine of heaven reflected in *Proslogion* 23–26 in relation to Anselm's broader concep-

---

4. Mackey does, however, engage these chapters briefly in his treatment of the rhetoric of the *Proslogion* (cf. *Peregrinations of the Word*, 103, 105–6).
5. Herrera, *Anselm's "Proslogion,"* 28.
6. P 1, Schmitt I 99:22–23.
7. P 18, Schmitt I 113:18.
8. P 26, Schmitt I 120:25–121:1.

tion of heaven, particularly as seen in his *Prayers and Meditations* and his letters. Then we turn to *Proslogion* 23, drawing attention to how divine simplicity functions for Anselm to identify each member of the Godhead as the *summum bonum* in *Proslogion* 23. We place particular emphasis on the tradition of interpretation of Luke 10:42 ("one thing is necessary") that precedes Anselm, that Mary's sitting at Christ's feet served as a type of the contemplative life of eternal enjoyment of God. Then we engage in a careful exegesis of *Proslogion* 24–26. In *Proslogion* 24, we explore the nature of Anselm's conjecture (*conjectatio*) about divine goodness, drawing particular attention to the recapitulation of themes and terms from earlier in the book, particularly *Proslogion* 1. We divide *Proslogion* 25 into three sections, suggesting that the final two of these especially (paragraphs 2–4 in Schmitt) comprise the climax of the book. We draw from the *Memorials of St. Anselm* to situate the fourteen beatitudes of the middle section of this chapter in relation to the rest of his teaching career, drawing upon Anselm's doctrine of friendship to account for his concluding emphasis on the infinite multiplication of love in heaven in the final section of this chapter. Finally, we explore how *Proslogion* 26 brings resolution to the book, as Anselm returns from self-address to a final prayer, summarizing the joy he has discovered and asking God that he might grow in it.

Heaven in Anselm's *Prayers and Meditations* and letters

Heaven is a significant feature of Anselm's thought and life. It is the object of intense yearning all throughout his *Prayers and Meditations*; a frequent topic of counsel in his letters; and it features prominently in Eadmer's descriptions of Anselm's daily life. The first thing we read about Anselm in Eadmer's *Vita* is the story of Anselm as a young boy who, having imagined heaven to be at the top of the mountains, has a vision in which he climbs to the top of the mountain, enters into the court of God, and eats white bread in

God's presence while talking with him.⁹ In its own way this vision is an apt metaphor for the whole thrust of Anselm's theology and the particular effort he makes in the *Proslogion*.

Nonetheless, there has been surprisingly little exploration of Anselm's doctrine of heaven, perhaps because Anselm's letters and devotional writings are often neglected in comparison to his better-known, more speculative writings. But any thorough assessment of Anselm's theology must involve an engagement with these works, particularly in light of the significance of friendship and prayer in Anselm's life and thought. In Anselm's own day, he was admired for his prayers, for his friendship, for his spiritual direction, as much as for his philosophical brilliance. In the later medieval era as well, as Southern notes, Anselm's *Prayers and Meditatons* were "the most influential and widely read of all his writings."[10] As Benedicta Ward has pointed out, in his immediate influence Anselm was not merely an *Augustinus minor*, a theologian whose innovative employment of reason paved the way for high medieval scholasticism, but also a *Bernardus prior*, a spiritual writer whose innovative stress on the inward-looking, emotive aspects of prayer popularized a new style that altered the flavor of medieval European spirituality.[11] It is only through the winnowing effect of the fame of the "ontological argument" that the intellectual side of Anselm's significance has displaced the social and spiritual.

Anselm's letters and devotional writings provide certain insights into his thought that are not available in his more strictly theological or philosophical works. We find certain emphases and nuances in, say, the warmth of a letter exchange with Gundulf or the agony of his second meditation that we never would have happened upon in the *Monologion* or *Cur Deus Homo*. Anselm's doctrine of heaven, in particular, surfaces repeatedly in his spiritual and personal writings, despite its relative infrequency in his better-known

---

9. Eadmer, *Vita Sancti Anselmi* 1:2, 4–5.
10. Southern, *Saint Anselm*, 91.
11. Ward, *Anselm of Canterbury: A Monastic Scholar*, 17–18.

works. *The Rule of Saint Benedict*, which formed the basis of much of Anselm's daily life as a monk during his years at Bec, enjoined its readers "to desire to eternal life with all spiritual longing."[12] It described prayer as designed to help the sinner shake off the "torpor" and dullness of sin, stir up "compunction and tears," and grow in the love of God.[13] Anselm's own prayers were written in the same vein, designed to stir up the mind to the love or fear of God or to self-examination.[14] For Anselm and the monastic tradition that preceded him, this love of God is ultimately realized in heaven, and thus all prayer has an undercurrent of heavenly longing.[15] As Ward notes, "like St. Gregory, Anselm is a doctor of *suspira*, the longing for heaven, for union in love with God. The end of all the prayers is the same, union with God, the blessed Trinity, in the bliss of heaven."[16] Given this heavenly thrust in Anselm's prayer life, is it not surprising that the *Proslogion*—which, after all, is a prayer—climaxes into a *conjectatio* on the goods of the heaven and the soul's joy in experiencing them.

Heaven functions in several important ways in Anselm's *Prayers and Meditations*. With striking regularity, Anselm's prayers conclude with a focus on heaven, often referencing the Trinity and God's eternal happiness (*benedictus in saecula*). This is the case in all but one of the prayers (*Oratio* 12), and all three of Anselm's meditations conclude with a vision of God's triune, heavenly happiness.[17] But heaven also works itself into the body of the prayers and becomes one of their primary themes. Just as the *Meditationes* fuel remorse for sin by appealing to the terror of hell (especially *Meditatio* 2), so the *Orationes* fuel longing for God by appealing to the joy of

---

12. R 4.46.
13. See the helpful discussion in Ward, *Prayers and Meditations*, 45–46, 53–56.
14. *Or. prologus*, Schmitt III 3:3–5.
15. Ward, *Prayers and Meditations*, 89. Southern also draws attention to the innovations in Anselm's conception of meditation, and the widespread impact of his *Prayers and Meditations* throughout the medieval era (*Saint Anselm*, 99–112).
16. Ward, *Prayers and Meditations*, 56.
17. E.g., *Med.* 3, Schmitt III 91:211.

heaven.[18] Heaven becomes a key focus for Anselm's spiritual yearning not simply because it represents the release from sin for which he longs but also the glorification of body and beatific vision for which he was created.[19] In his *Oratio ad Christum*, for instance, Anselm exclaims:

Quando venies consolator meus quem expecto? O si quando videbo gaudium meum quod desidero! O si satiabor cum apparuerit gloria tua quam esurio! O si inebriabor ub ubertate domus tuae ad quam suspiro! Si potabis me torrente voluptatis tuae quam sitio!

When will you come, my consoler for whom I wait? O, if only I might see my joy, which I desire! O, if only I might be satisfied when your glory appears, for which I hunger! O, if only I might drink from the abundance of your house, for which I sigh! If only you would let me drink in the torrent of your pleasure, for which I thirst.[20]

The heightened tone achieved by repetition with variation here is reminiscent of the prayers of *Proslogion* 1, just as several of the biblical references (Psalm 17:13/16:15 and 35/36:8) are utilized again in *Proslogion* 25 in the same close sequence. As in the *Proslogion*, one is struck by the intensity of Anselm's longing, and his articulation that heavenly joy is the chief aim of his existence (consider his language, "my joy, which I desire").

The notion of confirmation in happiness—the permanent and perfect happiness of heaven for which each human being was created, which cannot be lost—is a key feature of Anselm's anthropology and receives a clear articulation in the final chapters of the *Monologion*. In *Monologion* 68, Anselm asserts that the rational creature was made for the purpose of loving God; then in *Monologion* 69, he clarifies that for this purpose to be achieved, the rational creature must love God without end, in a state of eternal security. "It is therefore

---

18. E.g., *Med.* 2, Schmitt III 82:69–83.
19. Anselm's interest in the resurrection of his body is striking, for instance, in *Or.* 3, Schmitt III 10:20–23.
20. *Or.* 2, Schmitt III 9:88–92.

clear that the human soul is such that if it maintains that for which it was made, it will finally live happily, truly secure from death itself and all other troubles."[21] The word *aliquando* ("finally" or "at some time") here indicates a new state of happiness that cannot be lost, in distinction to the happiness of the saints in this life, comparable to Augustine's fourth state of humanity in relation to sin, *non posse peccare*.[22] This notion of confirmation in happiness is teased out further in the several following chapters, in contrast to the final state of misery of the wicked. In *Monologion* 73, for instance, Anselm stipulates that every human soul is either always miserable or at some time truly happy (*semper misera aut aliquando vere beata*).[23] The contrast between "final" misery or happiness again sheds light on Anselm's anthropology—in his mind, because every human being was created specifically to love God, a state of permanent happiness or a state of permanent misery are the only two options possible for an eternal soul, depending on whether this end is achieved.

Anselm's prayers to the saints reflect a clear awareness that they are already in a state of perfect, glorified, confirmed happiness, and Anselm emphasizes the distinctness of this state from that of the saints on earth. In his prayer to Stephen, Anselm can even declare that his sins are against Stephen and all the saints as well, and the mercy he receives is from them as well as from God. He writes, "I know fully, lord, Stephen, beloved of God, that when I offend God, I offend you also, and all of his holy ones."[24] He then acknowledges that the saints in heaven are so full of goodness that they can free those whom they are able to condemn and petitions Stephen for his merits to suffice for Anselm.[25] But above all, Anselm emphasizes the *joy* of the saints' current heavenly experience. Later in the same prayer, for instance, Anselm references Stephen's "falling asleep" in

21. *M* 69, Schmitt I 80:4–6.
22. E.g., see *Enchiridion* 118.
23. *M* 73, Schmitt I 82:15–18.
24. *Or.* 13, Schmitt III 51:52–53.
25. *Or.* 13, Schmitt III 51:55–52:57.

Acts 7:60, and then writes: "O sleep with rest, rest with security, security with eternity! You rest, O happy one, in joy; you rejoice in rest. You glory, O secure one, in satisfaction; you are satisfied in glory. Your happiness will not change, your light will not fail."[26] Anselm then goes on for some amount of space (fourteen further lines in Schmitt's edition) marveling at the perfection and fullness of Stephen's heavenly joy, before lamenting his own distance from that joy and petitioning Stephen that Anselm could experience that same heavenly joy one day.[27] One notes again, as in *Oratio* 2 and *Proslogion* 25, the reference to drinking from the torrent of God's pleasure from Psalm 35/36:8.

The longing for heaven is also a recurrent theme in Anselm's letters. His characteristic opening is something like "brother Anselm, [hoping] to live sacredly in this life with prosperity, and happily in the future one with eternity."[28] The wording varies slightly, and sometimes Anselm will express this desire for heavenly bliss as a description of himself rather than a wish for the recipient of the letter. But this construct of earthly "prosperity" (*prosperitas*) and eternal happiness (*felicitas*), whether wished to his recipient or sought for himself, is a regular opening formula.[29] Heaven is also a theme throughout the body of the letters. Three themes, in particular, might be drawn out.[30]

First, Anselm repeatedly casts life as a journey from earth to heaven. One might call this the *pilgrimage* motif in his doctrine of heaven. In an early letter to a fellow monk, he depicts all earthly

26. *Or.* 13, Schmitt III 53:110–54:113.
27. *Or.* 13, Schmitt III 54:114–41.
28. *Ep.* 6, Schmitt III 107:2–3.
29. *Ep.* 2, 6, 39, 48, 50, 59, 62, 63, 65, 143, etc.
30. I have been helped in my understanding of the role of heaven in Anselm's letters by David Hogg, Richard Southern, and Gregory Sadler, though I draw these three motifs from my own survey through them. Though I have looked at all of Anselm's letters, I have drawn more from those earlier in his life, since those after he became archbishop in 1093 tend to focus more on matters of state. Southern argues that the letters from Anselm's time as prior and abbot at Bec (1070–1093) should be "sharply distinguished" from his later letters for this very reason (*Saint Anselm*, 138).

saints as traveling together on a common path toward their heavenly home, expressing his need to call out for help to those further down the path than him.³¹ Later, in his counsel to a young man named William about the dangers of loving the world, Anselm admonishes him to abandon the Jerusalem on earth, as well as the treasures of Constantinople and Babylon, and "begin the path to the heavenly Jerusalem," where he will find treasures that can be received only by despising the earthly ones.³² Closer to the end of his life, he speaks of our earthly life as a race and heavenly crowns as the reward, drawing from Paul's imagery.³³ These images of a pilgrimage, or a long journey or race, recur again and again in his letters,³⁴ and his readers are often exhorted to walk *in via aeterna*³⁵ or *in via caelestis patriae*.³⁶

In the pilgrimage from earth to heaven, Anselm conceives of good deeds as the primary mechanism by which one makes progress, somewhat as stairs are the means by which one progresses from one floor to another. In his letter to Abbess Eulalia and the nuns of St. Edward, Shaftesbury, Anselm writes, "indeed, as long as a man lives, he is either ascending into heaven by living well or descending into hell by living poorly. If, therefore, you desire to attain to what you have vowed, it is necessary that you advance (*proficere*) there by holy actions (*sanctis actionibus*), as if by certain steps."³⁷ Anselm emphasizes the gradual, step-by-step nature of the saints' progressive movement toward heaven by good deeds. He often describes the saints journey to heaven as "from strength to strength" (*de virtute in virtutem*),³⁸ a reference to Psalm 83:8/84:7 that is occasionally qual-

---

31. *Ep.* 3, Schmitt III 102:9–12.
32. *Ep.* 117, Schmitt III 254:66–71.
33. *Ep.* 335, Schmitt V 271:12–15.
34. E.g., *Ep.* 35, Schmitt III 143:14–18.
35. E.g., *Ep.* 46, Schmitt III 160:21.
36. E.g., *Ep.* 51, Schmitt III 165:34.
37. *Ep.* 183, Schmitt IV 68:9–12. Fröhlich translates *quasi quibusdam passibus* "as if step by step" (*Letters* vol. 2, 102).
38. E.g, *Ep.* 55, Schmitt III 169:2; *Ep.* 60, Schmitt III 174:2.

ified with "from progress to progress" (*de profectu ad profectum*).[39] Because Anselm depicts all of life as a journey to heaven, he encourages his readers to make it the object of their constant and lifelong striving. He repeatedly quotes Ecclesiasticus 19:1, "whoever despises little fails little by little," for instance, warning his readers not to deviate from their heavenly journey in the slightest way.[40]

Second and very much related, Anselm emphasizes the fierce tension between the saints' earthly life and their heavenly life. He frequently admonishes his readers to reject making this world their home, frequently encouraging them amidst earthly sorrows and difficulties that their true home is in heaven. One might call this the *exile* motif in his doctrine of heaven. Whereas the *pilgrimage* motif entails a sense of always striving toward heaven, the *exile* motif emphasizes that heaven can only be obtained by forsaking the world. As Anselm warns his fellow monk Herluin, "think very frequently, my brother, and know very certainly, that eternal bitterness seizes those whom the sweetness of the world entices; and perpetual happiness (*perpetua beatitudo*) satisfies those whom the sweetness of God attracts."[41] Anselm repeatedly enjoins his readers to give up on earthly glory, happiness, and wealth and instead seek holiness in this life, so that they may one day inherit heavenly glory, happiness, and wealth.

There is a fierce, dialectical contrast between these two realms: one is either at home in the world or in heaven, never both. In the opening of his letter to Albert the physician, Anselm will refer to himself as "brother Anselm, despising earthly things for heavenly things, seizing heavenly things instead of earthly things."[42] Anselm will often appeal to this dialectic between earth and heaven in order to encourage his readers both to become a monk or a nun or to continue in the monastic way of life amidst worldly temptation. A

39. *Ep.* 231, Schmitt IV 137:26.
40. E.g., *Ep.* 450, Schmitt V 398:26.
41. *Ep.* 8, Schmitt III 110:4–6.
42. *Ep.* 44, Schmitt III 156:2–3.

frequent verse on this vein is James 4:4—because friendship with the world is enmity with God, we must abandon worldly friendships and seek instead friendship with "God and his friends, the angels."[43] There are frequent references to the fact that few will be saved and many will be lost, as well as the doctrine of election. At one point, quoting Christ's words that "few are chosen," Anselm declares, "whoever therefore does not yet live as the few must either join himself to the few by correcting his life, or fear reprobation with certainty."[44]

This *exile* motif can lead Anselm to seemingly harsh counsel at times and could seem to reflect a rather dismal view of the world. But it must be seen as a product of Anselm's anthropology, in which human beings were created for the supreme happiness of heavenly union with God in love, and no other happiness can replace this function. For Anselm, the happiness of heaven is not simply superior to that of this life, but it is the fulfillment and goal of every other form of happiness. The sacrifice of earthly happiness is necessary to the larger end of receiving the greater happiness of heaven. As he counsels his cousin Peter, "hasten toward such a profit, so that by relinquishing those things which are of the world, you may receive a hundred-fold, and possess eternal life."[45] In a letter to the nun Gunhilda, urging her to resume the monastic life, Anselm contrasts the spiritual pleasures of union with Christ with the carnal pleasures of extramarital sex, emphasizing how far superior are the pleasures of pure devotion to Christ, both in this life and the next.[46] This letter and its even sterner follow-up letter are striking for their high doctrine of the soul's union with God in heaven, as an alternative to all worldly love, particularly sexual love, and as the highest object of the soul's striving.[47] If the *pilgrimage* motif showed how

---

43. E.g., *Ep.* 405, Schmitt V 350:22–25.
44. *Ep.* 2, Schmitt III 100:42–44.
45. *Ep.* 56, Schmitt III 171:17–19.
46. *Ep.* 168, Schmitt IV 44:17–29.
47. E.g., *Ep.* 169, Schmitt IV 50:103–6.

expansive Anselm's doctrine of heaven was, structuring his vision of the Christian life as a whole, the *exile* motif shows how penetrating and intense it was, requiring the deepest human passions and fulfilling the deepest human desires.

Third, there is a communal thrust to Anselm's vision of heaven. Earlier we mentioned Anselm's image of saints travelling together on the road to heaven, where he spoke of his need for help from those walking ahead of him.[48] Likewise, Anselm will counsel others not to notice those whom they may surpass "on the road to the celestial country" (*in via caelestis patriae*) but to keep moving resolutely forward.[49] Nonetheless, it is not simply the journey to heaven that Anselm depicts in communal terms but the arrival in heaven. We might call this the *reunion* motif. Anselm frequently expresses his longing to be reunited with others in heaven, and, for him, much of the joy of heaven consists in the perfected love among the saints and angels that will be present there, not only toward God but also toward one another. Anselm opens his letter to Lonzo the novice, for instance, by appealing to heaven in order to comfort himself regarding their physical separation. "When I consider, most beloved, your desire and mine, by which we long for one another, there is one thing which consoles me about our separation: that through divine mercy I hope for our eternal union (*aeternam nostram coniunctionem*) in the life to come."[50] Anselm then defines this "eternal union" as two souls being bound together as one through love (*caritas unam conficiat*), which they already experience despite their geographical distance and consequent longing for one another.[51] He then reflects upon the nature of their heavenly reunion: "but when the pilgrimage (*peregrinatione*) of this life is over, with the help of the one toward whom we strive and in whom we hope, we shall come together in the country for which

---

48. *Ep.* 3, Schmitt III 102:9–12.
49. *Ep.* 2, Schmitt III 100:47–50.
50. *Ep.* 37, Schmitt III 145:3–6.
51. *Ep.* 37, Schmitt III 145:6–9.

we sigh, as if by different paths (*quasi diversis itineribus*)."⁵² Finally, Anselm states that the more patiently they bear their current separation, the greater will be the joy of their reunion.

This image of different paths into the same country (*patria*) is a good encapsulation of the *reunion* motif, and it is a surprisingly prominent theme in the doctrine of heaven in his letters. For example, in his letter to Abbot Paul, Anselm commends him for his godly example to the saints, which God has "made as a guide to those proceeding from earth to heaven through the narrow way of virtue."⁵³ He then encourages him to rejoice, not only because of his own heavenly reward, but because the joy of eternal happiness will be multiplied (*multiplicetur*) for many others as a result of his example.⁵⁴ This theme of the multiplication of joy in heaven through perfect love will come to a fuller expression in *Proslogion* 25. In the letter to Hugh the Hermit, which we referenced at the beginning of chapter 3, Anselm emphasizes several others themes that will also surface in *Proslogion* 25: especially (1) that the saints will be omnipotent in heaven because their wills will be united with God's, and (2) that the saints will love each other as they love themselves and love God more than they love themselves.⁵⁵ In this letter Anselm goes on in some detail about the nature of heavenly love, emphasizing that it is as different from earthly love as a stench is from a scent and as darkness is to light.⁵⁶ It is clear that he regards love as the fundamental dynamic of heavenly joy—and not just the love of saints and angels for God but also for each other.

Anselm's high view of love among the saints (and angels) helps explain the intensity of his expressions of yearning in his letters. Some have seen erotic or sexual tones in his language, but it is better to read them in light of Anselm's view that two souls can be

---

52. *Ep.* 37, Schmitt III 145:9–13.
53. *Ep.* 80, Schmitt III 203:5–6.
54. *Ep.* 80, Schmitt III 203:6–8.
55. *Ep.* 112, Schmitt III 245:24–31.
56. *Ep.* 112, Schmitt III 246:56–57

spiritually united as one through love. As Southern notes, Anselm knew that his letters would be widely circulated and read, and thus they "were not intended to convey private emotional attachments, still less forbidden yearnings. They were public statements about the rewards of the life dedicated to God."[57] Anselm's high view of friendship, moreover, was common in both the medieval as well as the ancient world. As Ward notes, "from Cicero and Cassian, to Bernard and Aelred, the ideal of the union of the souls of good men in the pursuit of virtue grew and achieved a place in Christian theology."[58]

What exactly was Anselm's doctrine of friendship? Essentially, Anselm held that two souls could be spiritually united to one another through love. To the monk Henry, Anselm speaks of "those whose minds are welded into one by the fires of love," expressing his frustration at their physical separation despite this union.[59] Writing to Lanfranc, Anselm states that the monk Osbern has become so attached to Anselm's soul that he cannot part from him without his heart being torn apart (*scissura*).[60] At times, Anselm's letters will express this union (or desire thereof) so strongly that it almost calls to mind notions of *perichoresis* (mutual indwelling or interpenetration), as in the relations among the Godhead. In a letter to Gundulf, for example, he says: "for since your soul and my soul can by no means endure to be absent from each other, but are incessantly entwined together, there is nothing in us that is missing from each other except that we are not present to each other bodily."[61] It is a strikingly high doctrine of spiritual friendship that can regard two souls as sharing everything but physical location in common ("there is nothing in us that is missing from each other"), and this view of friendship helps explain why the

---

57. Southern, *Saint Anselm*, 147.
58. Ward, *Prayers and Meditations*, 72.
59. *Ep.* 5, Schmitt III 106:2–8.
60. *Ep.* 66, Schmitt III 186:12–13.
61. *Ep.* 41, Schmitt III 152:6–9.

reunion motif of heaven is such a recurrent motif in Anselm's letters. Heaven is the place, in Anselm's thinking, where the intense longing of physical distance will be finally ended, where this intertwining (*amplectentes*) of souls will be completed and cemented—not just among two saints, but among all the saints and angels, as they are reunited together in their true home at the end of their respective pilgrimages. Southern notes that friendship was central to Anselm's theological program because it is the only relationship that continues unaltered into heaven.[62] This heavenly thrust in spiritual friendships must be kept in mind when interpreting Anselm's strong expressions of love and longing for other monks. As Southern suggests, after exploring Anselm's theology of friendship, he suggests, "when (Anselm) spoke in ecstatic terms about friendship, he was thinking of individuals, not primarily on earth, but in Heaven."[63] This is perhaps also one reason why Anselm included friendship as one of the fourteen beatitudes of heaven (which we will discuss more thoroughly below).[64]

Seen together, these three motifs of pilgrimage, exile, and reunion illustrate how important Anselm's doctrine of heaven is in his overall theology. Their respective implications are that heaven for Anselm is (1) the fundamental interpretation of the Christian life, (2) the deepest longing of Christian desire, and (3) the ultimate expression of Christian love and community. In this third principle two of the greatest themes of Anselm's letters—love for others in friendship and the longing for God and heaven—come together. Interestingly, these two themes also join together in *Proslogion* 23–26, particularly, as we will see, in the climax of the entire book, the final paragraph of *Proslogion* 25.

---

62. Southern, *Saint Anselm*, 155.
63. Southern, *Saint Anselm*, 158.
64. *Mem.*, 60–61, 282.

Proslogion 23: The Trinity as the *unum necessarium*

Proslogion 23 is marked by its compactness and compression. In the *Monologion* Anselm had spent some thirty-five chapters developing his doctrine of the Trinity (29–63) and another seventeen to relate human rationality and happiness to the Trinity (64–80). Now here in *Proslogion* 23 he will draw both doctrines together in little more than two hundred words. But he is drawing from this larger discussion in the *Monologion*—one is best poised to understand *Proslogion* 23 and the chapters that follow by keeping in mind Anselm's prior assertions, for instance, that the rational mind is the principal means by which we know God (*Monologion* 66–67), that rational creatures were created to love God (*Monologion* 68), that loving God is true happiness (*Monologion* 69), that disdaining God is eternal misery (*Monologion* 71), and that happiness or misery are the only alternative states for immortal souls (*Monologion* 73). The anthropology reflected in these chapters of the *Monologion*, and specifically the doctrine of human happiness, will now funnel into Anselm's conception of the beatific vision as it now comes into focus in these final chapters of the *Proslogion*.

Anselm has two goals in *Proslogion* 23: first, to identify each person of the Trinity (and the Trinity as a whole) as the *hoc bonum* he has arrived upon at the end of *Proslogion* 22; second, to identify this *hoc bonum* as the *unum necessarium* of human happiness. The first of these goals is pursued in the first paragraph in four lengthy sentences of tightly condensed reasoning; the second goal is pursued in the second paragraph, in two brief sentences of biblical reference (Luke 10:42) and application. The introduction of *unum necessarium* at the end of the chapter serves as an important transition in the book into the self-examination and joy in *Proslogion* 24–26.

The first paragraph of *Proslogion* 23 reflects self-consciously orthodox language with respect to the doctrine of the Trinity. Anselm introduces "God the Father" (*deus pater*) as the direct object of his prayer, and begottenness (*nasci*) and procession (*procedens*) are

THE CLIMAX OF THE *PROSLOGION*

used to define the respective relations of Word/Son to the Father, and Spirit/Love to both Father and Son. But unlike the *Monologion*, where Anselm spends a great deal of energy in establishing the various relations of the divine persons, Anselm here simply invokes them. Anselm seems more interested in using the doctrine of the Trinity in his movement toward the beatific vision than exploring it directly: if in the *Monologion* the doctrine of the Trinity is like a field to be mined, here it is more like a bridge to be crossed. (Hence the collapsing from thirty-five chapters to two hundred lines.) The most outstanding fact about *Proslogion* 23, and most fundamental to its interpretation, is its role in this larger sweep of thought: Anselm is interested in God as simple and God as triune in the context of his more basic concern of God as *summum bonum*. Here, as all throughout, the *Proslogion* reflects Anselm's deep interest in human happiness.

In the first paragraph of *Proslogion* 23, Anselm wants to identify each person of the Trinity and then the Trinity all at once, as the *hoc bonum* he has been pursuing in the previous chapters. To do this, Anselm's tool is once again divine simplicity—but there are subtleties in how divine simplicity functions in this chapter. In sentence 1, Anselm specifies that both God the Father and God the Son are *hoc bonum*—though significantly, God the Son is introduced first as God's Word (*verbum tuum, id est filius tuus*).[65] In sentence 2, Anselm elaborates on this claim of identification, and then justifies it by appealing to divine truth: "for your word is as true as you are truthful, and for this reason it is truth itself, just as you are."[66] Only then is divine simplicity explicitly invoked: "and you are so simple that nothing can be born from you other than what you are."[67] A similar move is then made with the Holy Spirit in sentence 3. As Anselm introduced God's Son as his self-expressive speech (*in verbo quo te ipsum dicis*), Anselm introduces the Spirit as

---

65. P 23, Schmitt I 117:6–7.
66. P 23, Schmitt I 117:8–9.
67. P 23, Schmitt I 117:10.

the love shared between the Father and the Son.[68] He then identifies the Spirit with both the Father and the Son by appealing to the nature of their love: "for you love yourself and him, and he loves you and himself, as much as you and he are." Once again, divine simplicity is then immediately invoked in order to further substantiate this identification: "for nothing is able to proceed from the supreme simplicity (*de summa simplicitate*) other than that from which it proceeds."[69] In other words: Anselm identifies the Son and the Spirit with the Father not by a generic appeal to divine simplicity but one mediated through the corollary doctrines of divine truth and love. God's Son is God because he is also God's Word, and God's Word is *true*, thus sharing in God's truth; the Holy Spirit is God because he is also the love that exists between the Father and the Son, and this love is real, thus sharing in the reality of the Father and the Son.[70]

The correlation of Son and Spirit with reason/speech and love was not unique to Anselm—it was common in medieval theology and could be traced back to Augustine.[71] But for Anselm, this identification functions in a particular way. In his thinking, the three persons of the Trinity are identified not only because they are "other" (*aliud*) from each other but also because they are not "greater or lesser" (*maius vel minus*) than each other. This language reflects the recurrent instincts of the *unum argumentum* and suggests that even here, in the doctrine of the Trinity, Anselm's conception of God is driven by his divine formula. A God whose speech or love was able to be separated from himself would not, in Anselm's thinking, be "that than which nothing greater can be conceived." Sentence 4 of *Proslogion* 23 is a climactic, summative conclusion to

---

68. *P* 23, Schmitt I 117:11–12.
69. *P* 23, Schmitt I 117:15–16.
70. Anselm makes clear his Western view of procession here (*ab utroque procedens*)—but again, he does not argue for it, as he will later in his career, especially in DIV.
71. Augustine, *De Trinitate* XV, 17, 31.

this first paragraph; here Anselm concludes, on the basis of divine simplicity, that each person of the Trinity is completely identified with the Trinity as all at once. Divine simplicity is cast in Anselm's typical chiasm: *summe simplex unitas et summe una simplicitas*.

Finally, in the second paragraph of *Proslogion* 23, Anselm identifies the Trinity with the *unum necessarium* of Luke 10:42. In context, these words are part of Christ's rebuke to Mary for being distracted and anxious about many things, while Mary sits at Christ's feet to listen to his teaching: "Martha, Martha, you are anxious and troubled about many things, but one thing is necessary. Mary has chosen the good portion (Vulgate: *optimam partem*), which will not be taken away from her" (Luke 10:41–42, ESV). In Anselm's text the paragraph reads as follows:

> Porro unum est necessarium. Porro hoc est illud unum necessarium, in quo est omne bonum; immo quod est omne et unum et totum et solum bonum.
>
> "Further, one thing is necessary. And this is that one necessary thing, in which is all good; rather, which is the complete, one, whole, and only good."[72]

Several factors make this passage one of the most perplexing and fascinating in the entire *Proslogion*. In the first place, the seeming incongruity of the contexts of Luke 10:42 and *Proslogion* 23 is perplexing. What does the Trinity have to do with Mary's sitting at Christ's feet? By what rationale can Anselm so deftly identify the *unum bonum* with the *unum necessarium*? The placement of this quote at such a crucial juncture of the book, combined with Anselm's lack of introduction and relatively brief comment on it, further combine to heighten the difficulty and importance of this paragraph.

There are at least three possibilities for seeking to understand the second paragraph of *Proslogion* 23. First, perhaps Anselm is not quoting Luke 10:42 at all. This would remove the difficulty of explaining the original context of the quote but raises other, more

---

72. *P* 23, Schmitt I 117:20–22.

severe difficulties. Anselm frequently sprinkles biblical quotations throughout his writing, as we have often seen, and the Latin here is identical to the Vulgate. Furthermore, if *porro unum est necessarium* were simply his own assertion, the paragraph reads quite clumsily— particularly the repetition of *porro* in rapid succession, the brevity of the first sentence, the introduction of the technical term *unum necessarium*, and then the subsequent qualification of this term with *illud unum necessarium*.[73] It is difficult to imagine, as virtually all commentators on the *Proslogion* recognize, that Anselm's identical wording to Christ's statement to Mary is simply coincidental here.

A second possibility is that Anselm is taking Luke 10:42 out of its context as a proof text for divine necessity. As a monk whose daily habits immersed him in the language of Scripture, perhaps Anselm is simply drawing upon the familiar wording of this passage to communicate God's unique necessity, presumably in contrast to creaturely contingency, without reference to the original import of Christ's words about Mary's sitting at his feet. But beyond having to attribute to Anselm an uncharacteristically clumsy usage of Scripture, this view labors to explain how divine necessity *as such* would meet Anselm's purposes at this juncture of the book. The doctrine has already been well established throughout earlier portions of the book, and the flow of the thought in *Proslogion* 23 concerns God's role as *summum bonum*, anticipating Anselm's conjecture on the greatness of the joy of possessing this good in *Proslogion* 24–25. A strict focus on divine necessity *without* reference to its meaning in Luke 10:42 would seem rather lonely here at the end of *Proslogion* 23, where Anselm is right on the brink of the beatific vision. Furthermore, the conclusion that Anselm himself draws from this quotation is that the Trinity (which is the *unum necessarium*) contains all good and is in fact *omne et unum et totum et solum bonum*.[74] It is not clear how a focus on divine necessity as such would warrant this conclusion regarding divine goodness.

73. *P* 23, Schmitt I 117:20.
74. *P* 23, Schmitt I 117:21–22.

The third and superior option is that Anselm is drawing on a prior tradition of thought regarding Luke 10:42 in which the Trinity is associated with the *unum necessarium* of human happiness. If this is right, then Anselm is citing Luke 10:42 with sensitivity to its original context but also in a way that fits with the flow of his argument. We must remember how steeped Anselm's mind was not only in Scripture but also in the interpretation of Scripture from earlier church tradition, especially Augustine. In the centuries between Augustine and Anselm, Mary and Martha were routinely interpreted as types of the two recognized lives of the church: the active life of earthly charity and service (Martha) and the contemplative life of heavenly enjoyment of God (Mary). In fact, Luke 10:38–42 was so frequently interpreted in light of this *vita activa et contemplativa* construct as to give the impression of a commonplace.[75]

In his usage of Luke 10:38–42 in several different sermons, Augustine interpreted Martha and Mary as figurative for earthly labor and heavenly enjoyment of Christ. "In these two women," he wrote, "two lives are figured: present and future, laborious and quiet, wretched and happy, temporal and eternal."[76] Augustine emphasized that the contrast between Martha and Mary is not that the service to the Lord represented by Martha is bad, whereas Mary's is good. Rather, both women are equally loved by the Lord, and both of them function in a paradigmatic way for the Christian.[77] The contrast, rather, is between the many labors of our temporal life and the one enjoyment of our eternal life. "In Martha was the image of the present, in Mary of the future. What Martha was doing, we

---

75. I provide my own documentation in what follows, but for further discussion of the Mary/Martha trope in medieval thought, see Giles Constable, *Three Studies in Medieval Religious and Social Thought: The Interpretation of Mary and Martha, the Ideal of the Imitation of Christ, the Orders of Society* (Cambridge: Cambridge University Press, 1995), 1–141.

76. Augustine, *Sermon* 104.4 (PL 38:617): "in his duabus mulieribus, duas vitas esse figuratas, praesentem et futuram, laboriosam et quietam, aerumnosam et beatam, temporalem et aeternam."

77. Augustine, *Sermon* 104.4 (PL 38:617); cf. also sermons 169, 179.

are now there; what Mary was doing, we hope for then."[78] Thus for Augustine, the "better part" represented by Mary is not simply humility and virtue but the enjoyment of God as the *unum necessarium* of human happiness.[79] Augustine emphasizes the heavenly location of this enjoyment of God, in contrast to the earthly and temporal labors of Martha.[80]

Augustine also identified the *unum necessarium* of heavenly happiness specifically as the Trinity:

> For one thing is necessary, that one celestial thing (*unum illud supernum*), the unity in which the Father and Son and Holy Spirit are one. See how unity is to be commended by us! Certainly our God is a Trinity. The Father is not the Son, the Son is not the Father, the Holy Spirit is neither the Father nor the Son, but the Spirit of both: and yet these three are not three gods, nor three omnipotents, but one omnipotent God; the Trinity himself is one God, because one thing is necessary. To this one thing nothing leads us, unless we who are many have one heart (*cor unum*).[81]

It is striking that Augustine would appeal to Christ's statement in Luke 10:42 to explain the unity of the Trinity, as he does in the second to last sentence here: "the Trinity himself is one God, because one thing is necessary." Evidently, the Trinity and human happiness are not unrelated topics in Augustine's thinking, but they are bound up with one another as *unum illud supernum*. This association of the Trinity and human happiness becomes particularly evident in the last sentence of this quote, where having "one heart" is necessary for finding the "one thing." Furthermore, Augustine's association of the Trinity with human happiness led him to speculate about the nature of divine goodness on the basis of the goodness of creaturely things. In one of his sermons on the Mary and Martha story, he

---

78. Augustine, *Sermon* 104.4 (PL 38:618): "in Martha erat imago praesentium, in Maria futurorum. Quod agebat Martha, ibi sumus: quod agebat Maria, hoc speramus."
79. Augustine, *Sermon* 255 (PL 38:1188-89).
80. E.g., Augustine, *Sermon* 104.4 (PL 38:617); *Sermon* 103.6 (PL 38:615).
81. Augustine, *Sermon* 103.4 (PL 38:614-15).

writes, "the things which were made are many, he who made them is one.... The things which he made are very good: how much better is he who made them?"[82] This is an identical kind of argumentation to that which Anselm will make in *Proslogion* 24, as we shall see, where many created goods entail a superior goodness in the one Creator.

Augustine was not alone in the late fourth to early fifth century in correlating the Trinity and the *unum necessarium* of human happiness. John Cassian, for instance, used the story of Mary and Martha as an illustration of the superiority of meditation on God even over other virtues. John identified the "one thing" typified by Mary as "the view (*intuitum*) of God alone," by which some saints rise above their actions and services and "are now fed by the beauty and knowledge of God alone."[83] Like Augustine, John also used the words "which shall not be taken away from her" to indicate the eternal, heavenly nature of this "one thing."[84] A century later, Gregory I would also appeal to the story of Mary and Martha in Luke 10:38–42 in his *Moralia* to demonstrate the superiority of the contemplative life over the active life, arguing that Mary and Martha function in the story to typify these different lives.[85] Like Augustine and John, he emphasized that the life of service typified by Martha is not bad in itself but simply inferior to the life of contemplation typified by Mary.[86] In his homilies, Gregory further specified that the contemplative life of Mary is superior because it is eternal, drawing as Augustine did from the words "which will not be taken from her" (*quae non auferetur ab ea*). For Gregory, the active life ends when the body fails, and the contemplative life begins in our heavenly home (*in coelesti patria*) when hunger, thirst, and death are no more and as we see the one whom we love.[87] Strikingly, for Gregory the "oneness" of the heavenly contemplation of God, typified in Mary's sitting at

82. Augustine, *Sermon* 104.3 (PL 38:617).
83. John Cassian, *Conferences* 1.8 (PL 49:492B).
84. John Cassian, *Conferences* 1.8 (PL 49:493A).
85. Gregory, *Moralia* 37, rec. 17 (PL 75:764C-746D).
86. Gregory, *Moralia* 37, rec. 17 (PL 75:764C).
87. Gregory, *Homily* 2.9 (PL 76:954A).

Christ's feet, is correlated with the unity of the church in its love for Christ. Thus, elsewhere Gregory will draw a correlation between the "one thing" of Luke 10:42 with the "one heart and soul" of the early church in its love for Christ in Acts 4:32.[88]

For Bede also, Martha stood as a type for the "active life"— feeding the hungry, teaching the ignorant, and caring for the sick, etc. Mary, in contrast, stood as a type of the "contemplative life"— whole-hearted love and longing for God alone, the cessation of earthly grief and activity, and the desire to take part in the worship of saints and angels in heaven.[89] Bede associates the activities of this contemplative life with heaven, and twice specifically with the beatific vision: (1) *ad videndam faciem sui Creatoris*; and (2) *in conspectu Dei incorruptione gaudere*.[90] He also draws attention to "oneness" of the contemplative life, associating it with the "one thing" David asks of the Lord in Psalm 26/27:4[91] and calling it "the perfection of uniformity" (*uniformis perfectio*).[92]

Further into the medieval era, it becomes difficult to find exceptions to this interpretation of Luke 10:38–42. Routinely the *unum necessarium* typified by Mary is taken as the contemplative enjoyment of God in heaven. So, for instance, in the writings of Leodegar,[93] Rabanus Maurus,[94] Odo of Cluny,[95] Radulfus Ardens,[96] Bruno of Segni,[97] Otloh of St Emmeram,[98] Franco of Affligem,[99] and Rupert of Deutz.[100] At times, following Augustine, the *unum neces-*

---

88. Gregory, *Commentary on I Kings*, chapter 2 (PL 79:49C-49D).
89. Bede, *Exposition on the Gospel of Luke* 3.10 (PL 92:470D-471A).
90. Bede, *Exposition on the Gospel of Luke* 3.10 (PL 92:471A).
91. Bede, *Exposition on the Gospel of Luke* 3.10 (PL 92:471D).
92. Bede, *Exposition on the Gospel of Luke* 3.10 (PL 92:471B).
93. Leodegar, *Letter of Consolation* (PL 96:376A).
94. Rabanus Maurus, *Commentary on II Chronicles* (PL 109:300A).
95. Odo of Cluny, *Sermon 5* (PL 133:716D-717A).
96. Radulful Ardens, *Homilies* (PL 155:1426A).
97. Bruno of Segni, *Commentary on Luke* (PL 165:392A-392B).
98. Otloh of St. Emmeram, *Book of Spiritual Course* (PL 146:83A).
99. Franco of Affligem, *On the Grace of God* (PL 166:783C-783D).
100. Rupert of Deutz, *On the Works of the Holy Spirit* (PL 167:1819B-1819C).

sarium is also associated specifically with the Trinity—for instance, in the writings of Gottfried of Admont.[101] Haymo of Halberstadt extends the typology of the passage even further: in addition to interpreting the sisters' two lives as "the two lives of the church, namely, the active and contemplative," he also interprets the village of Mary and Martha as a type of the world and Christ's visit to their village as a type of the incarnation.[102] By the thirteenth century, Aquinas devotes an entire Question in the *Summa Theologiae* to exploring the relation of the active life to the contemplative life, drawing from this tradition of interpretation with respect to Luke 10:42.[103]

The presence of this tradition of interpretation with respect to Luke 10:38–42 goes a long way to help explain Anselm's usage of this text in *Proslogion* 23. Specifically, the suggestion that he is drawing on this association of the *unum necessarium* with the contemplation of God in heaven fits his purposes perfectly of identifying God as the *summun bonum*, leading into his discussion of heaven in the next chapter. There is a more basic observation with which we close our discussion of *Proslogion* 23. Why is it only here, in identifying the *summum bonum* as the *unum necessarium* of the human soul, that Anselm turns to the Trinity? One might have supposed that the Trinity would have been relevant at an earlier stage of the project, especially in light of its prominence in the *Monologion*. It is interesting that the Trinity comes in so late and so briefly, in the context of a carefully defined movement toward human happiness. *Proslogion* 23 seems to function as a pivotal chapter, in which the *unum argumentum* finds its terminus in the Trinity of Anselm's faith, and it turns out that *aliquid quo nihil maius cogitari possit* is nothing other than the Father, Son, and Holy Spirit. Nonetheless, it is also clear that *Proslogion* 23 does not bring to resolution Anselm's highest concerns. That is why it is not the conclusion of the book but rather pivots Anselm from his identification of God as the *sum-*

101. Gottfried of Admont, *Homilies* (PL 174, coll. 963C–964A).
102. Haymo of Halberstadt, *Homilies* (PL 118:768C).
103. Aquinas, *ST* II, q. 182.

mum bonum in *Proslogion* 22 to the application of this identification to his soul's desires in *Proslogion* 24–26. It is in these final chapters, in both their tone and content, that the most basic movement of the *Proslogion* comes to fruition.

Proslogion 24: Anselm's "Conjecture" about Divine Goodness

At the start of *Proslogion* 24, for the third time in the book, Anselm turns *alloquium* to *soliloquium*, from addressing God to addressing his own soul: *excita nunc, mea anima* ("now, rouse yourself, my soul").[104] As we have seen, in *Proslogion* 1 Anselm called himself to an *excitatio mentis*, retreating into solitude and contemplation in order to seek God; then, in *Proslogion* 14, halfway through the book, Anselm paused to examine what progress he had made thus far. Now in *Proslogion* 24 and continuing through the end of *Proslogion* 25, Anselm turns to self-address once again—and to vocabulary that is reminiscent of these earlier sections. The word *excita* recalls the *excitatio mentis* of the title of *Proslogion* 1, while the following injunction, "and raise your whole understanding" (*et erige totum intellectum tuum*), recall the *persona* of the *proœmium* seeking "to raise his mind to contemplate God" (*erigere mentem suam ad contemplandum deum*).[105] Similarly, Anselm's reference to himself as a *homuncio* in the first paragraph of *Proslogion* 25 recalls his use of this term in the first paragraph of *Proslogion* 1.[106] These features, combined with the urgency of tone that returns in this section, recalling that of *Proslogion* 1, 14, and 18, suggests the importance of *Proslogion* 24–25 as an answer to these earlier sections in the book.[107]

---

104. *P* 24, Schmitt I 117:25.

105. *P prooemium*, Schmitt I 94:1.

106. *P* 25, Schmitt I 118:15. Logan suggests that the repetition of this term constitutes an "allusion" to *Proslogion* 1 (*Reading Anselm's "Proslogion,"* 111).

107. Karl draws attention to Anselm's return to self-address here, rightly emphasizing that the way Anselm opens *Proslogion* 24 demarcates a new unit of text within the book (*Ratio und Affectus*, 971).

Nonetheless, *Proslogion* 24–25 surpasses these earlier sections even while drawing from them. In several respects, *Proslogion* 24–25 are unparalleled in the entire book, like a range of mountain peaks that rises higher than the rest. In the first place, as Cattin observes, *Proslogion* 24–26 is one of the few sections of the book that has no precedent in the *Monologion*.[108] In *Monologion* 68–80, Anselm draws implications from his meditation on the divine essence for the human soul, but nothing there resembles the detailed, energetic, *exploration* of the soul's joy in heaven of *Proslogion* 24–26, with its detailed list of beatitudes and its communal focus. More basically, the self-address of *Proslogion* 24 reflects a fundamentally different posture from those earlier in the book and serves a different purpose. In both *Proslogion* 1 and 14, Anselm is still basically grieving God's distance and yearning to discover how to find him. Still in *Proslogion* 18 he remains in this state of fundamental angst and confusion. But by *Proslogion* 24, Anselm has identified the *summum bonum* of his soul with the Trinity of his faith, and so the purpose of his self-address is not to seek God but to explore the implications of having found him. The difference between the *excitatio* of *Proslogion* 1 and the *coniectatio* of *Proslogion* 24, in other words, is this stark: one is lamenting the absence of God, the other is celebrating the discovery of God. The clarity to which Anselm has here broken through, however, as Karl emphasizes, does not abolish the mystery in Anselm's doctrine of God in the earlier sections of the book.[109] Rather, Anselm's joy has now been ratcheted up to the same incomprehensible status as God: a being who is greater than can be thought (*Proslogion* 15) issues forth into a joy that is greater than can be thought (*Proslogion* 24).

The significance of the achievement Anselm has arrived upon in *Proslogion* 24 helps explain why his self-address here continues on in one long, sustained *soliloquium* through the end of *Proslogion* 25, the climax of the book. *Proslogion* 1 and 14, by contrast, are

---

108. Cattin, *La preuve de Dieu*, 138.
109. Karl, *Ratio und Affectus*, 971.

punctuated with self-address in a larger flow into prayer. Cattin's summary reflects this difference, slicing the book's form of address into three fundamental camps rather than two:

- *Proslogion* 1 and 14: both *je-tu* and *je-je*
- *Proslogion* 2–13, 14–23, and 26: *je-tu*
- *Proslogion* 24–25: *je-je*[110]

The upshot of this schematization is to underscore the uniqueness of *Proslogion* 24–25, for although Anselm here returns to self-address that characterized both his initial *excitatio mentis* and his self-examination halfway through, he now pushes this self-address further and for more ambitious purposes. From the flow of the argument into this chapter, its title and contents, and the presence of the word *nunc* at its outset, it becomes clear that Anselm is no longer calling his soul to search for God but rather calling his soul to consider the result of having found God. This is a fundamentally different kind of *excitatio* from that of *Proslogion* 1 and 14. One might say that in *Proslogion* 1, Anselm is at the bottom of the mountain, rousing his soul to climb up toward the *visio Dei*; in *Proslogion* 14, he is halfway up, asking his soul how far he has climbed and urging his soul to continue the ascent; finally, in *Proslogion* 24, he has reached the top and now invites his soul to look around and consider the landscape that he has arrived upon.

In the remaining part of the first sentence of *Proslogion* 24, Anselm specifies the exact nature of the object he seeks to grasp: "consider, as much as you are able, both what kind of good this is, and how great it is" (*et cogita quantum potes, quale et quantum sit illud bonum*).[111] The *illud bonum* refers back to what Anselm has just identified as the *unum necessarium* of the human soul at the end of *Proslogion* 23, namely, the *omne et unum et totum et solum bonum*.[112] As Logan puts it, "the *unum argumentum* has led to the

110. Cattin, *La preuve de Dieu*, 9.
111. P 24, Schmitt I 117:25–26.
112. P 23, Schmitt I 117:21–22.

unum necessarium, which is the *unum bonum*."[113] The words *quale et quantum* are repeated here from the title of the chapter. Anselm uses these words frequently; Gilbert suggests that Anselm draws them from Aristotle, as transmitted through the commentaries of Boethius.[114] In particular, he argues, Anselm has drawn from the *Isagoge* a particular understanding of the quality of a substance (as evidenced from his treatment of this topic in *De Grammatico*), and that this meaning is in view here.[115] Whether this is right or not, these words certainly indicate a more comprehensive thrust to Anselm's interest in this chapter, particularly when seen in relation to the word *coniectatio* in the chapter title, which can be translated "conjecture" or "guess."[116] Anselm has identified the *summum bonum* in *Proslogion* 23, and now, having done so, he wants to offer a further speculation or guess concerning the nature (*quale*) and extent (*quantum*) of its goodness.

In the second sentence of *Proslogion* 24, Anselm stipulates the principle by which he will be able to offer such a guess. Essentially, he identifies the goodness of created things, and then he traces it back to the superior goodness of their Creator and source: "for if particular goods are delightful (*delectabilia*), consider intently how delightful that good is which contains the pleasantness (*iucunditatem*) of all goods; and not such as we have experienced in created things, but as different as the Creator differs from the creature."[117] In this assertion the complexity of Anselm's Creator/creation relationship is seen, as we have noticed elsewhere: here he emphasizes the absolute difference between Creator and creation in the exact

---

113. Logan, *Reading Anselm's "Proslogion,"* 111.
114. Gilbert, *Le "Proslogion" de S. Anselme*, 215.
115. Gilbert, *Le "Proslogion" de S. Anselme*, 217.
116. Lewis and Short, *A Latin Dictionary*, 422. This is a relatively rare term in Anselm, and different from the usual terms with which Anselm starts his chapter titles (quod, quomodo, etc.). According to Ian Logan, the comma after the word *coniectatio* in the title is probably derived from the later scribes and not intrinsic to Anselm himself (personal conversation, July 28, 2015).
117. P 24, Schmitt I 117:26–118:3.

THE CLIMAX OF THE *PROSLOGION*

same movement by which he draws inferences about the Creator from creation. Thus, on the one hand, we can grasp something of how delightful God is from considering delightful things in the world; on the other hand, God's delightfulness must infinitely surpass their delightfulness, as much as *differt creator a creatura*. Anselm's terminology (*delectabilia, iucunditatem*) here seems to reflect not just the state of creaturely happiness in general but the pleasure and enjoyment of particular created objects.

If the second sentence of *Proslogion* 24 is the principle of Anselm's conjecture, sentences 3–5 exhibit three particular expressions of this principle in question form.

1. For if created life is good, how good is creative life?
2. If salvation made is pleasant, how pleasant is the salvation that makes all salvation?
3. If wisdom in the knowledge of created things is loveable, how loveable is the wisdom which created all things from nothing?[118]

Anselm's language and syntax are very carefully crafted here. Each sentence takes the same form but with stylistic variation (e.g., the word for "created" in sentence 1 is different from sentence 3). As Gilbert notes, the three nouns here—life (*vita*), salvation (*salus*), and wisdom (*sapienta*)—are often linked earlier in the *Proslogion* (chapters 11, 12, 18, and 22), often in a longer list alongside terms like *bonum* or *veritas* or *lux*.[119] The purpose of these questions is to present an argument from the lesser to the greater, on the principle that the source is greater than the result. Anselm is not interested, however, in God's generic greatness as Creator and Savior but specifically that he is pleasant (*iucunda*) and loveable (*amabilis*). This reflects once again his abiding concern for creaturely happiness.

In the final sentence of *Proslogion* 24, Anselm then returns to an abstract, summative assertion of this principle: "for if there are

118. P 24, Schmitt I 118:3–7.
119. Gilbert, *Le "Proslogion" de S. Anselme*, 222.

many and great delights in delightful things, what kind of how great (*qualis et quanta*) a delight is in him who made these delightful things?"[120] Variations of this term *delectatio* occur four times in this sentence, which may perhaps be regarded as the key term throughout *Proslogion* 24. The whole thrust of this chapter is concerned with God's delightfulness, and thus, in the larger flow of the book, this chapter serves as a transition from the identification of God as the *summum bonum* to the implications of this identification for human happiness. Anselm has offered a conjecture concerning God's supreme delightfulness and is now ready to apply this conjecture to the needs of the human soul.

Proslogion 25: An Infinite Multiplication of Joy

Proslogion 25 sustains the self-address of *Proslogion* 24 rather than revert to prayer—but it also extends this address outwards to all of those who share Anselm's condition, opening with the words *O qui hoc bono fruetur*.[121] At times Anselm will speak directly to himself in this chapter: "for what do you love, O my flesh, what do you desire, O my soul?"[122] But the overall focus of the chapter is broader, including the entire company of saints and angels who enjoy the *unum bonum*. This chapter is essentially an application of the conjecture of *Proslogion* 24 to this class of people. Anselm's goal is to articulate the comprehensiveness and fullness of their joy. *Proslogion* 25 is the lengthiest chapter after *Proslogion* 1 and contains the most significant crescendo of energy in the entire book, concluding in a fit of ecstasy that matches and surpasses the longings of *Proslogion* 1, 9, 14, and 18. Evans goes so far to say, after quoting this chapter, "nowhere else in his writings does Anselm reach a peak of joyous affirmation like this."[123] At the same time, *Proslogion* 25

120. *P* 24, Schmitt I 118:7–9.
121. *P* 25, Schmitt I 118:12.
122. *P* 25, Schmitt I 118:18.
123. Evans, *Saint Anselm of Canterbury*, 55.

brings the deepest themes of the book—the greatness of God and the joy of the saints—into climactic resolution. Here we will explore this chapter in three movements.[124]

1. The Infinite Happiness of Heaven

In paragraph 1, Anselm articulates a doctrine of infinite happiness among those who possess God and, as a consequence, chides those who attempt to pursue joy anywhere else. He says, in effect, "in light of my conjecture that the *unum bonum* contains all other goods, why would I ever look for happiness in anything else?" He begins, "O he who enjoys this good! What will be his, and what will not be his! Certainly he will have whatever he wishes, and he will not have whatever he does not wish."[125] Anselm here articulates the happiness of heavenly creatures in that their desire exactly corresponds to their will. Those who possess the *unum bonum* possess all goods and thus whatever they could possibly want. This description recalls the doctrine of sin Anselm had articulated in *Proslogion* 1, where the human fall had caused the frustration of the will through the loss of the *unum bonum*.[126] Throughout the *Proslogion* Anselm has traversed this vast distance, from bewailing the misery of completely thwarted desire (*O misera sors hominis, cum hoc perdidit ad quod factus est*)[127] to exulting in the joy of comprehensively fulfilled desire (*O qui hoc bono fruetur: quid illi erit*).[128] This is the

---

124. Gilbert divides the chapter into four sections, corresponding to the four paragraphs in Schmitt's critical edition: first, Anselm proposes the general form of his argument; second, he speaks of goods of body; third, he speaks of goods of the soul; fourth, he concludes in joy (*Le "Proslogion" de S. Anselme*, 225). This is an instructive breakdown, particularly as most English translations combine paragraphs 2 and 3 into one paragraph. Nonetheless, because of the similarity of these two middle paragraphs (both here and later in Anselm's career), we will engage them together.
125. *P* 25, Schmitt I 118:12–13.
126. E.g., *P* 1, Schmitt I 99:10–15.
127. *P* 1, Schmitt I 98:16.
128. *P* 25, Schmitt I 118:12.

arc from beginning to ending, from *excitatio* to *coniectatio*, that fundamentally characterizes the *Proslogion*.

In the third sentence of *Proslogion* 25, Anselm specifies that the goods of heaven are for both body and soul, quoting I Corinthians 2:9 to assert their transcendence over human experience and understanding.[129] Anselm will refer to both his body and soul again later in this paragraph, and, as we will see, the beatitudes listed in the next paragraph are divided into two categories, those for the body and those for the soul. The effect of this dual focus, combined with the reference to I Corinthians 2:9, is to emphasize further the infinite quality of the joy of heaven. Anselm frequently quotes I Corinthians 2:9 to describe the joy of heaven elsewhere in his writings[130] and will quote it again in *Proslogion* 26 twice to emphasize that the joy of heaven is greater than can be imagined.[131] The reference to *bona* (plural) here and in the chapter title widens the focus from the previous chapter's focus on *hoc bonum*, facilitating Anselm's focus on the saints' *experience* in heaven, which he will develop in the next paragraph.[132] In the remainder of this paragraph, Anselm chides himself for seeking joy in any place other than the *unum bonum*, in light of the comprehensive joy it contains within itself. Referring to himself once again as *homuncio*, as he did at the beginning of the book, Anselm questions why he wanders through many things (*per multa vagaris*) to seek the goods of his soul and body, instead summoning himself to love the *unum bonum*, which contains all other goods, because whatever he desires is there.[133]

---

129. *P* 25, Schmitt I 118:13–15.

130. E.g., *Ep.* 59, Schmitt III 174:12–13; *Mem.* 127, 274.

131. *P* 26, Schmitt I 121:7–8, 11–12.

132. Gilbert draws attention to this movement from *bonum* in *Proslogion* 24 to *bona* in *Proslogion* 25 (*Le "Proslogion" de S. Anselme*, 214). While this observation is helpful for highlighting the flow Anselm's argument, *hoc bonum* and *bona* should not be seen as separate topics, because here in *Proslogion* 25 (as well as earlier in *Proslogion* 23) Anselm has defined that the *unum bonum* is that which contains all other goods: *unum bonum, in quo sunt omnia bona (P* 25, Schmitt I 118:16).

133. *P* 25, Schmitt I 118:15–19. Karl observes the repetition of *homuncio* here,

This juxtaposition of "one thing" versus "many things" recalls Anselm's usage of Luke 10:42 at the end of *Proslogion* 23, along with the tradition of interpretation preceding Anselm in which "one thing" is associated with heavenly happiness and "many things" with earthly labor.

2. The Fourteen Beatitudes of Heaven

The second and third paragraphs of *Proslogion* 25 (often combined into one paragraph in English translations) are an extended meditation on the infinite scope of the joys of the *unum bonum*, which Anselm has established in the first paragraph. Here Anselm lists 14 beatitudes, each of which is described as an object of human longing, and then he asserts by means of a biblical quotation that each will be fully realized in heaven. With the exception of a few explanatory phrases, which at times function instead of a biblical quotation, each sentence follows the same formula: if (*si*) _____, [biblical quotation]. For example, the first sentence reads: *si delectat pulchritudo: fulgebunt iusti sicut sol* ("if beauty delights, 'the just shall shine like the sun'").[134] The particular beatitudes and Scriptures/assertions listed are:

1. beauty (*pulchritudo*): Matthew 13:43.
2. speed or strength (*velocitas aut fortitudo*): Matthew 22:30, I Corinthians 15:44.
3. freedom of the body (*libertas corporis*): Matthew 22:30, I Corinthians 15:44.
4. long and healthy life (*longa et salubris vita*): Wisdom 5:16, Psalm 36:39/37:39.
5. abundance (*satietas*): Psalm 16:15/17:15.

---

highlighting also the similarity of Anselm's *Prayers and Meditations* with the self-address form of prayer in *Proslogion* 1 (*Ratio und Affectus*, 788).

134. P 25, Schmitt I 118:20.

6. drunkenness (*ebrietas*): Psalm 35:9/36:8.
7. music (*melodia*): none, but the assertion, "there the choirs of angels sing without end to God" (*ibi angelorum chori concinunt sine fine deo*).
8. pleasure of any kind, not impure but pure (*quaelibet non immunda sed munda voluptas*): Psalm 35:9/36:8.
9. wisdom (*sapientia*): none, but the assertion, "the very wisdom of God will show itself to them" (*ipsa dei sapientia ostendet eis seipsam*).
10. friendship (*amicitia*): lengthy explanation, anticipating the reasoning of the third paragraph.
11. unity (*concordia*): none, but the assertion that all will have one will because all will have the will of God.
12. power (*potestas*): none, but the assertion that all will be omnipotent by being united to God's will.
13. honor and wealth (*honor et divitiae*): Matthew 25:21, 23, Matthew 5:9, Romans 8:17.
14. true security (*vera securitas*): theological affirmation of the confirmation in good of those in heaven.

It is worth noting this list because it is not only in *Proslogion* 25 that Anselm will describe heavenly joy by listing a series of fourteen beatitudes. We have already referenced in chapter 1 Margaret Healy-Varley's observation that the 14 beatitudes listed in *Proslogion* 25 were commonly used for instruction on the doctrine of heaven in the cathedral schools during and after Anselm's lifetime.[135] But we may now add that Anselm himself appears to have developed and refined this construct of fourteen beatitudes in his teaching and preaching on heaven in the years following the *Proslogion*, though he did not write again on the subject. There are three primary texts included in the written memorials of Anselm's teaching by his disciples (particularly Eadmer and Alexander): *Scriptum*

---

135. Margaret Healy-Varley, "Anselm's Afterlife and the Middle English *De Custodia Interioris Hominis*," in *Saint Anselm of Canterbury and His Legacy*, 241.

de beatitutudine de perennis vitae (hereafter, simply *De beatitutudine*), *Liber Anselmi Archiepiscopi De Humanis Moribus Per Similitudines* (hereafter, simply *De Moribus*), and Alexander's *Liber Ex Dictis Beati Anselmi* (hereafter, simply *Dicta*). While *De beatitutudine*, *De Moribus*, and the *Dicta* should not be taken as having the same authority as Anselm's own writings, it would also be a mistake to ignore them or regard them with excessive suspicion. As Schmitt and Southern argue, "the substance of what they report can confidently be accepted as a record of Anselm's thoughts,"[136] and this is particularly the case when all three documents converge in agreement on a subject with Anselm's prior writings. In this case, all three of these works employ a similar list of beatitudes to describe heaven, and by looking at them one can detect how Anselm's doctrine of heavenly joy, as articulated in the second paragraph of *Proslogion* 25, developed and became more systematized throughout his career.

De beatitutudine was written by Eadmer based upon a sermon of Anselm's on the joys of eternity delivered at Cluny and then filled out on the basis of Eadmer's recollection of Anselm's broader teaching on heaven, probably either in 1097 or 1100.[137] This work not only employs a similar list of beatitudes to describe the heavenly life but shares the same overall method of reasoning of *Proslogion* 25 in moving from earthly goods to the superior joys of eternal life. It also shares many of the same Scripture references (e.g., I Corinthians 2:9).[138] The fifteen chapters are divided into various beatitudes that correspond with only minor differences to the fourteen beatitudes of *Proslogion* 25 (with the misery of the reprobate added as a fifteenth chapter):

1. On beauty (*De pulchritudine*)
2. On speed (*De velocitate*)
3. On strength (*De fortitudine*)

---

136. *Mem.* 2.
137. *Mem.* 31–32.
138. E.g., *Mem.* 275.

4. On freedom (*De libertate*)
5. On the incapacity of suffering (*De impassibilitate*)
6. On pleasure (*De voluptate*)
7. On length of life (*De vitae diuturnitate*)
8. On wisdom (*De sapientia*)
9. On friendship (*De amicitia*)
10. On unity (*De concordia*)
11. On power (*De potestate*)
12. On honor (*De honor*)
13. On security (*De securitate*)
14. On joy (*De gaudio*)
15. On the misery of the reprobate (*De miseria reproborum*)[139]

The *Dicta* was written by Alexander sometime in the early twelfth century, compiled from Anselm's words *in commune*, which means, according to Schmitt and Southern, "either in the monastic chapter or in formal sermons."[140] It is lengthier and more diverse than *De beatitutudine*, but chapter 5 is strikingly similar, treating "the fourteen parts of eternal fitness or happiness (*beatitudinis*)," which are further divided into seven goods for the body and seven goods for the soul.[141] Chapters 48–71 of *De Moribus*, written sometime after the *Dicta* on the vices and virtues of the religious life, sharpens the list of fourteen beatitudes further, adding fourteen corresponding pains of hell to Anselm's list of the fourteen joys of heaven.[142] Although the exact order and nature of these various lists differ, substantial overlap exists among them. Schmitt and Southern, for instance, compare the first seven beatitudes of the body in *De beatitutudine*, *Dicta*, and *De Moribus* with *Proslogion* 25.[143]

---

139. *Mem.* 275–91.
140. *Mem.* 19.
141. *Mem.* 127.
142. *Mem.* 57–63. For a helpful overview of this work, see Schmitt and Southern's introduction in *Mem.* 4–18.
143. *Mem.* 10.

THE CLIMAX OF THE *PROSLOGION*

ANSELM'S BEATITUDES

Proslogion	*De beatitudine, Dicta,* and *De moribus*
1. pulchritudo	1. pulchritudo
⎧ velocitas	2. velocitas (agilitas *De moribus*)
2. ⎨ fortitudo	3. fortitudo
⎩ libertas corporis	4. libertas
3. ⎧ longa ⎫ vita	7. diurnitas (longaevitas *De moribus*)
⎩ salubris ⎭	5. sanitas
4. satietas	
5. ebrietas	6. ⎰ voluptas
6. melodia	
7. voluptas	

Many of the beatitudes in the second half have overlap as well.

One might summarize the development of Anselm's fourteen beatitudes from the *Proslogion* to the memorials in three ways: first, the exact beatitudes and their order becomes more fixed; second, they are explicitly divided into two halves, with seven beatitudes listed for the body and seven others for the soul; and finally, fourteen pains of hell corresponding to the fourteen joys of heaven are developed. These developments help shed light on Anselm's usage of this construct in *Proslogion* 25 in several ways. First, they underscore his emphasis on the dual nature of heavenly joy as involving both body and soul. This was affirmed in the first paragraph of *Proslogion* 25 multiple times and was also implicit in kinds of beatitudes listed but becomes more explicit as the fourteen beatitudes developed throughout his career. Anselm very clearly regards heaven as the place where both physical and spiritual desires are comprehensively fulfilled, and this helps account for his rather surprising emphasis on goods like speed, pleasure, and drunkenness (*ebrietas*), as well as his continual reference to Psalm 35:9/36:8 to describe heaven, in *Proslogion* 25 and elsewhere.[144] Once again, this vision of heaven at the end of the *Proslogion* brings resolution to

144. E.g, as discussed above, *Or.* 2, Schmitt III 9:88–92; *Or.* 13, Schmitt III 54:114–15.

the doctrine of sin at the beginning of the book, where Anselm describes the fall of Adam as resulting in the comprehensive loss of happiness and consequent death.[145]

Second, the developments in Anselm's fourteen beatitudes throughout his teaching and preaching career testify further to his close association of creaturely goods (*multa bona*) and divine goodness (*unum bonum*). For all his emphasis on divine transcendence over creation, he repeatedly draws inferences about the heavenly enjoyment of God on the basis of created goods. Moreover, these goods appear to be as diverse as human experience, as we have noted—Anselm conceives of God as the comprehensive source and explanation of all good, the *unum bonum, in quo sunt omnia bona*.[146] Finally, Anselm's use of these fourteen beatitudes serves to increase the sense of heaven's desirability and perfect happiness. The rhetorical force of this extensive list of beatitudes is to encourage the love and desire of God, since all goods—even those as diverse as drunkenness and wisdom, speed and friendship—are contained in him. "It is there, it is there, whatever you love, whatever you desire" (*Ibi est, ibi est quidquid amatis, quidquid desideratis*).[147]

3. The Perfect Love of Heaven

In the final paragraph of *Proslogion* 25, Anselm turns to consider the communal nature of the joy of heaven. It is only here that the full import of the conjecture initiated in the title of *Proslogion* 24 is realized, as Anselm finally comes to a vision of the joy of heaven as not just infinite but infinitely multiplying.[148] Anselm begins by correlating the greatness of human joy with the greatness of divine goodness: "truly what kind or how great (*quale aut quantum*) a joy there is where there is such and so great (*tale ac tantum*) a good!"[149]

145. *P* 1, Schmitt I 98:16–99:7.
146. *P* 25, Schmitt I 118:16.
147. *P* 25, Schmitt I 118:18–19.
148. Cf. Gilbert, *Le "Proslogion" de S. Anselme*, 233.
149. *P* 25, Schmitt I 120:1. I have chosen not to smooth out this rather laborious

THE CLIMAX OF THE PROSLOGION

This is a kind of summary of what he has established thus far in the chapter, which till now has focused more on human pleasures and delights than on joy per se, and provides the most explicit link yet in the chapter between divine *bonum* and human *gaudium*, which is Anselm's driving theme in these chapters. Here, as elsewhere, it is clearly visible that Anselm's pursuit of God's greatness has never been an abstraction but always to the end of his desirability.

The second and third sentences of this paragraph demonstrate that Anselm has not yet emerged from *soliloquium* into *alloquium*— here he speaks directly to the human heart (*cor humanum*) and then summons the reader to interrogate their inmost self (*intima tua*). In sentence 2, the joy of possessing God is again cast as a contrast and answer to the sadness and emptiness that formerly prevailed: apart from God, the human heart is fundamentally lacking (*indigens*) and thus overwhelmed with troubles (*obrutum aerumnis*); now possessing God, it rejoices (*gauderes*) because it overflows (*abundares*).[150] The completeness of the contrast from *Proslogion* 1 to *Proslogion* 25 is again visible here. In sentence 3, Anselm then calls upon himself to ponder whether he can even comprehend the joy of such a great happiness.[151] This exhortation, combined with the quotation of I Cor. 2:9 at the beginning of *Proslogion* 25, conveys Anselm's perception that however much he has grasped of heavenly joy, it remains ultimately beyond his comprehension. This doctrine of joy here at the end of the *Proslogion* seems to draw from, and correspond to, the doctrine of God that has been operative throughout the earlier portions of the *Proslogion*. One might say: as the fundamental engine that drives the *Proslogion* is a doctrine of God as "that than which nothing greater can be thought," so the fundamental consequence into which the *Proslogion* terminates is a doctrine of heaven as "a joy greater than which nothing greater can be thought."

---

translation so as to make visible the apposition of *quale aut quantum* and *tale ac tantum* here.

150. *P* 25, Schmitt I 120:2–3.
151. *P* 25, Schmitt I 120:2–4.

But at this point Anselm's meditation takes a sudden turn, as he ratchets up the happiness of heaven even further by appealing to the communal joy of love and unity among the saints and angels. This transition may initially appear a bit abrupt in the text, coming in the middle of the paragraph, and at the conclusion of a book, which is essentially a solitary, introspective meditation. Nonetheless, given what we have seen in his letters (recall the *reunion* motif) and in his *Prayers and Meditations*, any description of the joy of heaven would be incomplete without an emphasis on its communal nature. Although this emphasis on the communal joy of love in heaven is not unique to Anselm—Augustine, for instance, may have influenced him in this regard—it seems to be a special hallmark of Anselm's thought.[152] In both his letters to the saints *in via*, as well as in his *Prayers* to the saints *in patria*, Anselm has exhibited the most intense yearnings for spiritual union with others, and his high doctrine of friendship has consistently been an essential ingredient in his view of heaven.[153] At first glance, this deep longing for spiritual unity among the saints may seem to be at odds with Anselm's equally strong emphasis on spiritual solitude. But as much as Anselm's prayers call for retreat into the secret chamber of the mind, they are at the same time cast as movements toward the community of heavenly joy—as Ward puts it, Anselm retreats from worldly interactions, not for the sake of total and final aloneness, but rather to enter "more deeply into the fullness of the people of God, where he talks with Christ and the saints as a man talks with his friends."[154] Thus, paradoxically, solitude and retreat into one's own mind is for Anselm the very means by which to approach the

---

152. Cf. the discussion in van Fleteren, "Augustine's Influence on Anselm's *Proslogion*," 68, in *Twenty-Five Years (1969–1994) of Anselm Studies: Review and Critique of Recent Scholarly Views*, ed. Frederick van Fleteren and Joseph C. Schnaubelt, Texts and Studies in Religion 70 (Lewiston, N.Y.: Edward Mellen Press, 1996).

153. On how Anselm expressed his unity with the saints in heaven in his *Prayers*, see Ward, *Anselm of Canterbury: His Life and Legacy*, 44–45.

154. Ward, *Prayers and Meditations*, 52.

THE CLIMAX OF THE *PROSLOGION*

richest experience of community and friendship. This is the movement of the *Proslogion*: he begins by calling himself to "enter into the chamber of your mind and shut out all else,"[155] and he ends "in that perfect love of countless happy angels and human beings."[156]

The essential principle throughout this final section of *Proslogion* 25 is that the perfect love among the creatures of heaven will multiply their joy. The paradoxical nature of this heavenly joy, as Karl emphasizes, is seen in that it has a quantitative, measurable aspect even while it remains ultimately incomprehensible—it is both infinite and expanding.[157] Anselm begins by envisioning one relationship in heaven: "but surely if someone else, whom you loved in every way just as yourself had the same happiness, your joy would be doubled, because you would rejoice no less for him than for yourself."[158] The joy would be further multiplied, Anselm then reasons, for two or three others who were also loved with the same love.[159] Thus, considering the sum effect of this multiplication of joy, Anselm concludes, "therefore, in that perfect love of countless happy angels and human beings, where no one loves anyone else less than himself, each one will rejoice no differently for each of the others as for himself."[160] Anselm then seems somewhat mesmerized by the dizzying stature of this infinite multiplication of joy among the angels and saints who possess God. If it is true, he wonders, that the human heart cannot comprehend its own joy in possessing so great a good, how can it possibly comprehend "so many and so great joys?"[161]

This conception of the ever-multiplying joy of love is then stretched even further upward as it is applied to God himself:

---

155. *P* 1, Schmitt I 97:5–10.
156. *P* 25, Schmitt I 120:9–10.
157. Karl, *Ratio und Affectus*, 991.
158. *P* 25, Schmitt I 120:4–7.
159. *P* 25, Schmitt I 120:7–9.
160. *P* 25, Schmitt I 120:9–11.
161. *P* 25, Schmitt I 120:11–13.

And surely, since the more one loves someone, the more they rejoice in their good, thus, just as in that perfect happiness (*in illa perfecta felicitate*) each one will love God incomparably more than himself and all others with him, so one will rejoice inconceivably more from God's happiness than from his own and all others with him.[162]

In the previous parts of this paragraph Anselm has been arguing that the heavenly environment of love (*in illa perfecta caritate*) motivates joy. Here Anselm further argues that the heavenly environment of happiness (*in illa perfecta felicitate*) will, in turn, motivate love. This conception of the *caritas* and *felicitas* of heaven as mutually reinforcing, combined with his depiction of the saints and angels loving God even more than they love themselves and each other, has the effect of further developing Anselm's view of the *gaudium* of heaven. In Anselm's thinking, the joy of heaven is not static but continually and infinitely multiplying by itself. This is because the joy of heaven is fundamentally centered in the joy of God: "one will rejoice inconceivably more from God's happiness than from his own and all others with him." In the final sentence of this chapter, Anselm concludes that the saints and angels of heaven will love God with their whole heart, mind, and soul, such that their whole heart, mind, and soul will be insufficient for the greatness of their love. As Karl notes, Anselm's depiction of the supreme love for God as involving human thinking, willing, and feeling draws from the biblical commandment in Matthew 22:37.[163] This surpassing love entails surpassing joy, so that the saints and angels will rejoice so much with their whole heart, mind, and soul, that therefore their heart, mind, and soul will be insufficient for their fullness of joy (*plenitudini gaudii*).[164] This reference to "fullness of joy" prepares for Anselm's exploration of John 16:24 in his concluding chapter.

It is difficult to overstate the significance of *Proslogion* 25 for the interpretation of the book as a whole and in Anselm's thought more

---

162. P 25, Schmitt I 120:13–17.
163. Karl, *Ratio und Affectus*, 994–95.
164. P 25, Schmitt I 120:17–20.

generally. Its exuberant tone stands out starkly against the yearning emptiness of the earlier prayers of *Proslogion* 1, 14, and 18, and its vision of human happiness in possessing God seems exactly matched to answer the misery at lacking God articulated in those chapters. It is therefore plausible to regard *Proslogion* 25 as the climax and resolution of the entire book. Furthermore, looking at Anselm's writings as a whole, it is reasonable to see *Proslogion* 25 as his definitive teaching on the subject of heaven, in light of (1) Anselm's frequent usage of the beatitudes of *Proslogion* 25 in his later teaching on heaven, (2) how he will direct people to the ending of the *Proslogion* in his letters in order to learn about heaven,[165] and (3) the relative paucity of systematic teaching about heaven anywhere else in Anselm's writings. The central importance of heaven in Anselm's theology and life, as evidenced by its continual recurrence in his letters and *Prayers and Meditations*, suggests that *Proslogion* 25 is not only the climax of the *Proslogion*, but a key peak in the landscape of Anselm's entire theology. This chapter exhibits, in many respects more clearly than anywhere else, Anselm's vision of the purpose of all of life, namely, the soul's union in love with God and other creatures in heaven.

Proslogion 26: Anselm's Summary and Concluding Prayer

Proslogion 26 represents a slight winding down from the energy of *Proslogion* 25, as Anselm returns from *soliloquium* to *alloquium*, and from future indicative verbs to present imperatives. Anselm has been envisioning what will be the case in heaven: now he returns to his present situation, petitioning that he might live in light of this vision. As Evans puts it, "the final chapter returns us to more familiar ground, as Anselm sinks back a little into longing and striv-

---

165. E.g., *Ep.* 112.

ing for that which has just been so vividly present to him."[166] The return to prayer is made clear from his opening invocation: "my God and my Lord, my hope and the joy of my heart."[167] The specific question that Anselm then poses is whether the fullness of joy he has discovered is to be identified with the promise of Christ for fullness of joy in John 16:24.[168] *Proslogion* 26 is thus like *Proslogion* 11 or 21 in that it deals with the interpretation of a certain passage of Scripture. But the more basic *function* of this chapter, in the larger flow of the book, is to summarize the joy that Anselm has discovered and then petition God that he will continue to grow in it. This summary is conducted in the first paragraph of the chapter; the petition is the focus of the second and final paragraph.

Anselm begins his summary of the joy of *Proslogion* 24–25 by asserting its paradoxical nature: it is both fully inside him and fully outside of him at the same time. He asserts, "for I have found a joy that is full, and more than full,"[169] then qualifying this description by asserting that even when the entire human being is full with this joy, there will still be joy left over "without measure" (*supra modum*).[170] He concludes, "therefore, that whole joy will not enter into those who rejoice, but those wholly rejoicing will enter into that joy."[171] This chiastic expression is more than merely stylistic; it makes an important theological assertion about the nature of heavenly joy, further drawing attention to its infinite, inexhaustible immensity. But whereas in the previous chapter Anselm emphasized the comprehensiveness and ever-multiplying nature of the joy of heaven, here he supplements these descriptions by emphasizing its objective, durable, inexhaustible nature. It is not a joy that the saints

---

166. Evans, *Saint Anselm of Canterbury*, 55.
167. P 26, Schmitt I 120:23.
168. P 26, Schmitt I 120:24–26. The only references to Christ in the *Proslogion*, outside of the explication of the Trinity in *Proslogion* 23, are here in *Proslogion* 26, with this quotation of John 16:24 repeated here and again in the second paragraph.
169. P 26, Schmitt I 120:26–121.
170. P 26, Schmitt I 121:1–3.
171. P 26, Schmitt I 121:3–4.

THE CLIMAX OF THE *PROSLOGION*

and angels possess but a joy that possesses them. Anselm may be drawing here from Augustine's reflections on whether joy comes from seeking or finding God, since God is incomprehensible and thus can never be finally found.[172] The effect of this paradoxical description of joy is once again to increase its desirability.

Anselm then asks that God would help him understand if this joy is to be identified with that referenced in Matthew 25:2, only to remind himself with another quotation of I Cor. 2:9 that this joy cannot be comprehended.[173] From this Anselm draws the conclusion, "therefore, I have not yet said or thought, Lord, how much your blessed ones will rejoice." Thus, Anselm's answer to the question posed in the title of this chapter (*an hoc sit gaudium plenum, quod promittit dominus*) appears to be, in a sense, in the negative— he believes that he has not yet articulated the fullness of the joy of the Lord, because that joy is both ineffable and incomprehensible in this life. Human joy does not only parallel divine greatness, it turns out, in being "greater than which nothing can be conceived," but also in being "greater than can be conceived." Anselm quotes I Cor. 2:9 yet again at the end of the paragraph to establish that the reason we cannot comprehend the extent of the joy of heaven is that, in this life, we cannot yet comprehend how much we will know and love God there.[174] This explanation coheres with the tight correlation of love for God and joy in God in *Proslogion* 25. It also draws from Anselm's spiritually determined anthropology, in which, as Karl observes, the fulfillment of human religious desire necessarily involves the correlation of both the love of God and the knowledge of God.[175] The incompleteness of Anselm's discovery of joy, even here at the end of the book, creates a forward-looking, eschatological tilt to the entire project. Anselm has been drawn up from the misery of Adam's fall into the heights of heavenly ecstasy,

---

172. Cf. the discussion in Logan, *Reading Anselm's "Proslogion,"* 113.
173. *P* 26, Schmitt I 121:4–8.
174. *P* 26, Schmitt I 121:9–13.
175. Karl, *Ratio und Affectus*, 979; cf. also 996–98.

but his journey has been nonetheless in the *cubiculum* of his mind: his joy is that of anticipation, not yet realization. This closing focus on future heaven then leads to the petition of the final paragraph.

Here Anselm prays that he would know and love God in order to rejoice in him.[176] Anselm recognizes the progressive, incremental nature of this request, asking that he would advance further each day until he arrives at the fullness of joy he desires.[177] Having drawn a correlation between knowing God, loving God, and rejoicing in God, Anselm now draws a further correlation between how these three activities function on earth with how they function in heaven. Specifically, he asks that his love and knowledge of God would grow in this life and there be full, so that his joy in this life would be great in hope (*in spe*), and his joy there will be great in reality (*in re*).[178] These several sentences reiterate from *Proslogion* 25 that Anselm regards joy in God as fueled by the love and knowledge of God and also indicate that, whatever the shortcomings of his current experience, he sees an essential continuity between the love, knowledge, and joy in God in this life and in heaven.

Finally, referencing again Christ's promise in John 16:24, Anselm makes one final request that one day he will receive the fullness of joy he has discovered and that until that point it would occupy all his energies.

Let my heart love it, let my mouth proclaim it. Let my soul hunger for it, let my flesh thirst for it, let my whole being (*tota substantia*) desire it, until I enter into the joy of my Lord, who is God three and one, blessed forever. Amen.[179]

The concluding benediction, drawn from Romans 1:25 (*trinus et unus deus benedictus in saecula*), recalls Anselm's *Prayers*, which fre-

---

176. P 26, Schmitt I 121:14.
177. P 26, Schmitt I 121:14–16. Williams renders *in dies usque* "day by day" (*Anselm*, 97).
178. P 26, Schmitt I 121:16–18.
179. P 26, Schmitt I 121:22–122:2.

quently end with a vision of God's eternal, triune happiness. Anselm's summoning of his *tota substantia* is also reminiscent of the *Prayers*,[180] and Cattin underscores how this language recalls that from the beginning of the *Proslogion*.[181]

It is striking that at the end of his book, having successfully achieved his aims, Anselm should nonetheless conclude in the same posture of earnest pursuit that has already characterized so much of his effort up to this point. For all the progress Anselm has made in the *Proslogion*, for the decisive exuberance of finding God to be the joy of the human soul, this discovery has not resulted in a relaxation of those impulses that led him to initiate his search for God, but—if anything—has only further aggravated them. It is somewhat fitting, given the dynamic, multiplying nature of heavenly joy articulated in the previous chapter, that Anselm's book should conclude in this way with a crescendo, rather than deflation, of energy. By concluding with an articulation of his love, desire, and hunger for God, Anselm underscores one more time the ultimate thrust of the entire *Proslogion*, which is not only to direct the mind to God as *summum* of all reality, but to direct the soul to God as the *bonum* of all happiness.

---

180. *Or.* 7, Schmitt III 18:6–7.
181. Cattin, "La prière de S Anselme dans le *Proslogion*," 392.

Conclusion

This book has urged a holistic reading of the *Proslogion*, with special attention given to Anselm's stated intentions throughout. Such an interpretative strategy—a close reading of the text, from start to finish—can hardly be considered a radical approach. But, as we have noted, much of the history of the *Proslogion* stands in contrast to such a procedure. Among both medieval and modern readers, Anselm's proof for God's existence has been regularly "extracted and anthologized;"[1] or at least the broader text has been subsumed under its interests. There are exceptions to this, of course, from medieval devotional use of the *Proslogion* to the "Anselm renaissance" of our own day. But even among those interpreters who stray into *Proslogion* 1 or *Proslogion* 5–26, the treatment is often piecemeal and/or systematically driven, so that the logical progression of the entire *Proslogion* is not visible. Thus, even the most rigorous engagements with the *Proslogion* often have little to say about how the prayers of *Proslogion* 1, 14, and 18 contribute materially to Anselm's argument; or how Anselm's doctrine of God develops logically from the divine formulae and attributes of the early chapters to the doctrines of eternity, simplicity, and Trinity in the later chapters; or even why the heavenly

---

1. This language is from Williams and Visser, *Anselm*, 73.

CONCLUSION

enjoyment of the vision of God in *Proslogion* 24–26 brings the ultimate resolution to Anselm's interests.

This book has pursued a more thoroughgoing exegesis of Anselm's entire text than is customary, exploring its purpose, development, and resolution, with sensitivity to Anselm's aims and context as an eleventh-century monk. Here it may be useful to summarize some of the more conspicuous results. To begin with several methodological issues, this book has proposed a solution to the long-standing debate concerning the alleged "contradictions" in Anselm's epistemology, suggesting that Anselm's stated method of arguing "by reason alone" (*sola ratione*) was not intended to exclude faith but rather the citation of authority. Claims that Anselm is a strong rationalist or is inconsistent in his procedure result from a misreading in which later distinctions between faith and reason are projected back into a context in which they would have been foreign. This thesis, advanced in chapter 1, has encouraged us to read the *Proslogion* with appreciation for its tight correlation of logic and yearning, its lack of appeal to authoritative texts, and its particular authorial *persona* (i.e, *fides quaerens intellectum*).

This book has proposed, secondly, to read the *Proslogion* in relation to Anselm's entire corpus, particularly his letters, *Prayers and Meditations* and the *Memorials of St. Anselm*. These texts are often neglected, and yet they convey certain qualities of Anselm's spirituality and practical life that are less visible in his speculative works. For instance, in Anselm's practical correspondences with fellow monks, as well as in his teaching ministry and his prayers to the saints in heaven, we gather a sense of the richness and intensity of his doctrine of friendship. Against this backdrop, Anselm's vision of the communal joy of heaven in *Proslogion* 24–25 appears less random—less like a turn into unfamiliar territory and more like a fitting arrival onto a central aspect of his thought. Much of the content of these chapters, in fact, will already be well familiar to us, such as the list of fourteen beatitudes in *Proslogion* 25, which are recapitulated throughout Anselm's teaching career as captured in

CONCLUSION

the *Memorials*. Finally, this book has engaged German and French scholarship on the *Proslogion*, especially that of Yves Cattin, Paul Gilbert, and Siegfried Karl. Their insights, which are often overlooked in the English-speaking world, have drawn attention not only to the structure and unity of the *Proslogion* but to its spiritual profundity. To use Gilbert's language, the *Proslogion* does far more than convince its readers of God's existence—it draws them up into the silent, secret desire of humanity.[2]

The most fundamental effort of this book, represented in chapters 3–5, is a close reading of Anselm's text that traces his argument through its various developments, seeking to keep apace with Anselm toward the resolution of *his* interests, rather than curtail the argument for our own purposes. Engaging the *Proslogion* in this way has yielded the consistent portrait of an author who is after far more than a proof of the divine, and it has opened up fresh insights into the text's genius and unity. In the first place, reading the *Proslogion* in light of Anselm's search for joy accords well with Anselm's established goals in the *prooemium*, especially his intention to prove that God is the *summum bonum* "which all things need for their being and well-being."[3] Here Anselm narrates the profound struggle he experienced in arriving upon the argument, as well as the joy it finally resulted in, stipulating that he wrote it down simply so that others might share in his pleasure.[4] Eadmer adds that Anselm produced the *Proslogion* only after losing much food and sleep, even wondering if the devil was tempting him. It finally arrived upon him, with greater emotional power, during prayer, as a kind of spiritual illumination.[5] This circumstantial backdrop has enabled us to appreciate the overarching unity that the *Proslogion* shares with the *Monologion*, even while it takes us into new territory. The sheer energy of the *Proslogion*, its ability to work upon its

2. Gilbert, *Le "Proslogion" de S. Anselme*, 8–9.
3. *P prooemium*, Schmitt I 93:8–9.
4. *P prooemium*, Schmitt I 93:21.
5. Eadmer, *Vita Sancti Anselmi* 1:19, 30.

readers at a deeply existential level, and its driving interest in human happiness all take on a new plausibility and significance when we recall that the *Proslogion* was occasioned by an intense spiritual crisis and resolution.

The spiritual profundity of the *Proslogion* is especially prominent in its first and lengthiest chapter. In the first paragraph of the book, Anselm summons himself to solitude and inwardness, as he has often done in his *Prayers and Meditations*. This address to his own soul (*soliloquium*), in contrast with the address to God (*alloquium*) that characterizes most of the book, recurs at crucial junctures in his argument—midway in *Proslogion* 14, where Anselm pauses to ascertain his progress, and finally in *Proslogion* 24, where Anselm considers the result of his achievement. This opening paragraph also sets up the essential problem of the book in moral terms—as a sinful *homuncio*, Anselm has been separated from the very purpose for which he was created, namely, seeing God. The bulk of *Proslogion* 1 is essentially an extended and anguished lament at this condition, followed by eager petitions for divine help as Anselm proceeds by faith seeking understanding. This introductory prayer is structurally and thematically foundational to the book, framing the *Proslogion* as a spiritual ascent toward the *visio Dei*, introducing its emotional character as an *excitatio* unto this goal, and establishing its method of procedure as *fides quaerens intellectum*.

In *Proslogion* 2–4 Anselm's interest in joy remains never far from view. These chapters advance an argument for God's existence, to be sure. But they are also filled with a range of nuances suggesting Anselm's interest in the whole quality and implication of God's existence, more than the bare fact of his existence. A mere ontological proof would in itself fail to accomplish Anselm's purpose here. Some generically existing "God" (*tu es*) will not do; Anselm wants the whole package that is affirmed by his faith (*tu es sicut credimus*). This is, as Anselm demonstrates, the God who exists so truly and so greatly that existence itself is his possession and thus whose nonexistence cannot even be thought. Only this God will fulfill the beatific vision, and Anselm describes his perception of such a God as a gift of divine illumination.[6] To see nothing more than God's existence in *Proslogion* 2–4 is not merely a slight deviation from Anselm's path but a movement against his intentions.

The structure of Anselm's ascent toward God throughout the middle and later chapters of the *Proslogion* furthers our awareness of his interest in joy. After establishing God's existence, Anselm immediately proceeds with the same argument to explore God's nature: "what therefore are you, Lord God, than which nothing greater can be thought?"[7] Having derived God's aseity, ultimacy, and supremacy as further consequences of the *unum argumentum* (*Proslogion* 5), Anselm proceeds to use these axioms to harmonize various perceived contradictions in the divine attributes (*Proslogion* 6–11), then identifying God's attributes with his utterly unique divine essence (*Proslogion* 12–13). All these various conclusions are logically derived from the same argument by which Anselm has established God's existence, albeit indirectly, through the divine axioms of *Proslogion* 5. Thus, divine aseity is a consequence of the divine name (*Proslogion* 5): divine simplicity is, in turn, a consequence of this (*Proslogion* 12). Or, divine supremacy is a consequence of the divine name (*Proslogion* 5): God's unique unbounded and eternal existence is, in turn, a consequence of this (*Proslogion* 13). The development is organic, and it arrives at emotional peaks as it touches Anselm's concern for happiness—for instance, in *Proslogion* 9, where Anselm punctuates his exposition of divine goodness with pleas to experience divine mercy: "O immeasurable goodness, which thus exceeds all understanding, let that mercy come over me which proceeds from your great wealth!"[8]

Proslogion 14 represents a spiral upward, recapitulating and furthering the prayers of *Proslogion* 1. At this point halfway through the book, Anselm summarizes what he has accomplished thus far,

6. *P* 4, Schmitt I 104:5–7.
7. *P* 5, Schmitt 1 104:11.
8. *P* 9, Schmitt I 107:27–108:1.

making no reference to establishing God's existence but instead recounting various claims he has developed about God's nature, including God's identity as "eternal happiness and happy eternity."[9] Yet Anselm laments that his originating prayer remains unanswered; his soul does not yet perceive God; his anguish is greater in *Proslogion* 14 than in *Proslogion* 1. Anselm therefore redoubles his requests to see God, paradoxically falling back upon God's incomprehensibility as the very light and truth by which he is seen. Divine incomprehensibility then functions as Anselm's tool by which to proceed toward the soul's perception of God in what amounts to the second spiraling upwards in the book, from "that than which nothing greater can be thought" (the divine name) to "that which is greater than can be thought" (divine incomprehensibility). In *Proslogion* 15 Anselm derives divine incomprehensibility as a consequence of the divine name; in *Proslogion* 16 he identifies divine incomprehensibility with the *lux inaccesibilis* that enshrouds God's essence; in *Proslogion* 17 he associates God's *lux* with God's happiness as the (still hidden) object of his soul's longing: "you are hidden from my soul in your light and happiness and for that reason it still dwells in its darkness and misery."[10] In this chapter sin is again identified as the cause of his distance from God.

The first paragraph of *Proslogion* 18 recapitulates the prayers of *Proslogion* 14 and 18, once again employing repetition, biblical quotation, and imagery to convey the anguish of his soul's distance from God and petitioning for God's illumination: "enlighten the eye of my soul, that I may look upon you."[11] Then Anselm recounts a number of the divine attributes he has discovered, lamenting that he cannot delight in them all "in one simultaneous view" (*uno simul intuitu*). Thus, whereas his previous treatments of divine attributes sought their harmony, he now pursues God's simplicity and eternality to establish their unity. This initiates the third spiral up into

9. P 14, Schmitt I 111:11–12.
10. P 17, Schmitt 1 13:8–9.
11. P 18, Schmitt 1 14:11–12.

CONCLUSION

the "higher" divine attributes in which Anselm is concerned with God's radically unique transcendence as that which contains all things within his eternity (*Proslogion* 19–21) and alone is what it is (*Proslogion* 22). This final claim results from divine simplicity: all other things are one thing in the whole and another in their parts, but God alone is wholly and always whatever he is. This, at last, leads Anselm to the successful completion of his stated goal in the *prooemium*—namely, establishing God as the *unum et summum bonum* "whom all things need for their being and well-being" (*bene sint*).[12]

In *Proslogion* 23, Anselm identifies this *unum et summum bonum* as equally the Father, the Son, and the Spirit. Anselm's concluding reference to the *unum necessarium* of Luke 10:42 ("one thing is necessary") draws from the preceding tradition of interpretation in which Mary and Martha serve as types of the contemplative and active lives, respectively. *Proslogion* 23 thus identifies the Trinity as the *unum necessarium* that the human soul obtains in the eternal heavenly rest and enjoyment of God. This results, at long last, in the achievement of Anselm's longing to see God in *Proslogion* 24–26. He returns to self-address (*soliloquium*) to offer a conjecture as to the nature and extent of the good he has discovered (*Proslogion* 24), then extending this conjecture into a meditation on the communal joy of the all the saints and angels in heaven, a joy that is not only infinite but infinitely multiplying because of the communal love of heaven (*Proslogion* 25). Finally, Anselm petitions that God will help him live in light of this staggering vision of heavenly joy and grow in it daily until it "comes to fullness" (*Proslogion* 26).[13]

Therefore, the driving purpose of Anselm's argument in the *Proslogion* is to arrive upon the *visio Dei* that is the object of his soul's desire. Anselm's argument for God's (unique) existence is, of course, an important step in this larger effort and an ingenuous accomplishment in its own right. But the ultimate concern animat-

12. *P* 22, Schmitt 1 16:24–17:2.
13. *P* 26, Schmitt 1 21:15–16.

CONCLUSION

ing the book is not God's existence as such, or even God's nature, but specifically God's existence and nature as the fulfillment of all human longing. The scope of Anselm's argument in the *Proslogion* involves this entire movement from fallen misery to heavenly joy. Within this larger development, the divine formula by which Anselm proves God's existence (*Proslogion* 2–4) is that same formula by which he ascends all the way up through his doctrine of God as the *summum bonum* of the human soul (*Proslogion* 5–23) and then into his anticipation of the heavenly beatific vision (*Proslogion* 24–26). Thus, God's existence is only the penultimate derivation of "that than which nothing greater can be conceived"; its ultimate consequence is the infinite human joy that is *entailed* by God's existence. The *Proslogion* must therefore be regarded as, far more than an argument for God's existence, a meditation on God as the chief happiness of the human soul.

Bibliography

Primary Sources

Anselm. *Ein neues unvollendetes Werk des hl. Anselm von Canterbury.* Edited by F. S. Schmitt. Beiträge zur Geschichte der Philosophie und Theologie des Mittelalters Bd. 33, Hft. 3. Münster: Aschendorff Press, 1936.

———. *S. Anselmi Cantuariensis Archiepiscopi Opera Omnia*, 6 vols. Edited by F. S. Schmitt. Edinburgh: Thomas Nelson and Sons, 1946–1961.

———. *Memorials of Saint Anselm.* Edited by F. S. Schmitt and Richard W. Southern. Auctores Britannici Medii Aevi. Oxford: Oxford University Press, 1969.

———. *The Prayers and Meditations of Saint Anselm with the "Proslogion."* Translated by Benedicta Ward. Penguin Classics. London: Penguin Books, 1973.

———. *The Letters of Saint Anselm of Canterbury.* 3 vols. Translated by Walter Frölich. Kalamazoo, Mich.: Cistercian Publications, 1990.

———. *Anselm of Canterbury: The Major Works.* Edited by Brian Davies and Gillian R. Evans. Oxford World Classics. Oxford: Oxford University Press, 1998.

Anselm of Canterbury: Works. Edited and translated by Jasper Hopkins and Herbert Richardson. 4 vols. Lewiston, N.Y.: The Edwin Mellen Press, 1974–1976.

———. *Anselm: Basic Writings.* Edited by Thomas Williams. Indianapolis: Hackett, 2007.

Santo Anselmo, "Proslogion" seu Alloquium de Dei existentia. Translated by José Rosa. Textos Clássicos de Filosofia. Covilhã: LusoSophia, 2008.

Aquinas, Thomas. *Faith, Reason, and Theology: Questions I-IV of His Commentary on the De Trinitate of Boethius.* Translated by Armand Maurer. Medieval Sources in Translation 32. Toronto: Pontifical Institute of Medieval Studies, 1987.

———. *Summa Theologica.* 5 vols. Translated by the Fathers of the English Dominican Province. Christian Classics. Notre Dame: Christian Classics, 1948.

Augustine. *The Confessions and Letters of Augustine With a Sketch of His Life and*

BIBLIOGRAPHY

Work. Vol. 1. Edited by Philip Schaff. Nicene and Post-Nicene Fathers, First Series. 1886. Reprint, Peabody, Mass.: Hendrickson, 2012.

———. *City of God, Christian Doctrine*. Vol. 2. Edited by Philip Schaff. Nicene and Post-Nicene Fathers, First Series. 1887. Reprint, Peabody, Mass.: Hendrickson 2012.

———. *Enchiridion*. Hyde Park, N.Y.: New City, 1999.

———. *On the Holy Trinity, Doctrinal Treatises, Moral Treatises*. Vol. 3. Edited by Philip Schaff. Nicene and Post-Nicene Fathers, First Series.1887. Reprint, Peabody, Mass: Hendrickson 2012.

Boethius. *De Consolatione Philosophiae, Opuscula Theologica*. Edited by Claudio Moreschini. Bibliotheca Teubneriana. Munich: K. G. Saur, 2000.

Bonaventure. *Disputed Questions on the Mystery of the Trinity*. Translated by Zachery Hayes, OFM. Works of St. Bonaventure III. 1979. Reprint, St. Bonaventure, N.Y.: The Franciscan Institute, 2000.

Descartes, René. *The Philosophical Writings of Descartes*. 2 vols. Translated by John Cottingham, Robert Stoofhoff, and Dugald Murdoch. Cambridge: Cambridge University Press, 1984.

Duns Scotus, John. *Philosophical Writings: A Selection*. Edited and translated by Allan Wolter. Indianapolis: Hackett, 1987.

Eadmer. *Vita Sancti Anselmi*. Edited and translated by R. W. Southern. Oxford: Oxford University Press, 1972.

Edwards, Jonathan. *The Sermons of Jonathan Edwards: A Reader*. Edited by Wilson H. Kimnach, Kenneth P. Minkema, and Douglas A. Sweeney. New Haven, Conn.: Yale University Press, 1999.

Kant, Immanuel. *Critique of Pure Reason*. Translated by J. M. D. Meikle. 1781. Reprint, N.Y.: Dutton, 1974.

Lanfranc, Archbishop of Canterbury. *The Letters of Lanfranc, Archbishop of Canterbury*. Edited and Translated by Helen Clover and Margaret Gibson. Oxford Medieval Texts. Oxford: Clarendon University Press, 1979.

Leibniz, Gottfried. *New Essays on Human Understanding*. Edited and translated by Peter Remnant and Jonathan Bennett. Cambridge Texts in the History of Philosophy. Cambridge: Cambridge University Press, 1996.

Ockham, William. *Philosophical Writings: A Selection*. Edited by Stephen F. Brown and translated by Philotheus Boehner. Indianapolis: Heckett, 1990.

Suárez, Francis. *On the Various Kinds of Distinctions*. Translated by Cyril Vollert. Mediaeval Philosophical Texts in Translation. Milwaukee: Marquette University Press, 1947.

Spinoza, Baruch. *The Collected Works of Baruch Spinoza*. 2 vols. Edited and translated by Edwin Curley. Princeton: Princeton University Press, 1985.

Wiclif, Joannis. *De Ente Praedicamentali*. Edited by Rudolf Beer. London: Truber and Co., 1891.

BIBLIOGRAPHY

Secondary Sources

Adams, Marilyn McCord. "Praying the *Proslogion*: Anselm's Theological Method." In *The Rationality of Belief and the Plurality of Faith*, edited by Thomas D. Senor. Ithaca, N.Y.: Cornell University Press, 1995.

———. "Was Anselm a Realist? The *Monologium*," *Franciscan Studies* 32 (1972): 5–14.

Archambault, Jacob. "The Teaching of the Trivium at Bec and Its Bearing upon the Anselmian Program of *fides quaerens intellectum*." Paper presented at Reading Anselm: Context and Criticism. Boston, Mass., July 29th, 2015.

Anselm: Aosta, Bec and Canterbury: Papers in Commemoration of the Nine-Hundredth Anniversary of Anselm's Enthronement as Archbishop, 25 September 1093. Edited by D. E. Luscombe and Gillian R. Evans. Sheffield, United Kingdom: Sheffield Academic Press, 1996.

Anselm Studies: An Occasional Journal II: Proceedings of the Fifth International Saint Anselm Conference: St. Anselm and St. Augustine—Episcopi ad Saecula. Edited by Joseph C. Schnaubelt, Thomas A. Losoncy, et. al. White Plains, N.Y.: Kraus International Publications, 1988.

Athayde, Emmanuel Roberto Leal de. *Teologia no "Proslogion" de Anselmo de Cantuária*. PhD diss., Universidade Presbiteriana Mackenzie, 2011.

Baark, Sigurd. "Anselm: Platonism, Language and Truth in *Proslogion*." *Scottish Journal of Theology* 63, no. 4 (2010): 379–97.

Barth, Karl. *Fides Quaerens Intellectum: Anselm's Proof of the Existence of God in the Context of His Theological Scheme*. Translated by Ian W. Robinson, 1931. Reprint, Eugene, Ore.: Pickwick, 2009.

———. *Church Dogmatics*. Edited by Geoffrey Bromiley and T. F. Torrance. Translated by G. W. Bromiley. Study edition. London: T&T Clark, 2009.

Baumstein, Paschal. "Anselm's Thought as a Fulcrum for Benedict's *Rule*." *Cistercian Studies* 26 (1991): 194–203.

———. "Benedictine Education: Principles of Anselm's Patronage." *The American Benedictine Review* 43 (March 1992): 3–11.

———. "Revisiting Anselm: Current Historical Studies and Controversies." *Cistercian Studies Quarterly* 28 (1993): 207–29.

Bencivenga, Ermanno. *Logic and Other Nonsense: The Case of Anselm and His God*. Princeton: Princeton University Press, 1993.

———. "A Note on Gaunilo's Lost Island." *Dialogue: Canadian Philosophical Review* 46 (Summer 2007): 583–87.

Biblia Sacra Iuxta Vulgatam Versionem. Edited by Robert Weber and Roger Gryson. 5th ed. Stuttgart: Deutsche Bibelgesellschaft, 1969.

Brown, Montague. "Faith and Reason in Anselm: Two Models," *The Saint Anselm Journal* 2 (Fall, 2004): 10–21.

BIBLIOGRAPHY

The Cambridge Companion to Anselm. Edited by Brian Davies and Brian Leftow. Cambridge: Cambridge University Press, 2004.

Campbell, Richard. *From Belief to Understanding: A Study of Anselm's "Proslogion" Argument on the Existence of God.* Canberra, Australia: The Australian National University, 1976.

———. "Anselm's Theological Method." *Scottish Journal of Theology* 33, no. 4 (1980): 317–43.

———. *Rethinking Anselm's Arguments: A Vindication of His Proof of the Existence of God.* Anselm Studies and Texts 1. Leiden: Brill, 2018.

Cattin Yves, *La preuve de Dieu: Introduction à la lecture du "Proslogion" d'Anselme de Canterbury.* Bibliothèque d'histoire de la philosophie. Paris: Librairie Philosophique J. Vrin, 1986.

———. "La prière de S Anselme dans le *Proslogion.*" *Revue des Sciences philosophiques et théologiques* 72, no. 3 (1988): 373–96.

———. "Dieu d'amour, Dieu de colère: Justice et miséricorde dans le *Proslogion* (ch. VI-XI) d'Anselme de Canterbury." *Revue d'Histoire et de Philosophie religieuses* 69, no. 4 (1989): 423–50.

Chadwick, Henry. *Boethius: The Consolations of Music, Logic, Theology, and Philosophy.* Oxford: Oxford University Press, 1981.

Charlesworth, M. J. *St. Anselm's "Proslogion."* 1965. Reprint, Notre Dame: University of Notre Dame Press, 1979.

Colish, Marcia L. *The Mirror of Language: A Study in the Medieval Theory of Knowledge.* Revised ed. Lincoln, Neb.: University of Nebraska Press, 1983.

———. *Medieval Foundations of the Western Intellectual Tradition, 400–1400.* The Yale Intellectual History of the West. New Haven, Conn.: Yale University Press, 1997.

Corbin, Michel. *Saint Anselme.* Paris: Éditions du Cerf, 2004.

Dalferth, Ingolf U. "*Fides Quaerens Intellectum*: Theologie als Kunst Der Argumentation in Anselms *Proslogion.*" *Zeitschrift für Theologie und Kirche* 81, no. 1 (1984): 54–105.

Davies, Brian and Brian Leftow, eds. *The Cambridge Companion to Anselm.* Cambridge: Cambridge University Press, 2004.

Deme, Daniel. *The Christology of Anselm of Canterbury.* Burlington, Vt.: Ashgate, 2003.

Evans, Gillian R. "The *Cur Deus Homo*: The Nature of St. Anselm's Appeal to Reason." *Studia Theologica* 31 (1977): 33–50.

———. *Anselm and Talking about God.* Oxford: Clarendon Press, 1978.

———. *Anselm and a New Generation.* Oxford: Oxford University Press, 1980.

———, ed. *Concordance to the Works of St. Anselm.* Iola, WI: Kraus International Publications, 1983.

———, ed. *The Medieval Theologians: An Introduction to Theology in the Medieval Period*. Malden, Mass.: Blackwell Publishers, 2001.
———. *Anselm*. Outstanding Christian Thinkers Series. N.Y.: Bloomsbury Academic, 2005.
Fendt, Gene. "The Relation of *Proslogion* and *Monologion*." *Heythrop Journal* 46 (2004): 149–66.
Fortin, John R., ed. *St. Anselm—His Origins and Influence*. Texts and Studies in Religion 91. Lewiston, N.Y.: The Edwin Mellen Press, 2001.
Gasper, Giles E. M. *Saint Anselm of Canterbury and His Theological Inheritance*. Burlington, Vt.: Ashgate, 2004.
———, and Helmut Kohlenberger, ed. *Anselm and Abelard: Investigations and Juxtapositions*. Toronto: Pontifical Institute of Mediaeval Studies, 2006.
———. "Envy, Jealousy, and the Boundaries of Orthodoxy: Anselm of Canterbury and the Genesis of the *Proslogion*." *Viator* 41 (2010): 45–68.
———, and Ian Logan, ed. *Saint Anselm of Canterbury and His Legacy*. Durham Medieval and Renaissance Monographs and Essays 2. Toronto: Pontifical Institute of Medieval Studies, 2012.
Gibson, Margaret, ed. *Boethius: His Life, Thought, and Influence*. Oxford: Basil Blackwell, 1981.
Gilbert, Paul. *Dire l'Ineffable: Lecture du "Monologion" de S. Anselme*. Paris: Éditions Lethielleux, 1984.
———. "Justice et miséricorde dans le *Proslogion* de saint Anselme." *Nouvelle Revue Théologique* 108 (1986): 218–38.
———. *Le "Proslogion" de S. Anselme: Silence de Dieu et joie de l'homme*. Rome: Pontifical Gregorian University, 1990.
———. "Entrez dans la joie: les ch. 24 à 26 du *Proslogion*." *Science et Esprit* 47, no. 3 (1995): 239–59.
Gilbert, Paul, Helmut Kohlenberger, and Edmar Salmann, ed. *Cur Deus Homo: Atti del Congresso Anselmiano Internazionale*. Rome: Center for the Study of Saint Anselm, 1999.
Gilson, Étienne. *The Spirit of Mediaevial Philosophy*. Translated by A. H. C. Downes. N.Y.: Scribner, 1936.
———. *Reason and Revelation in the Middle Ages*. N.Y.: Scribner, 1948.
———. *History of Christian Philosophy in the Middle Ages*. N.Y.: Random House, 1995.
Glare, P. G. W., ed. *The Oxford Latin Dictionary*. Oxford: Oxford University Press, 1976.
Goodchild, Philip. "*Proslogion*." In *Phenomenology of Prayer*, edited by Bruce Ellis Benson and Norman Wirzba. Perspectives in Continental Philosophy 46, 232–43. N.Y.: Fordham University Press, 2005.
Gracia, Jorge J. E., and J. J. Sanford. "*Ratio quaerens beatitudinem*: Anselm

on Rationality and Happiness." In *Rationality and Happiness: From the Ancients to the Early Medievals*, edited by Jiyuan Yu and Jorge J. E. Gracia. Rochester, N.Y.: University of Rochester Press, 2003.

Grant, Colin. "Anselm's Argument Today." *Journal of the American Academy of Religion* 57, no. 4 (Winter 1989): 791–806.

Grzesik, Tadeusz. "What Anselm Owes to Boethius and Why He May Be Regarded as the Initiator of the Boethian Age." *Studia Anselmiana* 128, *Cur Deus Homo*. Rome, 1999.

Hall, Douglas C. *The Trinity: An Analysis of St. Thomas Aquinas' Expositio of the De Trinitate of Boethius*. Leiden: Brill, 1992.

Hartshorne, Charles. *The Logic of Perfection and Other Essays in Neoclassical Metaphysics*. Lasalle: Open Court, 1962.

Healy-Varley, Margaret. "Anselm's Fictions and the Literary Afterlife of the *Proslogion*." PhD diss., Harvard University, 2011.

Henry, Desmond P. "Saint Anselm's *De Grammatico*." *Philosophical Quarterly* 10 (1960): 115–26.

———. *The Logic of St. Anselm*. Oxford: Clarendon Press, 1967.

———. *Commentary on De Grammatico: The Historical-Logical Dimensions of a Dialogue of St. Anselm's*. Boston: D. Reidel, 1974.

———. "St. Anselm and the Linguistic Disciplines." *Anselm Studies* 2 (1988): 319–32.

Herrera, Robert A. *Anselm's "Proslogion": An Introduction*. Washington D.C.: The Catholic University of America Press, 1979.

Hick, John, and Arthur C. McGill, eds. *The Many-Faced Argument: Recent Studies on the Ontological Argument for the Existence of God*. N.Y.: Macmillan, 1967. Reprint, Eugene, Ore.: Wipf & Stock, 2009.

Hoenen, Maarten J. F. M., and Lodi Nauta, eds. *Boethius in the Middle Ages: Latin and Vernacular Traditions of the Consolatio Philosophiae*. N.Y.: Brill, 1997.

Hogg, David S. *Anselm of Canterbury: The Beauty of Theology*. Great Theologians Series. Burlington, Vt.: Ashgate, 2004.

Holopainen, Toivo J. *Dialectic and Theology in the Eleventh Century*. N.Y.: Brill, 1996.

———. "The *Proslogion* in Relation to the *Monologion*," *Heythrop Journal* 50 (2009): 590–602.

Hopkins, Jasper. *A Companion to the Study of St. Anselm*. Minneapolis: University of Minnesota Press, 1972.

Kane, Stanley G. "*Fides Quaerens Intellectum* in Anselm's Thought" *The Scottish Journal of Theology* 26 (1973): 40–62.

Kapriev, Georgi. *Ipsa Vita et Veritas: Der "Ontologische Gottesbeweis" und die Ideenwelt Anselms von Canterbury*. Studien und Texte zur Geistesgeschichte des Mittelalters. Leiden: Brill, 1998.

Karl, Siegfried. *Ratio und Affectus: Zum Verhältnis von Vernunft und Affekt in den Orationes sive Meditationes und im Proslogion Anselms von Canterbury*. Rome: Studia Anselmiana, 2014.

Kendrick, Nancy. "The Non-Christian Influence on Anselm's *Proslogion* Argument." *International Journal for Philosophy of Religion* 69, no. 2 (2011): 73–89.

Kienzler, Klaus. "Das *Proslogion*-Argument Anselms und die Confessiones des Augustinus." In *The European Dimension of St. Anselm's Thinking*, edited by Josef Zumr and Vilém Herold, 38–55. Prague: Institute of Philosophy, 1993.

———. "*Proslogion* 1: Form Und Gestalt." In *Anselm: Anselm: Aosta, Bec and Canterbury*, edited by D. E. Luscombe and G. R. Evans. Sheffield: Sheffield Academic Press, 1996.

Leff, Gordon. *Medieval Thought: From St. Augustine to Ockham*. London: Humanities Press, 1958.

Leftow, Brian. *Time and Eternity*. Ithaca: Cornell University Press, 1991.

Logan, Ian. "Ms. Bodley 271: Establishing the Anselm Canon?" *The Saint Anselm Journal* 2 (2004): 67–80.

———. "'Whoever Understands This...': On Translating the *Proslogion*." *New Blackfriars* 89:1023 (September 2008): 560–74.

———. *Reading Anselm's "Proslogion": The History of Anselm's Argument and Its Significance Today*. Burlington, Vt.: Ashgate, 2009.

Losoncy, Thomas A. "Chapter 1 of St Anselm's *Proslogion*: Its Preliminaries to Proving God's Existence as Paradigmatic for Subsequent Proofs of God's Existence." In *Greek and Medieval Studies in Honor of Leo Sweeney, SJ*, 171–79. N.Y.: Peter Lang, 1995.

Lubac, Henri, de. "'Seigneur, je cherche ton visage': Sur le chapitre xiv du *Proslogion* de saint Anselme," *Archives de philosophie* 39, no 2 (1976): 201–25.

Luscombe, D. E., and G. R. Evans, eds. *Anselm: Aosta, Bec and Canterbury: Papers in Commemoration of the Nine-Hundredth Anniversary of Anselm's Enthronement as Archbishop, 25 September 1093*. Sheffield, United Kingdom: Sheffield Academic Press, 1996.

Mackey, Louis. *Peregrinations of the Word: Essays in Medieval Philosophy*. Ann Arbor, Mich.: University of Michigan Press, 1997.

Maitzen, Stephen. "Anselmian Atheism." *Philosophy and Phenomenological Research* 70, no. 1 (January 2005): 225–39.

Majeran, Roman, and Edward Iwo Zieliński, ed. *Saint Anselm: Bishop and Thinker: Papers Read at a Conference Held in the Catholic University of Lublin on 24–26 September 1996*. Lublin: University Press of the Catholic University of Lublin, 1999.

Malcolm, Norman. "Anselm's Ontological Arguments." *The Philosophical Review* 69 (1960): 41–62.

The Many-Faced Argument: Recent Studies on the Ontological Argument for the Existence of God. Edited by John Hick and Arthur C. McGill. N.Y.: Macmillan, 1967. Reprint, Eugene, Ore.: Wipf & Stock.

Mar, Gary. "The Modal Unity of Anselm's *Proslogion*." *Faith and Philosophy* 13, no. 1 (1996): 50–67.

Matthews, Gareth B. "Inner Dialogue in Augustine and Anselm." *Poetics Today* 28, no. 2 (Summer 2007): 283–302.

McCracken, George E., and Allen Cabaniss, eds. *Early Medieval Theology*, vol. ix. The Library of Christian Classics. Philadelphia: The Westminster Press, 1957.

McIntyre, John. *St. Anselm and His Critics: A Re-Interpretation of the* Cur Deus Homo. Edinburgh: Oliver and Boyd, 1954.

Nagasawa, Yujin. "A New Defense of Anselmian Theism." *The Philosophical Quarterly* 58:233 (October 2008): 577–96.

Nault, Jean-Charles. "The First Chapter of St. Anselm's *Proslogion*." In *A Man Born Out of Due Time: New Perspectives on St. Anselm of Canterbury*. Edited by Dunstan Robidoux, 33–41. N.Y.: Lantern, 2013.

A New Latin Dictionary: Founded on the Translation of Freund's Latin-German Lexicon, Revised, Enlarged, and in Great Part Re-Written. Edited by Lewis Charlton T. Lewis and Charles Short. N.Y.: American Book Company, 1879.

Oberman, Heiko Augustinus, ed. *Forerunners of the Reformation: The Shape of Late Medieval Thought*. Translated by Paul L. Nyhus. N.Y.: Holt, Rinehart, and Winston, 1966.

Pelikan, Jaroslav. *The Christian Tradition: A History of the Development of Doctrine, vol. 3: The Growth of Medieval Theology*. Chicago: University of Chicago Press, 1980.

Plantinga, Alvin, ed. *The Ontological Argument: From St. Anselm to Contemporary Philosophers*. Garden City, N.Y.: Anchor Books, 1965.

———. *The Nature of Necessity*. Oxford: Clarendon Press, 1974.

Principe, Walter Henry. *William of Auxerre's Theology of the Hypostatic Union*. Studies and Texts 7. Toronto: Pontifical Institute of Mediaeval Studies, 1963.

Rogers, Katherin. *Anselm on Freedom*. Oxford: Oxford University Press, 2008.

Sadler, Gregory B. "The Ontological Proof, the Option, and the *Unique Nécessaire*: Maurice Blondel's Examination of the Proof in Anselm, Descartes, and Malebranche." *The Saint Anselm Journal* 2 (Spring 2005): 88–100.

———. "Saint Anselm's *Fides Quaerens Intellectum* as a Model for Christian Philosophy." *The Saint Anselm Journal* 4 (Fall 2006): 32–58.

Schnaubelt, Joseph C., and Thomas A. Losoncy, et. al., eds. *Anselm Studies: An Occasional Journal II: Proceedings of the Fifth International Saint Anselm*

Conference: *St. Anselm and St. Augustine—Episcopi ad Saecula*. White Plains, N.Y.: Kraus International Publications, 1988.

Schufreider, Gregory. *Confessions of a Rational Mystic: Anselm's Early Writings*. West Lafayette, Ind.: Purdue University Press, 1994.

Sharpe, Richard. "Anselm as Author: Publishing in the Late Eleventh Century." *Journal of Medieval Latin* 19 (2009): 1–87.

Slotemaker, John T. *Anselm of Canterbury and the Search for God*. Mapping the Tradition. Minneapolis, Minn.: Fortress Academic, 2018.

Smalley, Beryl. *The Study of the Bible in the Middle Ages*. Oxford: Clarendon Press, 1941.

Southern, Richard W. *Saint Anselm and His Biographer: A Study of Monastic Life and Thought 1059–c. 1130*. Cambridge: Cambridge University Press, 1963.

———. *St. Anselm: A Portrait in a Landscape*. Cambridge: Cambridge University Press, 1992.

Stock, Brian. "Self, Soliloquy, and Spiritual Exercises in Augustine and Some Later Authors." *The Journal of Religion* 91, no. 1 (January 2011): 5–23.

Stolz, Anselm. "Zur Theologie Anselms im *Proslogion*." *Catholica: Vierteljahrschrift fur Kontroverstheologie* 2. (Paderborn: 1933): 1–24.

———. "'Vere esse' im *Proslogion* des hl. Anselm," *Scholastik* 9 (1934): 400–409.

———. "Das *Proslogion* des hl. Anselm," *Revue Benedictine* 47 (1935): 331–47.

Orrin F. Summerell, ed. *The Otherness of God*. Studies in Religion and Culture. Charlottesville, Va.: University of Virginia Press, 1998.

Sweeney, Eileen C. "Anselm's *Proslogion*: The Desire for the Word." *The Saint Anselm Journal* 1 (Fall 2003): 17–31.

———. *Anselm of Canterbury and the Desire for the Word*. Washington, D.C.: The Catholic University of America Press, 2012.

———. "Anselmian Meditation: Imagination, Aporia, and Argument." *The Saint Anselm Journal* 9 (Fall 2014): 1–14.

Van Fleteren, Frederick, and Joseph C. Schnaubelt, ed. *Twenty-Five Years (1969–1994) of Anselm Studies: Review and Critique of Recent Scholarly Views*. Texts and Studies in Religion 70. Lewiston, N.Y.: Edward Mellen Press, 1996.

Vaughn, Sally. *Anselm of Bec and Robert of Meulan: The Innocence of the Dove and the Wisdom of the Serpent*. Berkeley: University of California Press, 1987.

———. *Archbishop Anselm 1093–1109: Bec Missionary, Canterbury Primate, Patriarch of Another World*. Burlington, Vt.: Ashgate, 2012.

———. "The Monastic Sources of Anselm's Political Beliefs: St. Augustine, St. Benedict, and St. Gregory the Great," in *Anselm Studies: An Occasional Journal II*, 71–74.

Vignaux, Paul. "La méthode de Saint Anselme dans le *Monologion* et le *Proslogion*." *Aquinas* 8 (1965): 110–29.

———. "Nécessité des raisons dans le *Monologion*." *Revue des Sciences philosophiques et théologiques* 64 (1980): 3–25.

Viola, Colomon Étienne. "Origine et portée du principe dialectique du *Proslogion* de saint Anselme. De l'argument *ontologique* à l'argument *mégalogique*." *Rivista di Filosofia Neo-Scolastica* 83 (1992): 339–84.

———, and Frederick Van Fleteren, ed. *Saint Anselm—A Thinker for Yesterday and Today: Anselm's Thought Viewed by our Contemporaries*. Texts and Studies in Religion 90. Lewiston, N.Y.: The Edwin Mellen Press, 2002.

Ward, Benedicta. *Anselm of Canterbury: A Monastic Scholar*. Fairacres 62; Oxford: Sisters of the Love of God, 1973.

———. *Anselm of Canterbury: His Life and Legacy*. London: Society for Promoting Christian Knowledge, 2009.

Williams, Thomas and Sandra Visser. *Anselm*. Great Medieval Thinkers. Oxford: Oxford University Press, 2009.

Wimmer, Reiner. "Anselms *Proslogion* Als Performativ-Illokutionärer und Als Kognitiv-Propositionaler Text Und Die Zweifache Aufgabe der Theologie." In *Klassische Gottesbeweise in der Sicht der gegenwärtigen Logik und Wissenschaftstheorie*, edited by Frido Ricken, Wilhelm K. Essler, et al., 174–201. Stuttgart: Kohlhammer, 1991.

Wolterstorff, Nicholas. "In Defense of Gaunilo's Defense of the Fool," in *Christian Perspectives on Religious Knowledge*, edited by C. Stephen Evans and Merold Westphal, 87–111. Grand Rapids, Mich.: Eerdmans, 1993.

Wood, Donald Dixon. "Anselm's Contribution to Barth's Doctrine of the Knowledge of God." Phd. diss., Fuller Theological Seminary, 1974.

Index

Abelard, 53
Adams, Marilyn McCord, 13, 34, 132n16
Anselm: beatitudes, 207–12; *Cur Deus homo*, 15, 20–22, 32–33, 36, 41, 47, 97, 103, 108, 116–17; *De casu diaboli*, 23–24; *De conceptu virginali*, 102; *De Concordia*, 20, 21, 100, 102; *De grammatico*, 2, 17, 40, 202; *De incarnatione verbi*, 15, 19, 21, 23, 28, 30–31, 33, 36, 40, 44–45, 89, 96, 108, 114, 116, 117, 123, 191; *De veritate*, 23–24, 155; doctrine of friendship, 185–88; letters, 181–88; *Memorials*, 208–12; *Monologion*, 6, 8, 11, 17–21, 23–27, 29, 34, 36–37, 39, 41, 44, 57, 59, 61, 70, 72, 74, 80–82, 84, 87–95, 100, 109, 114–15, 119, 121, 126, 131–34, 140–41, 143, 149, 162, 177, 179–180, 189–190, 198, 200, 225; *Prayers and Meditations*, 1, 9, 17, 59, 74, 75, 89–91, 97–99, 145, 176–181; *Reply to Gaunilo*, 32, 48, 116
Aquinas, Thomas, 1, 12, 16, 38, 39n107, 54–55, 198
Archambault, Jacob, 86n27
attributes, divine. *See* God
Augustine, 15, 23, 35–40, 81–82, 90, 96–97, 100, 102, 108, 151, 141, 180, 191, 194–97, 214, 219
authority: religious, 34–40

Barth, Karl, 2–3, 12n5, 12n6, 13n17, 16n22, 23, 40–41, 54n22, 56–57, 59n48, 65–66, 72, 76, 81, 85n20, 88, 90n40, 119n139, 121
beatific vision. *See visio Dei*
beatitudes, of Anselm. *See* Anselm
belief. *See* faith
Bencivenga, Ermanno, 13n17
Benedictine. *See* Rule of St. Benedict
Boethius, 16n23, 38–40, 81n6, 86n27, 87, 167–68, 202
Bonaventure, 53–54
Boso, 20, 22, 32, 92, 97
by reason alone. *See sola ratione*

Campbell, Richard, 33, 58n45
De casu diaboli. *See* Anselm
Cattin Yves, 4n16, 5, 17n24, 42, 62, 64–73, 76–77, 90n38, 128n9, 136–38, 143, 164–65, 200–01, 221, 225
Charlesworth, M.J., 2n5, 6, 11–12, 22, 51–52, 54n25, 59, 88, 104n95, 116n126
Clayton, John, 91, 116
Colish, Marcia L., 39n109, 81n6, 114n120, 116n125, 117
De Concordia. *See* Anselm
De conceptu virginali. *See* Anselm
Confessions. *See* Augustine
Consolation of Philosophy. *See* Boethius

241

INDEX

Corbin, Michel, 5n16, 13, 16n23, 64n73, 150n54
Cur Deus homo. *See* Anselm

Davies, Brian, 3n11, 13n13, 88
Descartes, René, 2, 54–56, 102
divine. *See* God
divine formula. *See* divine name
divine name, 48, 72–73, 115, 119, 127–130, 134, 139–143, 151, 157, 161–63, 166, 191, 227–28, 230
Duns Scotus, John, 54

Eadmer, 19, 28, 84–86, 91–93, 176–77, 208–09, 225
epistemology. *See* faith
eternity. *See* God
Evans, Gillian R., 2n6, 3n11, 13, 34, 52n17, 53, 56, 59–60, 86n24, 126, 133n18, 204, 217–18
Eucharist, 35, 37
existence. *See* God
experience: of Anselm, 33–34, 91–92

faith: versus reason, 11–23; necessity of, 29–34; seeking understanding, 40–43, 91–95
fides quaerens intellectum. *See* faith
fool: in the *Proslogion*, 40–43, 115–18, 122–23
French scholarship on the *Proslogion*, 4–5, 47, 64–74, 76, 150n54, 225
friendship, Anselm's doctrine of. *See* Anselm
Fröhlich, Walter, 79n3, 182n37

Gasper, Giles E. M., 38n101, 51n12
Gaunilo of Marmoutiers, 1, 23, 32, 46–51, 53
German scholarship on the *Proslogion*, 4n12, 5, 47, 56, 62–64, 74–76, 150n54, 225

Gilbert, Paul, 4n16, 5 62, 70–74, 76–77, 87–88, 101, 116, 128n8, 131–33, 139, 141, 161, 162–63, 202–03, 205, 206n131, 212n147, 225
Gilson, Étienne, 12n6, 13n17, 30, 60n48, 72
God: attributes of, 72, 77, 85, 11, 124, 127–31, 133, 138, 141–49, 151, 153, 160, 162–71, 223, 227; eternity of, 131, 149–50, 152, 162–63, 166–69, 171–72, 181, 209, 223, 228–29; existence of, 1–3, 111–23, 157n66, 169–70, 226–27, 229–30; justice of, 65, 70, 72, 85, 97, 124, 134, 141, 142–49; goodness of, 85, 134, 145–48, 150–51, 155, 157, 166, 171, 176, 180, 193, 195, 196, 199–204; incomprehensibility of, see *lux inaccessibilis*; knowledge of, 25, 27–28, 31, 33–34, 40–43, 74–75, 108, 112, 134–35, 143, 152–56, 219–220; mercy of, 65, 70, 72, 124, 134–35, 142–49; simplicity of, 24, 54, 83, 124, 127, 129, 148–49, 155, 166–67, 169, 171–72, 176, 190–92, 223, 227–29
goodness. *See* God
De grammatico. *See* Anselm
Gregory the Great, 38, 178, 196–97
Grzesik, Tadeusz, 38n106, 40n110
Gundulf, 177, 187
Gunhilda, 184

Hartshorne, Charles, 3, 58, 118n134
Healy-Varley, Margaret, 52, 53n19, 208
heaven, 7–9, 42, 44, 47, 59, 72, 74–76, 78–80, 103, 111, 124, 125, 130, 132, 135–36, 173–86, 207–17, 224, 229–30
Henry, Desmond P., 2n2, 39n106, 40n110, 76, 143
Henry, the monk, 187
Herrera, Robert A., 60, 171, 175

242

INDEX

Hogg, David S., 42n119, 61n54, 81n8, 91n42, 181n30
Holopainen, Toivo J., 13, 37n99, 62, 86–87, 88n35
Hopkins, Jasper, 2n6, 3n11, 5n16, 13, 20n33, 32n75, 33n79, 55n31, 59, 70n102, 88n33, 89n37
Hugh the Hermit, 78, 186

De incarnatione verbi. See Anselm

justice. *See* God

Kapriev, Georgi, 5n17, 13, 40, 62–64, 92n46
Kant, Immanuel, 2, 55, 59n46, 102
Karl, Siegfried, 5, 62, 74–76, 131, 134–35, 199n106, 200, 206n132, 215–16, 219, 225
knowledge, of God. *See* God

Lanfranc, 20, 35n89, 36–37, 116, 187
language, theological, 4n15, 26, 28, 66, 71, 102, 143–44
Leibniz, Gottfried, 2, 55, 102
Logan, Ian, 4n13, 5n18, 13, 49n9, 51n12, 53n21, 54n25, 54n26, 55n30, 58n44, 61, 64n75, 76, 108n112, 116n123, 119n136, 119n137, 120n142, 141n31, 169, 199n105, 201, 202n115, 219n171
logic, Anselm's use of, 2n6, 38–40, 86–87,
Lonzo, 185
love: of God, 30–34, 98–109, 177–78; of heaven, 212–217
lux inaccessibilis, 156–61

Mackey, Louis, 4n15, 69n99, 92n47, 118n135, 174–75
Malcolm, Norman, 3, 58, 118n134
McGill, Arthur C., 13, 49n8, 52n14, 57n39, 113

McIntyre, John, 12, 22
mercy, of God. *See* God
monasticism, 17–19, 34–35, 52, 59, 90–92, 99–100, 116, 173, 176, 183–84
mysticism, 3, 13n17, 57–58, 66, 71, 87, 102

necessary existence, 58, 118–23, 169

Ockham, William, 54
ontological argument, 1–10, 111–23

persona, 21, 29, 44, 61, 92–95
philosophical interpretations of the *Proslogion*, 3, 51–56, 58, 102
Plantinga, Alvin, 55n32, 58n46
Proslogion: climax of, 173–221; codicology of, 49–51; method of, 11–45; nature of chapters, 136–38; purpose of, 78–124; reception of, 46–77; structure of, 125–72; prayer, the *Proslogion* as, 4, 27, 90–96, 99, 106, 110, 112, 114, 128–30, 150–56, 162–66, 199, 213, 226

quo maius cogitari non potest (and variants). *See* divine name

rationalism. *See* reason
reason, 11–15, 18, 20–22, 25, 28, 29–34, 38–39, 40–43, 90–94, 100, 191, 224
remoto Christo, 12, 15, 20–24
Rogers, Katherin A., 13n17
Roscelin, 23n45, 29–31
Rule of St. Benedict, 116, 178,

Sadler, Gregory B., 181n30
Schmitt, F. S., 2n6, 5n18, 67, 209–210
scholasticism, 34–35, 177
Schufreider, Gregory, 13n17, 53n19, 60–61, 87n29, 100, 102, 119n136, 119n138, 164

INDEX

Scripture: Anselm's use of, 15, 18–20, 22–24, 28, 36, 147–48, 168–69, 192–99, 207–12, 217–21; in medieval theology, 35–36
simplicity, of God. *See* God
sin, 33–34, 74–75, 95–111, 163–65, 178–80, 205, 211–12, 226, 228
Smalley, Beryl, 35
sola ratione, 11–44, 88–89, 92n46, 224
Southern, Richard, 2n6, 13, 17n26, 27n55, 28, 34, 37n97, 38n103, 76, 85, 88, 177, 178n15, 181n30, 187, 188, 209–10
Spinoza, Baruch, 2, 55
spirituality, of Anselm, 14, 27–29, 33–34, 43, 100–101, 177
Stolz, Anselm, 3, 13n17, 56–58, 59n48, 66–67, 71–72, 87, 91n42, 118, 128n9
Sweeney, Eileen, 3n10, 13–14, 36n94, 61, 70n102, 76, 86n23, 87n29, 110, 116, 117n129, 158

that than which nothing greater can be thought. *See* divine name
Trinity, 9, 39, 47, 68, 72, 77, 87, 100, 111, 124, 129, 133, 162, 172–74, 178, 189–98, 200, 223, 229
truth, God as: 155–56, 158, 163, 166, 190–91, 228

unbeliever: Anselm's engagement with, 21, 32–33, 40–43, 117
unum argumentum, 59–60, 62–64, 74, 80–87, 91, 124, 126–27, 140–41, 157, 175, 191, 198, 201–2, 227
unum necessarium, 83, 174–75, 189–99, 201–02, 229

van Fleteren, Frederick, 5n18, 82n9, 96n59, 102n84, 214n151
Vaughn, Sally, 38n101, 38n104
De veritate. See Anselm
Viola, Colomon Étienne, 19–20, 21n35, 38n102
visio Dei, 8–9, 42, 44, 63, 74–75, 94, 102–04, 108–11, 117, 123–24, 128, 130, 134, 150, 153–54, 156, 159–61, 163–66, 171, 175, 179, 189–90, 193, 197, 201, 226–27, 229–30
Visser, Sandra, and Thomas Williams, 13, 22, 43, 53n19, 61n55, 93, 140, 223n1
Vita Anselmi. See Eadmer

Ward, Benedicta, 59, 60n48, 90n41, 91n42, 97n64, 98n69, 98n70, 99n72, 173, 175, 177–78, 187, 214
Williams, Thomas. *See* Visser, Sandra
worship, 27, 95, 110, 123, 197

Anselm's Pursuit of Joy: A Commentary on the Proslogion was designed in Arno
and composed by Kachergis Book Design of Pittsboro, North Carolina.
It was printed on 55-pound Natural Offset and bound by
Maple Press of York, Pennsylvania.

www.ingramcontent.com/pod-product-compliance
Lightning Source LLC
Chambersburg PA
CBHW022046290426
44109CB00014B/1002